DRYLAND AGRICULTURE

DRYLAND AGRICULTURE

By

Dr. Pradeep Shrivastava

Department of Zoology

Vikram University

Ujjain (India)

DISCOVERY PUBLISHING HOUSE PVT. LTD.

NEW DELHI-110 002

Published by:
Tilak Wasan

DISCOVERY PUBLISHING HOUSE PVT. LTD.
4383/4B, Ansari Road, Darya Ganj
New Delhi-110 002 (India)
Phone : +91-11-23279245, 43596064-65
Fax : +91-11-23253475
E-mail : discoverypublishinghouse@gmail.com
sales@discoverypublishinggroup.com
parul.wasan@gmail.com
web : www.discoverypublishinggroup.com

First Edition: **2014**

ISBN: 978-93-5056-389-2

Dryland Agriculture

Printed at:
Dynamic Printers
Delhi

Preface

Agriculture is predominantly related to rainfed agriculture under which both dry farming and dryland agriculture are covered. In dryland areas, variation in amount and distribution of rainfall influence the crop production as well as socio-economic conditions of farmers. The dryland areas of the country contribute about 42 percent of the total food grain production. The coarse grains like sorghum, pearlmillet, fingermillet and other millets are grown in drylands. The attention has been paid in the country towards the development of dryland farming. Crop varieties for dryland areas should be of short duration through resistant tolerant and high yielding which can be harvested within rainfall periods and have sufficient residual moisture in soil profile for post-monsoon cropping.

—*Editor*

Contents

1

Rainfed/Dryland Agriculture

BACKGROUND

The Rainfed/Dryland area under cultivation is about 85 million hectare which is 60 per cent of the total net sown area. The Sub-Mission on Rainfed/Dryland agriculture of the National Mission for Sustainable Agriculture attempts to devise strategies to make Indian agriculture more resilient to climate change. A number of technologies such as short duration drought resistant varieties, genotypes resistant to drought, conservation of initial soil moisture technologies and farming systems approach to Dryland farming etc are available. However, further research is required to develop more such technologies and refine them by testing for adoption. The Sub-Mission intends to support the convergence and integration of traditional knowledge and practices systems. The priority areas as conceived by NAPCC and by the Ministry of Agriculture are given below:

AREAS OF PRIORITY

- Development of drought and pest resistant crop varieties and also encouragement/promotion of adoption of low input and water efficient agricultural technologies and existing stress tolerant varieties.
- Improving methods to conserve soil and water to ensure theirs optimal utilization.
- Generate awareness through stakeholder consultations, training workshops and demonstration exercises

for farming communities, for agro-climatic information sharing and dissemination

- Financial support to enable farmers to invest in and adopt relevant technologies to overcome climate related stresses.

STRATEGY

TECHNOLOGY ADAPTATION

The potential of rainfed farming system will be harnessed through farming systems comprising crop, livestock, horticulture, agro forestry, fishery, bio mass and alternate income generating activities. Region specific farming system models having low input sustainable agriculture for different rainfed agro ecologies, waterlogged/flood frequented areas and overstressed irrigated areas will be inventorised and promoted for its wider adoption.

Enhancing productivity of water with distribution and application of irrigation water using micro-irrigation, supplemental and deficit irrigation, less water demanding crop and varities, resource conservation tillage, improved soil fertility and *in-situ* moisture conservation practices and multiple water use based farming systems will be promoted. Farming system models when integrated with watershed development will reduce risk and improve resilience towards adaptation to climate change.

Declining productivity as a result of excessive fertilizer use, physical and agro-chemical soil degradation, excessive withdrawal of groundwater and inefficient water use are serious concerns. Knowledge dissemination about rational and efficient use of resources and incentivization for saving resources through labour and/or material for promoting conservation agriculture, on-farm biomass generation and incorporation, cover cropping with leguminous crops, tree based farming systems, efficient water and fertilizer saving practices, integrated nutrient management, adoption of stress tolerant varities, crop-livestock integration and bio-mass recycling should form part of policy and investment portfolio. Wider adoption of these interventions taken on mission mode would help in adaptation and mitigation of climate change.

On development front, a two-pronged strategy is suggested to cope-up with impact of climate change on Dryland agriculture, i.e.:

- Build the capacity of the primary and secondary stakeholders through various training programmes, workshops and exposure visits; and
- Strengthen the existing government programmes of watersheds, micro-irrigation systems, etc. and adopt relevant technologies to overcome climate change related stresses.

Among the most important approaches is the adopting of farming system which combines crop production with animal resource development, agro-forestry and resource conservation technologies. Attempt will be made for updating and inventorization of available region-wise technologies for farming system.

RESEARCH

The Sub-Mission will have a two pronged strategy, viz.:

- Short term and long term research on climate change; and
- Capacity building of scientists on research methodologies in climate change, demonstration/ training of farmers through Model Field Units (MFU) on coping with climate change.

The strategies for addressing the themes of the Sub-Mission on Dryland agriculture are given in the following table:

S.No.	Theme	Strategy
1.	• Promotion for adoption of drought and pest resistant crop varieties • Improving methods to conserve soil and water	Short term and long term research on adaptation and mitigation through a net-work mode: — Promotion of existing varieties suitable for different agro-climatic zones at a faster pace. — Develop more technologies and refine them for adoption.

(Contd...)

2.	Stakeholder consultations, training workshops and demonstration exercises for farming communities, for agro-climatic information sharing and dissemination	Capacity building of scientists on research methodology; training of farmers on technologies to cope with climate change and use agro-climatic information, through Model field units in 50 pilot districts.

Research will be carried out on specific projects under the umbrella of the over all programme by Institutions of NARS and few relevant Institutions outside through a net-work mode. Research on mitigation will cover identification of Germplasm, development of crop varieties, soil and water management, conservation agriculture, energy use efficiency, livestock and fisheries management to reduce the impact of climate change on productivity and to decrease the GHG emissions from agricultural livestock sector.

FINANCIAL OUTLAY

DEVELOPMENT

The details of the fund requirement for the various activities proposed are given in Annexure—IV. The following table gives a summary of financial outlays for eight years (during XI Plan (2009-12) and XII Plan (2012-2017):

S.No.	Activities	Financial Outlay (₹ in Crore)
1.	Training/ capacity Building	313.00
2.	Workshops	17.00
3.	Farmers Field Schools	50.00
4.	Financial Support to Farmers to overcome Climate related stresses in targeted area of 35.00 million ha.	12,000.00
5.	Efficient use of water and nutrients (40 million ha)	45,000.00
	Total	**57,380.00**

RESEARCH

The total cost of the research component is estimated to be ₹ 1383.0 crore for the 3 years of the XI Plan and complete XII Plan period. The year-wise and head-wise break up is given below.

(₹ in crore)

Component	XI Plan				XII Plan						Grand Total
	2009-10	2010-11	2011-12	Total	2012-13	2013-14	2014-15	2015-16	2016-17	Total	XI + XII
Short term and long term research in network mode	80	133	80	293	80	150	80	80	100	490	783
Cost of MFUs in 50 districts under KVKs	60	20	20	100	300	50	50	50	50	500	600
Total	140	153	100	393	380	200	130	130	150	990	1383

Note: The cost of one MFU is one crore for the full plan period. It is proposed to set up 100 MFUs during XI Plan and 500 during XII Plan, which will cover most of the KVKs in the country. These MFUs will serve as training and capacity building centres and operational research and providing feedback to the research Institutes on the adoption and mitigation technologies generated by the NARs.

PLAN OF ACTION

DEVELOPMENT

The action plan for the next eight years envisages human resource development to cope up with climate change through conservation and efficient management of natural resources. For this, a bottom-up approach is suggested, which involves training of farmers mainly from the 100 core rainfed districts during the first phase, followed by trainers from 73 core rainfed National ARP zones out of the total 131 Agro-Climatic Zones. These training programmes are to be supported by capacity building of policy makers, administrators to come-up with suitable guidelines and policies to deal with climate change.

The developmental effort needs a constant support of research for this, core researchers have to build their capacities through a three-week training programme. All HRD programmes need to be in tune with global efforts. For this, exposure visit of higher-level officials are required.

The summary of activities proposed is below:

S.No.	Target Group	Training Duration (Days)
A.	Capacity Building	
	• Farmers (4,80,000) • Trainers (58,400) • Policy Makers, Administrators And Research Managers (1600) • Core Researchers (2880) • Exposure Visit (240)	5 7 3 21 14
B.	Workshops	
	• Workshop at District Level (100 Distt.) • State Level (Core Rainfed Zone-73 Zones) • National Level	03 03 03
C.	Farmer's Field School (one in each core rainfed distt.) in numbers	100
D.	Area in which financial Support to Farmers is proposed to be given to overcome climate related stresses (adoption of new verities of crops, minimum tillage, contingent plan measures, organic farming, water conservation, etc.)	35.00 million ha

Note: The figures in parentheses indicate number of participants Systematic plans be prepared for wasteland development from dovetailing funds from NREGA, SGRY, RKVY, etc. For this purpose, state level land development fund may be created and used. Such developed lands may be allotted to landless agricultural labourers, SC/ST farmers and their SHGs, with specific guidelines.

With a view to utilizing large fallow lands, states to develop and encourage land lease markets under their respective laws to optimum use of privately owned fallow lands. The lease system should ensure that the land owner does not risk of losing land, the cultivator has enough incentive to invest and continue his farming activity.

The studies of the Geo-spatial Data and Earth observation through use of communication technology and Remote Sensing Tools have shown the signs of climate change. It has also become possible to map, monitor and model the impact of climate change on earth resources and environment. Synergy of these will be suitably used in the implementation of proposed programme.

Water conservation, groundwater re-charge and rainwater harvesting by adopting appropriate technologies and funding mechanism. 12 lakh water harvesting structures in rainfed areas *i.e.* 3-4 structure in each village be taken up in mission mode.

To enable farmers to invest in and adopt relevant technologies to overcome climate related stresses, the additional activities such as introduction of new varieties of crops resistant to temperature, minimum tillage, contingent plan measures to mitigate effects of extreme weather events, organic farming for carbon sequestration, additional surface storages and groundwater recharge, etc would be undertaken for adaptation and mitigation of the adverse effects of climate change. It is proposed to undertake these activities including farming system and livelihood support in about 5.00 million ha area in the already developed watersheds of X Plan at the ₹ 6000.00 per ha. The above activities will be also undertaken in the 30.00 million ha of Rainfed/Dryland areas in a period of 8 years (remaining 3 years of XI plan and XII Plan) at the rate of ₹ 3000.00 per ha. This will be additional to the existing unit cost norms under the existing watershed schemes.

Efficient Use of Water and Nutrients Application

The low water use efficiency, water scarcity and droughts will further aggravate the situation in rainfed areas due to climate change. Efficient water management of the available/ created water resources is one of the key areas to address the water scarcity issue. The availability of nutrients is limited in rainfed areas due to the limiting soil moisture. Therefore, application of the fertilizers should be done in judicious manner for its potential use. The application of liquid fertilizer and soil amendments along with water application will not only helpful in providing nutrients to crop but also help in efficient use of soil moisture. For efficient water management and to encourage liquid fertilizer application, it is proposed to bring 30 million ha under pressurized and non-pressurized water application system in the remaining years of XI Plan and XII Five year Plan in the country.

The proposed targets and outlays are:

- Pressurized irrigation system (Drip/Sprinkler) in 20 million hectare
  - Assistance up to ₹ 25,000 per hectare or 50% of the actual cost whichever is lower for installation of drip/ sprinkler systems including water lifting devices in 10 m. ha. (Total cost ₹ 25,000 crore).
  - Assistance up to ₹ 10,000 per hectare or 50% of the actual cost whichever is lower for installation of drip/sprinkler system to the farmers who have the tube-wells/ water lifting devices and other infrastructure excepting the application system, in 10 m. ha. (Total cost ₹ 10,000 crore).
- Non-pressurized irrigation system in 10 million hectare

Developing distribution system through box and conduit systems and pre-fabricated water conveyance system in 10 m. ha is proposed for improving the water application. Farmers would also be advised for adopting ridge and furrow method of irrigation, raised bed method of farming, field Bunding and levelling etc. for efficient use of water. Assistance to farmers up to ₹ 10,000 per hectare or 50 per cent of the actual cost whichever is minimum will be supported (Total cost ₹ 10,000 crore).

In addition, following also are to be suitably adopted:

- Model codes on drought, floods and good weather be prepared bringing out short term and long term mitigation measures, such as ensuring availability of quality seeds, planning for crops/varieties resistant to heat, floods, etc.
- The National Seed Grid will be strengthened to ensure supply of seed across the country as per area specific requirements.
- Issuance of Soil Health Pass Book to each farmer with soil testing advisories within next five years.

- Bio-fertilizers, liquid fertilizers and compost should be included in the subsidy regime. Their production and marketing needs to be undertaken in an organized manner.
- Guidelines may be put in place for rotational grazing, scientific lopping and pollarding and conserve fodder resources.

RESEARCH

Considering the 4th assessment report of the IPCC released in 2007, the impact of climate change on Indian agriculture is expected to be more severe than realised earlier. Particularly, Dryland agriculture is likely to face more risks and uncertainties due to predicted changes in rainfall patterns and increased droughts. Sectors like livestock production and fisheries are also likely to be significantly affected. While the impacts of climate change are regional and global, the adaptation and mitigation measure have to be evolved locally by blending traditional wisdom and modern technologies. Although many of the technologies developed by NARS in the past like short duration varieties and soil and water conservation measures are potentially useful for adaptation and mitigation, the scale and magnitude of the problem cutting across all sectors requires an exclusive and dedicated research programme.

The indirect effects of climate change on water resources are likely to be more significant than the present. Likewise, soil organic carbon and other basic soil processes will be affected. A comprehensive research programme is therefore required which should address natural resource management issues, development of crops and cropping systems that cope with increased temperature and rainfall aberrations, energy efficient production technologies and crop management practices which reduce the emission of green house gases.

The Sub-Mission on Dryland agriculture intends to address these critical gaps in addition to studying the effects on livestock, fodder production and fisheries in a comprehensive manner. Strategic research be taken up for evolving suitable cropping systems for various agriculture climatic conditions to enhance yield levels. The Sub-Mission activities will form part of overall activities of the National mission on Sustainable Agriculture which in turn will work in coordination with other missions like water and energy under National Action Plan on Climate Change. The suggested research programmes such as cataloguing of germplasm of crops, livestock and fisheries evolving short duration varities, study of pests and diseases with respect to weather relationships and use of micro-organism based technology will be taken up for adaptation and mitigation. The details are at Annexure—IV.

COLLABORATING AGENCIES

Development: Adoption of Technologies

Past experience has shown that working in partnership and in a consortium mode has proved to be more effective, resulting in cost reduction and resource sharing by avoiding duplication. It is, therefore proposed to develop strong linkages with National Organizations like ICAR, ISRO, IMD (NCMRWF), NRSC, SAC, NABARD and other institutions and NGO's and Line Departments besides improving the existing linkages with SAUs. It is also proposed to strengthen linkages with international organizations like CGIAR Institutes, UNDP, FAO, WMO, etc.

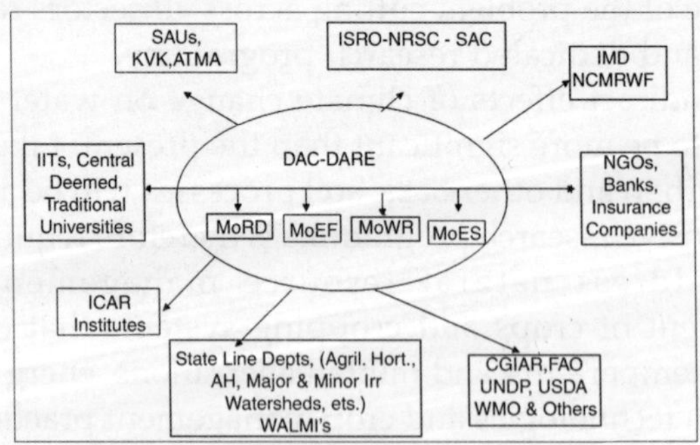

Fig 1.1 Proposed Linkages and Collaborating Institutions

In the coming years, linkages are to be strengthened further to exploit the synergistic power of institutions and organizations to cope up with climate change. The following figure depicts an illustrative outline of proposed collaboration.

DRYLAND IN INDIA

CONCEPT

Indian agriculture is predominantly a rainfed agriculture under which both dry farming and dry land agriculture is included. Dry faring was the earlier concept for which amount of rainfall (less then 500 mm annually) remained the deciding factor for more then 50 years. In modern concept, dry land areas are those where the balance of moisture is always on the deficit side. In other words, annual evapotranspiration exceeds precipitation. In dry land agriculture, there is no consideration of amount of rainfall. It may appear quiet strange to a layman that even those areas which receive 1100 mm or more rainfall annually fall in the category of dry land agriculture under this concept. To be more specific, the average annual rainfall of Varanasi is around 1100 mm and the annual potential evapotranspiration is 1500 mm. thus the average moisture deficit so created comes to 400 mm. this deficit in moisture is bound to affect the crop production under dry land situation ultimately resulting into total or partial failure of the crops. Accordingly the production is either low or extremely uncertain and unstable which are the real problems of dry land in India.

The success of crop production in these areas depends on the amount and distribution of rainfall, as these influences the stored soil moisture and moisture used by crops. The amount of water used by the crop and stored in the soil is governed by the water balance equation: ET = P-(R+S). When the balance of the equation shifts towards right, precipitation (P) is higher then ET, so that there may be waterlogging or it may even lead to run off (R) and flooding. On the other hand, if the balance shifts to the left, ET becomes higher then the precipitation, resulting in drought in the various severity. Taking the country as a whole, as per meteorological report, severe drought as large area is experienced once in 50 years and partial drought in five years while folds are expected every year in one part of the country or the other, especially during rainy season. In fact the balance of the equation is controlled by the weather, season, crops and cropping pattern.

STATUS

Out of 14.2 million ha of net sown area in the country, rainfed agriculture is practiced in 95 million ha (67 per cent). Nearly 67 m ha of rainfed area falls in the mean annual precipitation range of 500-1500 mm.

The average annual rainfall of the country is 1200 mm amounting to 400 million ha meter of rain water over the country's geographical area (329 m ha). However, the distribution across the country varies from less than 100 mm in extreme arid areas of western Rajasthan to greater than 3600 mm in NE states and 1100 mm from east coast 2500-3000 mm in the west coast. The broad area of the summer monsoon activity extends between 30^0 N to 30^0 S and from 30^0 W to 16.5^0 E. the detail information on rain fall and monsoonal pattern in India has been summarized in the following table:

Table 1.1 Rainfall and Monsoonal Pattern in India

Season/Period	m ha m	Percent
Winter (Jan-Feb)	12	3
Pre-monsoon (Mar-May)	52	13
South-west monsoon (Jun-Sept)	296	74
North-east monsoon (Oct-Dec)	40	10
Total for the year	**400**	**100**

Rainfed farming comprises about 91 per cent area of coarse cereals (sorghum, pearl millet, maize and finger millet), 91 per cent pulses (chickpea and pigeon pea), 80 per cent of oilseeds (groundnut, rape seed, mustard and soybeen), and 65 per cent of cotton. Also, about 50 per cent area under rice and 19 per cent area under wheat is rainfed.

During the past 25 years there occurred significant changes in the area and yield of imported crops of rainfed farming areas. The area under coarse cereals decreased by about 10.7 million ha and most of this was under sorghum. The area under oilseeds increased by 9.2 million ha and most of this increase was due to irrigated rapeseed and mustard and soybeen. The total area under pulses and cotton remained constant but more of cotton became irrigated and shifts in the area under occurred from one agro-ecological region to others. Area under chickpea in the northern belt decreased but increase in the central belt. This change occurred due to increase in area under rice-wheat cropping system which displaced chickpea and also pearl millet to a great extent and maize to a small extent.

According to the present concept, there are 128 districts in the country which face the problems of dry land of these 25 districts covering 18 m. ha of net area sown with 10 per cent irrigation receive 375-750 mm rainfall annually spread over Central Rajasthan, Saurashtra region of Gujarat and rain shadow region of Western Ghats in Maharashtra and Karnataka. Twelve districts have irrigation covering 30-50 per cent of the cropped area and do not pose serious problems. The remaining 91 districts covering mainly Madhya Pradesh, Gujarat, Maharashtra, Andhra Pradesh, Karnataka, Uttar Pradesh, parts of Haryana, Tamil Nadu etc., represent typical dry land area. The total net sown area in these districts is estimated to be 42 million hectares of which 5 m ha are irrigated. Rainfall in these districts varies from 375 to 1125 mm. therefore, more and more efforts are to be made for enhanced and stable production in these areas so that the recurring droughts do not stand in the way of meeting the growing food demands.

It is not that no attention has been paid in the country towards the development of dryland farming. Efforts were made right from 1923 to improve crop yields with the establishment of a research projects at Manjari in Maharashtra and later at Solapur, Bijapur, Raichur and Hagari in Deccan and Rohtak (Haryana) in the north. An All India Coordinated Research Project for Dry land Agriculture was launched by ICAR in 1970 in collaboration with Government of Canada and later Central Research Institute for Dry land Agriculture (CRIDA) was established in 1985 at Hyderabad. These projects generated technology, which, if followed, can bring marked improvement in cropping intensity, productivity and stability in production.

Problems

In dry land agriculture, scarcity of water is the main problem. Apart from the low and erratic behaviour of rainfall, high evaporative demand and limited water holding capacity of the soil constitute the principle constraint in the crop production in dry land area. Yield fluctuations are high mainly due to vagaries of weather, often much behind the risk bearing capacity of the farmers. It is surprising to a layman that even humid areas with 2000 mm of annual rainfall not only suffer from moisture stress, but also face drinking water scarcity. Monsoon starts in the month of June and ends in last week of September or sometimes in the first week of October. Most of the rainfall is received during this period. With undulating topography and low moisture retention capacity of the soil, major portion of the rain water is lost through run-off, causing erosion and adding to the waterlogging of low lying areas. After the rain stops, very little moisture is left in the profile to support plant growth and grain production.

In dry land area deficiency and uncertainty in rainfall of high intensity causes excessive loss of soil through erosion which leaves the soil infertile. Owing to erratic behaviour and improper distribution of rainfall, agriculture is risky, farmers lack resources, tools become inefficient and ultimately productivity is low.

Vertisoles have high clay content and high moisture retention capacity. Owing to its swelling and shrinking characteristics, permeability is low and hence the rate of infilteration of water is minimum. This causes more surface and high soil loss from the top layer owing to surface erosion. It is estimated that 68.5 tones/ha per year soil is lost from*vertisoles*. Due to high clay content it develops cracks during Rabi season at flowering stage of crops.

Alfisols are, by and large, light textured soils which have low moisture holding capacity but high water intake. The rain water falling in such areas gets soaked up and saturates the profile. The soil water percolation is more and therefore, is lost for crop use. Owing to faster intake of water in the profile the surface run-off is limited and soil loss from erosion is low (3.05 t/ha/year).

Soil crusting is a common problem in low rainfall areas.

Entisols are generally loamy sand or sandy loam. Depth in these soils is not a constraint. These soils have very low clay content and hold water up to 200 mm per meter of soil profile. Its nutrient holding capacity is poor. In low rainfall areas monsoon cropping is practiced and in high rainfall areas double cropping is possible.

Submontane soils are medium in texture and depth is medium to deep as well as moderate in clay content. Moisture retention capacity is high (300 mm/m. profile). These soils are poor in nitrogen but in other nutrients. Phosphorous may be limiting in high production system. Due to high rainfall double cropping is possible in these soils.

Sierozems are extremely light soils, effectively depth being influenced by the $CaCo_3$ concentration in soil profile. Its moisture holding capacity is low (150 mm water.m). Sierozemic soils are low in nitrogen and sometimes inadequate in phosphorous. Subsoil salinity is common. These soils are mostly monsoon cropped, except in deep sandy loams where post-monsoon cropping is also possible. Crusting is very frequent.

IMPROVED DRYLAND TECHNOLOGY

The improved techniques and practices, which have so far been generated and recommended for achieving the objective of increased and stable crop production in dryland areas, have been summarized in following lines.

CROP PLANNING

The farmers of the dry land areas, prior to the development of dry land techniques, were growing a crop either on rainwater in kharif or on conserved soil moisture during the winter. The crop varieties grown when moisture is sufficiently available. Such varieties have low genetic potential for yield. Selecting suitable crops and varieties capable of maturing with in actual rainfall periods will not only help in enhancing production of a single crop but in intensifying the cropping intensity. Many criteria have been laid out for selecting a crop variety for drylands. The capacity to produce a fairly good yield under limited soil moisture conditions is the most desirable criteria. The duration of kharif crops/varieties should not normally exceed the number of rainy days. In other words, crop varieties for dryland areas should be of short duration, through resistant tolerant and high yielding which can be harvested with in rainfall periods and have sufficient residual moisture in soil profile for post-monsoon cropping.

Under dry land agriculture determination of length of growing period (LPG) *i.e.,* moisture availability of a given soil type, provides better index than total rainfall based crop planning. LPG is defined as the period when the moisture and temperature regious are suitable for crop growth and the period is determined by the FAO method (1983). The LPG is computed as the sum of the period when P is more than 0.5 PET plus time taken to utilize stored soil moisture (assured 100 mm) after P falls short of PET. For example 'Nagpur' and Ratnagiri in Maharashtra receive mean annual rainfall of 1120 mm and 2500 mm, respectively but LPG determination indicates that both the places have LPG of 210 days in deep black soils. Therefore, both the places are suitable for single long duration on a short duration crop with a relay rabi crop.

PLANNING FOR ABERRANT WEATHER

Dryland agriculture is subject to high variability in areas sown, yields and output. These variations are the results of aberrations in weather conditions, especially rainfall. Delays in normal monsoonal pattern causes problems of timing and the organization of preparatory tillage and other initial activities for commencing cultivation processes for the season. Such monsoonal delays have repercussions on the programme of activities for the entire agricultural year. Even after the onset of monsoon and the commencement of planting, there may be monsoonal withdrawal causing moisture stress on plants and creating difficulties in the adoption and timing of approval cultural practices ultimately causing reactions in yields and outputs. Some crops are highly susceptible to such mid-season variations in moisture availability such as at the flowering stage in rice. Major crops like rice and maize get seriously affected if monsoonal rains cease early.

The need for modifying and introducing and introducing new technology for increasing and sustaining yield in dry land areas can hardly be overemphasized. Equally urgent is the need to decelerate and ultimately eliminate the process of damage to agricultural assets which are proceeding unbated in dry land areas. Erratic rainfall results in fluctuating production. This in turn leads to frequent scarcities, like the ones experienced in Indonesia and Vietnam in 1977 which created severe food shortages.

Droughts in China in 1972, 1974 and 1985 brought depression of foodgrain production by up to about 25 million tones. Frequent droughts in India during 1966, 1968, 1972, 1974, 1979, 1982 and 1987 seriously affected the food and fodder production in the country. Hence, it is necessary to understand the distribution of South-West monsoon within the season to determine the extent to which the crop productions are likely to be affected by the vagaries of monsoon.

Several attempts have been made to understand the behaviour of South-West monsoon rainfall in different agro-climatic regions on the basis of historical rainfall records.

These studies have brought out that

- There is large variation in dates of commencement of South-West monsoon from year to year in different parts of the country;
- The monsoon rainfall is of sequential nature with long dry spells or breaks extends sometimes to the period of even one month or more;
- There is large year to year variation in dates of withdrawal of South-West monsoon;
- There is variation in quantum of rainfall received from year to year; and
- High intensity rainfall occurs in association with movement of cyclones or depression resulting in sizeable loss of rainwater through run-off and deep drainage. Thus, crop production in dry lands

fluctuates widely from year to year due to vagaries of weather.

An aberrant weather can be categorized under three heads i.e.

- Delayed onset of monsoon;
- Long gaps or breaks in rainfall; and
- Early stoppage of rains towards the end of monsoon season. Therefore, to mitigate such weather situations, farmers should make some changes in normal cropping schedule for getting some production in place of total crop failure.

CROP SUBSTITUTION

Alternate crop strategies have been worked out for important regions of the country for *vertisols, alfisols, entisols, submontane* and *sierozemic* soils. Strategy has also been evolved for normal onset of rains, breaks in rains, early withdrawal, its uneven distribution; through selection of uneven crops/ varieties which are inefficient utilize of the soil moisture, less responsive to production input and potentially low producers should be substituted by more efficient ones. Appropriate crops, suiting varying rainfall situations, have been identified for most of the dry land regions of India (*See Table 1.2 on next page*).

Crops which do not under normal rainfall years may not do so under abnormal years. Studies conducted in agro climatic conditions of Varanasi (eastern U.P.) revealed that under normal monsoon crops like short duration upland rice, maize, pearl millet, blackgram, greengram, sesame, pigeon pea etc. should be taken up on the basis of needs. These crops should be followed by chickpea, lentil, barley, mustard, safflower, linseed etc. on residual moisture during winter season.

If monsoon sets in as late as second week of july, short duration upland rice (variety—NDR-97 and NDR-118) may be included in place of Akashi and Cauvery is recommended. If the rains are delayed beyond the period but start somewhere in last week of July or first week of August and growing season is reduced to 60-7- days, then cultivation of hybrid pearl millet (NHB 3-4, B.J. 104), blackgram (Type 9), greengram (var-Jagriti and Jyoti) may be included in pace of T-44 and k-851 etc. should be grown. Yet another alternative could be to harvest a fodder of either pearl millet, maize, sorghum or a mixture of cowpea, blackgram and one of the above fodder crops.

In case monsoon rains stop early towards the end of season, normal sowing of short duration upland rice, blackgarm and sesame may be taken up. If the rain stops very early, *i.e.* by the end of August or first week of September, only fodder crops or grain legumes could be harvested. Depending upon the soil moisture condition, relay sowing of crops like chickpea, lentil, mustard, linseed and barley could be done in rabi season.

Table 1.2 Traditional and Alternate Efficient Crops in Different Dryland Regions of India

S. No Crop	Region Crop	Traditional Efficient	Alternate
1.	Deccan Rabi season	Cotton, wheat	Safflower
2.	Malwa Plateau	wheat	Safflower, Chick pea
3.	Uplands of Bihar Plateau and Orissa	Rice	Ragi, Black gram, Groundnut
4.	South-easy Rajasthan	Maize	Sorghum
5.	North Madhya Pradesh	Maize	Soybean
6.	Eastern UP	Kalitur	Chick pea
7.	Sierozems of North-west India	Wheat	Mustard, Taramira (Eruca sativa)

During the recent drought, it was found that farmers in Karnataka, Andhra Pradesh and Maharashtra who went in for sunflower cultivation were in gainers. Sunflower succeeded where other crops failed. In other dry land regions, alternative efficient crops can profitably substitute the traditional ones (*See Table 1.3 on next page*).

Table Relative Yield of Traditional and Efficient Crops in Dryland Areas

Region	Traditional (q/ha)	Yield Crops	Efficient	Yield (q/ha)
Bellary	Cotton	2.0	Sorghum	26.7
Varanasi	Wheat	8.6	Chickpea	28.5
Ranchi	Upland Rice	28.8	Maize	33.6
Indore	Green gram,	11.8	Soybean	33.3
	Wheat	11.0	Safflower	24.2
Agra	Wheat	10.3	Mustard	20.4
Hisar	Wheat	3.0	Taramira	16.0
Udaipur	Maize	18.0	Hybrid sorghum	29.0

Dry land research has remained confined to important traditional crops such as sorghum, millet, pulse and oilseeds and has not explored the possibility of growing non-traditional crops such as dye-providing crops {*e.g.* Henna (Lawsonia inermis: mehadi) and jaffra(Bixa ovellana) species (*e.g.* cumin), and medicinal value crops (*e.g.* eitronella, lemon grass, senna and isabgol)}. These crops need to find an important place in research aagenda of dry land farming.

Time has come for the relevant researchers to plan a joint integrated research programme for maximizing the profitability, productivity and sustainability of learning systems of rainfed areas. Sericulture offers great promise in rainfed farming strategy, particularly of the watershed approach in peninsular India.

EFFICIENT CROPPING SYSTEM

Besides putting various measures to increase the productivity levels of dry land crops, efforts would also be needed to increase the cropping intensity in dry land areas which was generally 100 per cent, implying that a single crop was taken during the year. Cropping intensities of these areas could be increased by practice of inter cropping and multi cropping (sequential) by way of more efficient utilization of resources. The cropping intensity would depend on the length of growing season which in turn depends on rainfall pattern and the soil moisture storage capacity of the soil. For example in Indore region, receiving 1000 mm annual rainfall, only single crop can be taken on shallow soils, inter cropping in medium depth soils and double cropping on deep soils. Similar crop combinations have been identified for different regions of the country. In dry land of Varanasi region upland rice-chickpea/lentil sequence can be practices with advantage.

Inter cropping of vegetables with grain crops was pursued vigorously in some centres such as Varanasi and Phulbani. At both the palces long duration pigeon pea was inter cropped with vehetables such as okra, radish and chilli. Such inter cropping systems would be very useful to get maximum returns from rainfall agriculture. Even at solapur, leafy vegetables and some short duration beans were grown as intercrops during the rainy season.

FERTILIZER USE

Soils of dry lands in the country are not only thirsty but hungry also because these soils are severely eroded horizontly as well as vertically. Whenever efforts are made towards bunding and levelling of the fields in dry land areas, it is the surface soil which is removed. The resultant effect is that the fields are rendered shallow in depth and completely deprived of plant nutrients, particularly nitrogen, phosphorus and potassium. It is, therefore, necessary to apply all the three major nutrients in adequate amounts. Since soil moisture is limiting in dry lands, the availability of nutrients becomes limited, attempt should always be made to apply fertilizers in furrows below the seed. If seed-cum-fertilizer drills drawn by bullocks or tractors are available, this very objective can be fulfilled. There has been belief among the farmers of dry land areas that use of fertilizer increases the chances of crop failure but recent findings have shown that the use of fertilizer is not only helpful in providing nutrients to crop but also helpful in efficient use of profile soil moisture (*See Table 1.4 on next page*). If dry land farmers are shown such results, they will be convinced to use ore and more fertilizers.

Studies on the management of legumes in crop sequences for their residual effect indicated that in alluvial soils an advantage of 25-30 kg N/ha could be obtained in barley or mustard grown after black gram or green gram. Another possibility for nitrogen management in cropping system is to use legumes as green

Table 1.4 Effect of N-levels on Yield and Moisture Use Efficiency (MUE) of Barley and Wheat (Varanasi Centres)

Nitrogen Levels (kg/ha)	Grain Yield (q/ha)	Total Moisture use (mm)	MUE (kg/mm)
Barley			
0	14.05	133.7	10.5
30 20.45	136.3	15.0	
60	30.00	142.3	21.0
90	37.20	141.6	26.3
Wheat			
0	9.55	145.5	6.6
30	13.55	144.4	9.3
60	18.35	153.6	11.9
90	24.15	155.1	13.6

manures either at flowering stage or after one picking. Studies conducted at Varanasi centres clearly showed that general yield levels of barley and mustard were greater when legumes raised in the previous season was incorporated I soil after first picking as compared to that harvested at normal maturity (*See Table 1.5*).

In dry land areas, a proper mixing of organic and inorganic would be desirable. Organics have low nutrient content, but help to improve the moisture holding capacity of soils. In addition to yield advantage, nutrients like potassium help to increase drought tolerance by affecting plant-soil relationship. Transpiration losses are reduced and productivity per unit water increases.

Table 1.5 Nitrogen Economy to Legume-Cereal System (4 years Average)

Nitrogen level (kg/ha)	Incorporated	Crop yield (q/ha) Unicorporated
Green Gram	1.89	2.23
Barley		
0	16.98	13.65
30	21.30	18.64
60	24.43	21.84
90	27.27	25.20

RAINWATER MANAGEMENT

Efficient management of rain water can boost agricultural production from dry lands. The broad bed and furrow system of the Inernational Crop Research Institute for the Semi Arid Tropics (ICRISAT) for managing rain water in vertisols made it possible to increase crop yields four to five times as compared to normal practice. However, this method could not be adopted widely by the farmers in India because it is costly and labour intensive. The vertical mulching developed at Bellary centres increases the infiltration of water in soil profiles and improves *in situ* moisture conservation. The scope for managing profile moisture is limited in alfisols but the surface run off in such soils can be reduced by ridge-and-furrow technique. Alternatively, application of compost and farm yard manure as well as raising legumes will add the organic matter to the soil and increase the water holding capacity.

The winter which is not retained by the soil flows out as surface run-off. The run-off-recycling holds immense prospects in deep black soils where the seepage losses are very much less. This run-off water, if not permitted to drain out safely, causes erosion. Therefore, safe disposal of excess water from the field drains to the disposal system should be planned properly. This excess run-off water can also be harvested in storing dug out ponds and recycled to donor area in the event of severe moisture stress during rainy season or for raising crops during the winter.

WATER-SHED APPROACH FOR RESOURCE IMPROVEMENT AND UTILIZATION

Watershed management is a holistic approach arrived at optimizing the use of lad, water and vegetation in an area and thus, providing solution to alleviate drought, moderate folds, prevent soil erosion, improve water availability and increase fuel, fodder and agricultural production on a sustained basis. On the basis of the experiences of ICAR Operational research Projects, which attracted the attention of our farmers, State departments, administrators and scientists, 47 model watersheds were established during the year 1983 for development, jointly by the Ministry of Agriculture, ICAR and various State Government

Department and Agricultural Universities, in 16 states and then the Department of Agriculture and Co-operation launched the National Watershed Development Project for Rainfall Areas (NWDPRA) covering almost the same states. Out of these 47 model watersheds, the Central research Institute for dryland Agriculture (CRIDA). Hyderabad has been entrusted with 30 watersheds. These activities were in micro and mini-watersheds covering 500-2000 ha.

Major components in these model watersheds are:

- Improvement of water resources;
- *In situ* soil and water conservation: rain water harvesting for safe disposal of surface run-off;
- Increase in cropping intensity; and
- Alternate land use system for efficient use of lands as per land capability to provide stability in productivity.

The model watersheds in operation have provided a fruitful experience of how development can lead to all round improvement in food and fodder production, economic condition of the farmers. Sakho-majori model, where creation of eater source worked as a catalyst and triggered the development process can be repeated under similar situations. Similar experiences have been gained a Tejpura (Jhansi), Ariel (Bareilly District) and Tejpura watersheds which have been awarded the First and Second Prizes respectively by the President of India on 14-11-1988 based on the recommendation of National Productivity Council.

ALTERNATE LAND USE SYSTEM

All dry lands are not suitable for crop production. Some lands may be suitable for range/pasture management, while others for tree farming, ley farming, dry land horticulture, agro-forestry systems including alley cropping. All these systems which are alternatives to crop production are called as alternate land use systems. This system not only helps in generating much needed off-season employment in mono crop dry land but also minimizes risk, utilizes off season rains which may otherwise go waste as run-off, prevents degradation of soils and restores balance in the ecosystem.

Crop production may be disastrous in the years of drought, whereas drought resistant grasses and trees could be remunerative. Scientists of dry land have developed many alternate land use systems which may suit different agro ecological situations. These are alley cropping, agri-horticultural system and silvi-pastoral systems which utilize the resources in better way for increased and stabilized production from dry lands.

- *Alley Cropping:* For imparting stability and providing sustainability to the farming system, a tree-cum-crop system will be one most appropriate for such situations. One such system called 'alley cropping' - a version of agro-forestry system, could meet the multiple requirements of food, fodder, fuel, fertilizer etc. Alley cropping is a system in which food crops are grown in alleys formed by hedge rows of trees or shrubs. The essential feature of the system is that hedge rows are cut back at planting and kept pruned during cropping to prevent shading and to reduce competition with food crops.

For example, fast growing leguminous trees such as *Leucaena leucocephala* or *liliricidia spp.* are planted in rows. During the cropping season, trees are lopped at about 0.5 metre height. These loppings are used as much to reduce moisture loss and improve the nutrient status of soil. Arable crops like maize, rice, pearl millet, legumes, oilseeds etc. are planted in the alleys formed by the two rows of threes. This is also known as agri-silvi culture. Alley cropping is also a form of conservation farming which enhances soil fertility and prevents erosion.

One very strong argument in favour of alley cropping is its ability to produce usable material even in years of severe drought. At Rajkot in 1985, rainfall received during the season was only 30 per cent of the normal. There was total failure of grain production of the three legume crops tried in the system. In sole crop plots production was limited to 5.0 q/ha to 17.0 q/ha of green fodder.

However, in alley cropped plots,- Leucaena hedge-rows produced over 50.0 q/ha of green fodder:

- *Agri-horticultural system:* Agri-horticultural system palys an important role in dry land areas, especially in semi-arid regions where production of annual crops is not only low but also highly unstable. Fruit trees if suitably integrated in dryland farming system could add significantly to overall agricultural production including food, fuel and fodder, conservation of soil and water and stability in production and income. Dry land fruit trees being deep rooted and hardy, can better tolerated monsoonal aberrations than short duration seasonal crops. Hence, in drought year when annual crops usually fail or their production is highly depressed, fruit trees species yield considerable food, fodder and fuel.

A suitable example of agri-horti-system is growing of cow pea/green gram/horse gram in inter space of *ber (Zizyphus mauritiaria)* at 6 x 6 m spacing at Hyderabad. Phalsa (*Grewia asiatica*) may be planted in between two ber plants in a row with a view to intensify the system. A well managed dry land orchard of *ber* should give 50 kg fruits per tree/year. There should be 250 plants/ha for optimized production. The grow income would touch around ₹ 50,000/ha (250 × 50 × 4), assuming that one kg *ber* fetches ₹. 4.

One could get an additional income of ₹. 800-₹. 1000 from green gram/cow pea (2.5-3.0 q/ha):

- *Silvi-Pastoral System*: This system is suited to marginal dry lands and is most preferable where the fodder shortages are experienced frequently. The system essentially consists of a top feed tree species carrying grasses on legumes (preferable perennial) as understorey crops. Dry land farmers having larger holdings and keeping a land follow for a longer period for one reason on the other, should go in for this system which could provide both fodder and fuel. In a survey carried out in Andhra Pradesh, Karnataka and Maharashtra by CRIDA scientists, it was revealed that after food it is the fodder which is of paramount importance for sustaining animal wealth in rural areas. In years to come, fuel will assume greater importance.

In August, 1981 *Leucaena leucocephalla* was planted in contour trenches 7.5 m apart, the plant to plant spacing being maintained at 2.0 m at CRIDA. Four strips at upper reaches of plot (2% slope) were put under *Cenchrus ciliaris,* while lower four strips were seeded with *Stylosanthes hamata.* The system has come up very well.

EFFICIENT IMPLEMENTS

In order to take full advantage of annual precipitation in dry land agriculture, higher doses of energy input is essential. Farmers in dry lands have been using traditional and outdated farm equipments which not only perform poorly but also demand a lot of energy and time and post-harvest operations. Farm implements can help to conserve as much rain water *in situ* as possible and to harvest rain water. Shallow off season tillage with pre-monsoon showers ensures better moisture conservation and lesser weed intensity. It has resulted in 20 per cent yield increase in sorghum in Andhra Pradesh. Deep tillage helps in increasing water in soils having textural profiles and hard pan.

This has resulted in 10 per cent yield increase in sorghum and 9 per cent yield increase in case of caster. For in-situ moisture conservation, land has to be opened so that it can cause hurdle to flow of rain water. Tillage machines of appropriate size and type matching the power sources need to be used. Location specific seeders have been developed for dry land areas and these have shown good prospects and promise. A feature of these machines is that the seeds and fertilizers are placed in the moist zone of the soil resulting in a high percentage of seed germination and good crop vigour. In deciding farm mechanization in dry land areas, where farmers are generally poor, and their socio-economic condition should always be kept in mind.

The foregoing discussions show that technology of crop production in dry land areas have been generated to a great extent. What is important now is to view it in socio-economic context of the farmers. Once the technology is adopted by the farmers, the contribution of dry land areas to the total production can be sizably improved and the living standards of the farmers of these areas can be improved. This has been clearly shown in selected watershed areas and what is needed is to have more watersheds identified, proper technology to be developed and implemented.

CHARACTERISTICS OF DRYLAND AGRICULTURE

Dry land areas may be characterized by the following features:

- Uncertain, ill-.distributed and limited annual rainfall;
- Occurrence of extensive climatic hazards like drought, flood etc;
- Undulating soil surface;
- Occurrence of extensive and large holdings;
- Practice of extensive agriculture *i.e.* prevalence of monocropping etc;
- Relatively large size of fields;
- Similarity in types of crops raised by almost all the farmers of a particular region;
- Very low crop yield;
- Poor market facility for the produce;
- Poor economy of the farmers; and
- Poor health of cattle as well as farmers.

PROBLEMS OF DRY FARMING IN INDIA

The major problem which the farmers have to face very often is to keep the crop plants alive and to get some economic returns from the crop production. But this single problem is influenced by several factors which are briefly described below.

MOISTURE STRESS AND UNCERTAIN RAINFALL

According to definition the dry farming areas receive an annual rainfall of 500 mm or even less. The rains are very erratic, uncertain and unevenly distributed. Therefore, the agriculture in these areas has become a sort of gamble with the nature and very often the crops have to face climatic hazards. The farmers also take up farming halfheartedly as they are not sure of being able to harvest the crops. Thus, water scarcity becomes a serious bottleneck in dry land agriculture.

EFFECTIVE STORAGE OF RAIN WATER

According to characteristics of dry farming, either there will be no rain at all or there will be torrential rain with very high intensity. Thus, in the former case the crops will have to suffer a severe drought and in the latter case they suffer either flood or waterlogging and they will be spoilt In case of very heavy downpour, the excess water gets lost as run-off which goes to the ponds and ditches etc. This water could be stored for providing life saving or protective irrigation to the crops grown in dry land areas. The loss of water takes place in several ways namely run-off, evaporation, uptake through weeds etc. The water could be stored for short period or long period and it can be preserved either in soil, pond or ditches based on situation and utilized for irrigation during dry periods.

DISPOSAL OR DRY FARMING PRODUCTS

In dry farming all the farmers grow similar crops which are drought resistant. These crops mature at the same time and the growers like to dispose off their products soon after the harvest. This results in a glut of products in the market and the situation is badly exploited by the grain traders and middlemen. Therefore, marketing becomes a serious problem in dry farming areas.

SELECTION OR LIMITED CROPS

Only drought resistant crops namely oilseeds, pulses and coarse grains like jowar, bajra, millets etc. can be grown in dryland areas. Thus, the farmers have to purchase other food grains and household commodities that unbalance their economic position.

CAREFUL AND JUDICIOUS MANURIAL SCHEDULING

In case of irrigated farming the farmers are at a liberty to apply [manures and fertilizers according to their availability and facility but in case of dry farming they have to be very careful in fertilizer application. Due to lack of available moisture, broadcasting or top dressing becomes wasteful and meaningless. These can be applied ' by only deep placement and foliar spray for an improved crop production.

UTILIZATION OF PRESERVED MOISTURE

Judicious and purposeful utilization of preserved moisture water depends upon soil type, plant type and other factors. The amount of available water to the plants depends upon the depth of plant roots, their proliferation and density. In case of limited moisture condition, the yield directly depends upon the rooting depth.

The rooting depth can be desirably increased by mechanical manipulation of the soil. If the planting is very dense and all the plants have same kind of rooting then there will be a tough competition among roots for moisture and scarce moisture condition will result in the wilting of plants. Therefore, utilization of preserved moisture is an art in dry farming. The water collected in ponds or brooks may be used to give protective or life saving irrigation.

The widely spaced crops can be intercropped with oilseeds or pulses for increasing the productivity of the land per unit area and per unit time. Therefore, the water., collected during the rainy season need special technique and skill for its efficient utilization.

QUALITY OR THE PRODUCE

The quality of the produce from dry farming areas is often found to be inferior as the grains are not fully developed or they are not filled properly; often mixed with other crop seeds owing to mixed cropping system prevalent in these areas and the fodder become more fibrous. All these factors reduce the market value of produce and the farmers do not get the profit of their labour and Investment.

WORK ON DRY FARMING IN INDIA

As it has already been stated, that crop production is highly risky in arid and semi-arid climates. In such conditions generally two types of agriculture is practised. One is crop production or arable farming and the other is mixed farming *i.e.* animal husbandry together with crop production and pasture management. But this type of agriculture holds true only in those countries where the population is limited and agricultural land is extensive such as Australia, South Africa and some states of the USA. In India, with high population and limited available land for agriculture, we have no other option than adopting arable farming.

The repeated and frequent crop failure in the past, resulting in short food grain supply, attracted the attention of our scientists and administration. Thus the scarcity of food grains in India were made the subject of enquiry in the year 1880 and the first Famine Commission was appointed in the same year. The commission after thorough study of the situation recommended the establishment of protective irrigation projects in South India and formation of department of agriculture in all the states. But nothing could be done till 1923 when the first systematic and scientific approach to the dry farming problem in India was made.

Thus, as a beginning, Bombay research scheme on dry farming was started in 1934 at Solapur and Bijapur after the establishment of Indian Council of Agricultural Research (ICAR) a. New Delhi in 1929. After some time the work on dry farming was started in Punjab, Madras and Hyderabad. Dry farming work in U.P. started in Jhansi and Agra at dry farming centres established—1943-44 and 1948-50, respectively. Since then the work has been in progress. Crop improvement brought out very promising strains during sixties which received our interest in finding out ways and means through which the crop production can be maximized in semi-arid and periodically dry areas of the country. Keeping this in view, the ICAR launched the All India Coordinated Research Project for Dry Land Agriculture in 1970 which was in active collaboration with government of Canada.

The project started with multi disciplinary research units at 23 coordinating research centres located in various typical agro climatic regions of India with Hyderabad as headquarter. The project started with the identification of the constraints responsible for lower yields in different regions: and then to develop a relevant location specific research programme to solve production constraints. Presently a joint team of senior scientists of India and Canada is working at Hyderabad. To make the programmes more effective it is expanded to 16 agro-economic research centres. These centres have been established with an obvious objective of accelerating the conservation development and efficient, long term use of basic resources of soil and water for a self sustaining production.

The main areas of investigations of these centres are given below:

- Identification of different crops and selection of high yielding varieties for different agro-climatic zones of the country.
- Developing cropping sequences and cropping systems suitable for dry farming.
- Determining the optimal crop population and planting pattern.
- Evaluating tillage implements and practices for water intake and storage in the soil profile, establishment of better crop stand and control of weeds.
- Designing and developing animal drawn implements for speedy and efficient cultural operations.
- Evaluating use of surface mulches, both organic and inorganic for short term moisture conservation.
- Determining ideal fertilizer doses and improving fertilizer use efficiency.
- Testing new planting materials for introduction/ substitution after they have proved their superiority over existing ones. -Harvesting and storing inevitable run off and recycling it as life saving or protective irrigation.
- Developing strategies for rneeting the challenges of an aberrant weather like skip or catch cropping etc.

PRINCIPAL DRY FARMING ZONES

Almost all the states have some area under rainfed culture depending upon topography and irrigation facilities, but only the major dry farming areas are discussed here.

THE INDO-GANGETIC PLAINS OF NORTH INDIA

This zone is the youngest in the geological formation. This zone includes districts of Rajasthan, Punjab, Haryana, North-western M.P., and V.P. This zone is characterized by two major soil types namely light loam and heavy loam. The land is nearly levelled with a modest slope of 2 ft/mile length. The soils are very deep and situated at about 700 to 800 ft. above sea level. Because of heavy sand and silt fractions in the soil it has large pore spaces. The soils are rich in essential nutrients like nitrogen, phosphorus, potash, calcium etc. and, therefore, quite good for raising the crop excepting few with high water requirements. The cropping intensity, in this zone, stands around 120 per cent and the major crops which are grown in this zone are millets, cereals, oil seeds and pulses.

As far as rainfall pattern in this zone is concerned, it is observed that about 60 per cent or more of the total rainfall is observed between the end of July to the end of August, and the rainfall in remaining months is quite poor. Thus, due to very high intensity of rainfall, floods are of frequent occurrence during the first week of September followed by a long spell of drought subsequently.

THE TRAPIAN PLATEAU OF PENINSULAR INDIA

This zone comprises the states of Maharashtra, Karnataka and Andhra Pradesh. The soil of this zone has been derived from the Deccan trap.The tract is undulating and consists of low ridges and valleys due to erosion which results in rapid run-off. About 40 per cent of the land of this zone is not fit for cultivation. This tract is situated; at an elevation of 1400 -2(XX) feet from sea level. The soil may be grouped into three types based on its depth as deep. medium deep and shallow soils. Leaching of lime has resulted in the formation of lime nodules or kanker on the surface soil. The soil is quite rich in total and available nitrogen. phosphorus and potash which favours production of crops if moisture is efficiently conserved.

In this zone. two high peaks of rain are observed because the area is affected by both south-west monsoon as well as northeast i monsoon. About 40-55 per cent of total annual rainfall is obtained from south-west monsoon and the rest from north-east monsoon. Mostly the millets and some oil seeds like groundnut. are grown in this zone.

PLATEAU OF GRANITE FORMATION

The soils of this zone are grouped as red soils and black cotton soils. Red soils are shallow while black cotton soils are very deep like clayey soils. The topography is of gentle undulations which favour run-off and soil erosion. The high pore space and high swelling of soil obstruct the permeability of rain water in to the lower layers of soil and its shrinkage results in hardening and clod formation on the surface which is unfavourable for plant growth. The red laterite and black cotton soils are deficient in nitrogen and phosphoric acids.

This zone also gets rain from two months namely south-west and north-east and the distribution pattern is more or less like peninsular group. Upland rice, millets, ragi, are the main crops of this zone. However. the yield of these crops is very low.

STEPS FOR RAISING PRODUCTIVITY IN DRY FARMING

To boost the crop production under dry farming, we will have to efficiently manage our soil and water resources in the respective areas as dry land fanning gets more complex and intractable when droughts occur frequently. An efficient soil and water conservation system will play a vital role in boosting the crop yield in dry fanning. The different interdisciplinary approaches which are recommended for dry land farming are categorized in to four major groups namely engineering, physiological, genetic and agronomic approaches.

ENGINEERING APPROACHES

These approaches are aimed at soil and moisture conservation through regulation of run-off, collection of surplus rain water checking evaporation and seepage losses of water. and recycling of collected water as irrigation in times of critical need.

Contouring Across the Slope

Contouring is practiced on the lands with 3-5 per cent slope. This system consists of constructing earthen bunds and the distance between the two bunds ranges from 30-50 m depending on the degree of slope. This is carried out with an object to provide a check to the flow of run-off water which then gets accumulated in the bunded area and is absorbed by the soil. Thus, contour bunding conserves moisture and prevents soil erosion.

Smoothening of Contour Inter-bund Areas

This is practiced only in those areas which have a slope of less than one per cent The smoothening may be achieved by running bullock drawn harrows or cultivators but small undulations are leveled during the process so that impounding of water may take place and maximum water absorption by the soil may be achieved.

Contour Border Strips Method

This method is suitable for areas having a slope of 3-4 per cent In this case parallel strips across the slope ranging from 10-15 m in width are laid down on contours and the soil surface is leveled by scrapping and placing the soil according to the need of the spot It is done to reduce the run-off and to conserve soil and water from the field. It is, however, an expensive method as it requires culling and filling up the soil from higher spots to lower ones.

Scooping or Land

In this practice, the land is generally scooped before the beginning of monsoon showers. By scooping, the soil is exposed for proper absorption and conservation of moisture. However, this is also a tedious as well as an expensive operation

Opening or Ridges and Furrows

In this practice, the entire land is laid out into ridges and furrows across the slope. The ridges and furrows are opened before onset of monsoon so that the flow of water may be reduced and erosion may be controlled to the minimum. During rainy season, crops like maize, jowar, bajra, etc. may be grown in the furrows and legumes like soybean, arhar, urd, mung, cowpea, etc. may be grown on the ridges. After the monsoon is over the land is again levelled. This way the furrows are used to accumulate maximum water which will supply moisture for winter season crops.

Compartmental Bunding

Areas having a slope of 1% or less are suitable for compartmental bunding. It helps in accumulation of more water and a uniform spread of water in the entire area. Levelling is also done with nominal or no additional expenditure.

Bedding System

In this system, small furrows are opened and the soil from the furrows is uniformly spread in space left between the furrows. Thus, inter furrow spaces form the raised beds of about 4-5 metres width. This method helps in the conservation of soil, moisture and checking the excess run-off of water.

The raised beds, in this practice, are used for growing such crops which need less water like legumes and oil seed crops, while the furrows are used for the crops which need more water.

Broadbased Bunding

This method is especially suitable for heavy black soil. Water is allowed to spread over a vast area by constructing a broadbased bund on a sloppy side. The water stays for a longer time because of high water holding capacity, lower leaching and seepage losses.

The stored water may be used for fish culture and also for providing life saving irrigation grown in surrounding areas of catchment portion. These bunds are also called check dams and are given a regulated drain or outlet for protecting the bunds from breaking.

Deep Summer Ploughing Followed by Surface Tilling

The field is ploughed deep by mould hard plough soon after harvesting rabi season crop with the objectives of:

- Exposing the soil for perfect drying;
- Killing the disease pathogens;
- Destroying eggs of insect pests; and
- Controlling weeds by sun drying. The surface tilling during other seasons forms natural mulch and thereby reduces evaporation loss of water from soil.

Water Harvesting

Water harvesting is a technology of utilizing the collected and conserved water for the purpose of crop production. It includes tillage practices for an efficient use of moisture between and within the crop rows. Frequent stirring of the land by surface tilling provides mulch and prevents the evaporation loss of water from the soil.

Besides harvesting moisture from between and within the crop rows, run off losses are considerably reduced. The store water is used for providing life sowing irrigation to the crops grown in the surrounding areas. The water harvesting of this type can be done in areas situated near hill and on greatly undulated lands.

In these cases, check dam tanks, and other reservoirs are constructed. The infiltration or percolation loss of water is prevented by spraying of asphalt compounds or by covering the bottom of the tanks or ponds through thin plastic sheets. The seepage loss may also be checked by providing a plastic lining. The evaporation loss of water is controlled by pouring some burnt crude oil over water surface.

On a highly eroded soil or soils having very high slopes, terraces are made for providing a gentle flow of run off water so that the soil is not further eroded and some crop may be grown on these terraces.

PHYSIOLOGICAL APPROACHES

Hardly one per cent of the water absorbed by the plant roots is used for the growth and development of plants and remaining 99 per cent is wasted through transpiration back to atmosphere. Thus one of the greatest causes of soil water wastage is loss of water through transpiration.

The extent of transpiration can be greatly influenced by using certain chemicals. These chemicals reduce transpiration, encourage root growth and protect the cytoplasmic proteins of the plants. These chemicals bring about more drought resistance in the plants. These compounds, according to their role, are classified as given below.

Anti-transpirants

Any chemical substance, which reduces rate of transpiration on its application to the plant surface, is called anti-transpirant.

Any substance which reduces the vapour pressure gradient in the stomatal cavity or increases stomatal resistance to water vapour diffusion, will act as anti-transpirant These substances have been used for arresting water loss from plant body with various degree of success. These are Phenylmercuric Acetate (PMA), Hydroxy Sulphonates (HS), Alkenyl Succinic Acid (ASA), Adol:-52 (a formulation of alcohol), and S-600 (a plastic transplanting spray).

Chemicals for Improved Cell Membrane Permeability of Water

Dry fanning areas are characterized by scarce rainfall and usually the roots have lipid layers which lower the absorption of water from the roots. Some chemicals like Alkenyl Succinic Acid (ASA) and Decenyl Succinic Acid (DSA), when applied, penetrate into the root and increase its water absorption power 8 times. Therefore, these chemicals are applied in the root zone for increased water absorption along with some chemicals to retard the transpiration from foliage.

Use of Plant Hormones and Growth Retardants

Some plant hormones like Indole acetic acid (IAA) and Abscissic acid (ABA) may be used for reducing the frequency and period of stomatal opening thereby minimizing the water loss from the plant body.

There are certain other chemicals known as growth retardants which either modify the plant structure or dwarf the plants by considerably reducing the total water requirement of the plants. The most important chemical of this group is cycocel or CCC (2- chlorocthyl trichloromethyl ammonium chloride). This chemical t\ also induces moisture stress tolerance in plants. Cycocel is presently used in cotton to encourage production of more fruiting branches (sympodial rather than monopodial or vegetative branches) and, Ii thereby even under drought condition it results in higher yield. In case of wheat, the use of Cycocel decreases the cell size and increases the density of the cytoplasm which ultimately results into a drought resistance into the plants.

Use of Chemicals

There are certain chemicals which are used for seed treatment to bring about drought resistance in plants right from seedling stage. Soaking of seeds in calcium chloride solution (0.25 per cent) for 20 hours soaking of seeds with frequent shaking results in better germination and drought resistance in the plants.

Boron solution is also used for soaking seeds. Agrosan is a fungicide but also induces drought resistance in the plants when seeds are treated with this chemical.

GENETIC APPROACHES

Because of scanty and unreliable rains the farmers of dry farming areas are still practicing crop husbandry on the basis of traditional approaches like low intensity cropping, little or no use of fertilizers or manures, raising low value crops. Crop varieties grown till the recent past were generally of long duration and slow growing. They were poor yielders too.

As nearly 70 per cent of our total agricultural land is rainfed and 45 per cent -of rainfed area is dryland, there is no way out but to evolve suitable varieties as well as appropriate technology for getting the most from our rainfed or dryland areas. As such, the concerted efforts of our plant breeders have resulted in the cultivation of several new plant types which possess all the characters needed for rainfed areas or dry lands. In terms of modem technology, such plant materials are called 'Ideo types'. These are the suitable strains of dry land crops which are characterized by short growth duration, effective and extensive root system, drought tolerance, high yield potential having altered morphology of plants which are conducive to dry lands.

According to breeders, an ideal 'Ideo type" should have following qualities to give desired results in dry farming:

- Early in growth duration and early vigour.
- Deeper root system with maximum branching at deeper zones.
- Dwarf plant types with lesser number of erect leaves.
- Moderate tillering; as profuse tillering causes competition. Very Good expression of ear heads even at higher planting density.

- Resistance to diseases.
- Bolder grains with moderate dormancy in them.
- Effective photosynthetic behaviour with greater sink capacity.

The following are some of the crop varieties recommended for commercial cultivation in different regions.

Black Cotton Soils

Jhansi Region

Sorghum -CSH-5, CSH-6, Spy -370
Pigeonpea -T-21, Pusa Ageti
Groundnut -Chandra \
Green gram -Kopergon
Maize -Satha, Diara
Soyabean -Ankur, J-231
Pearl millet -BJ-I04

Rajkot Region

Sorghum -CSH-6
Black gram -T-9
Green gram -Gujarat -2
Sesamum -Purva -1
Sunflower -EC-68414 f:
Pearl millet -J-1399

Akola Region "

Cotton -DHY -286, H-4, AKH-4,5
Sorghum -CSH-l,5,9, SPV-I02
Pigeon pea -C-ll,T-21
Green gram -Kopergaon, T-44
Black gram -T-9
Groundnut -JL-24
Sunflower -EC -68414
Safflower -N- 7-

Solapur Region

Pearl millet -BJ- 104, BK-560, Rahuri-
Foxtail millet *(Setaria italica)* Arjun, IS-279-

Groundnut -M-13,TMV-I0,SB-Il JIIJ-;:'(Jreengram -S-8,J-781

Sunflower -EC-69874, EC-68414

Sorghum -M-35-1, SPY-86, CSH-8R

Safflower -Tara, N-628, Bhima (S-4)

Bengal gram -Chafa, N-59

Indore Region

Maize -Ganga-5, Satha

Sorghum -CSH-5, CSH-6

Pigeon pea -No. 148, Khargone-2, HY-4 Soyabean -Bragg, JS- 72-44, Ankur

Groundnut -AK-12-24, Jyoti

I Sunflower -JSN-l

Wheat -Narmada-4, Narmada-112, Swati

I Bengal gram -Ujjain 21,24

Rewa Region

Rice (uplands) -DR-92, IR-28, Cauvery

Rice (low lands) -Ratna, Jaya

Soyabean -J-231,JS-17, Black soyabean Sorghum -CSH-l, CSH-5, 604, Swarna Pigeonpea -T-21, BS-l, Prabhat,JA-17

Green gram -ML-5, Jawahar-45

Groundnut -Jawahar, Jyoti, M-13, J-.J 1

Wheat C-3~,Narmada-4,112,Lok-l,Sujata, Swati

Bengal gram. -BG-200, H-208, Pink-2

Linseed -T-397, R-157

Bijapur Tegion

Green gram -PS-16 Black gram -K-3

Cowpea -C-152

Pigeon pea.C-28, PE-221

Cotton -Suyodhar

Sorghum -M-35-l

Bengal gram -A-I

Udaipur Region

Maize -Ganga -5, Ganga-2

Sorghum -CSH-5, Spy -245

Pigeonpea -Gwaliar-3, Hyderabad-l, Hyderabad-4
Green gram -S-9, Pusa Baisakhi, K-85l
Black gram -T-9
Cowpea -C-152
Safflower -N-62-8, JSF-2, JSF-5
Mustard -Durga Mani, T -59, Prakash
Bengal gram -C-235, Dohad, BG-203
Wheat -Narmada-4, Narmada-l 12, MP-175
Linseed -Chambal

Rabi Black Soils

Bellari region
Sorghum -SPV-86, M-35-l I
Safflower -S-144, A-300
Bengal gram -A-I, N-52
Cowpea -CO- 7, CO-8

Alluvial Soils

Agra Region

Pearl millet -BJ-l04
Black gram.T-9
Green gram -T -44, Jawahar -45
Pigeon pea.Pusa Ageti, T -21
Cow pea -C-152
Groundnut -T-64
Safflower -A-300, JSF-5
Barley -RS-6, Ratna I Mustard -T-59, RT-16, Bengal gram -G-24, G-130

Varanasi Region

Rice -Aka5hi, Cauvery, Ratna
Maize -Ganga safed-2, Ganga-5
Pearl millet -Jaunpuri, NHB -3-4, BJ-I04
Black gram -T-9, H-I0, B-76
Green gram -Varsha, K-851, PS-16, T-44 Sesamum -T-13, T-4, T-12
Pigeon pea -T -21

Wheat -C-306, Malviya-12
Barley -DL-3, K-125, Ratna
Bengal Gram -T-l, T-3, T-6, BG-l, BG-2 Mustard -T-59, T-5909
Linseed -T -397, Neelum, Mukta

Semi Arid Red Soils

Anantpur Region

Pearl millet -BJ-I04
Sorghum -CSH-5, SPV-I04
Castor -Aruna
Pigeonpea -PDM-l
Groundnut -TMV-2, Kadiri-l, Kadiri-3

Hyderabad Region

Sorghum -CSH-5, CSH-6
Pigeonpea -Hy-2 and 4

Subhumid Red Soils

Bhubaneswar Region

Upland rice -Subhadra, Parijat, CRM-13-32 41
Green gram -Kopcrgaon, K-8S1, PS-16
Pigeonpea -R-60,Kanka-9,T-21
Cowpea -C-20, C-170, FS-68
Groundnut -M-13,Polachi-1,NG-386
Maize -A-S1-S4, Jawahar, Diara

Ranchi Region I

Rice -Bala, Brown Gora, Kiran
Sorghum -CSH-S, CSH-6
Maize -Ganga safed-2
Arhar -BR-6S, Laxmi, BR-183
Groundnut -AK-12-21
Sesamum -Kanke white
Wheat -C-306, Kalyansona,HD-238S and2402
Barley -BR-1, BR-32, Ratna, K-12S –
Lentil -Pant-209, PL-8, Pant-406

Linseed -T-397, LC-267
Green gram -Sunaina
Black gram -Madhu, BR-10

Sierozemic Soils I

Anand Region

Pearl millet -CJ-104, BJ-104
Sorghum -CSH-S, CSH-6
Green gram -Gujarat-1
Tobacco -Gujarat-4, Anand-2

Hissar Region

Pearl millet -BJ-104 C",
Sorghum -CSH-S, CSH-6 '
Green gram -5-9
Moth -T-2
Castor -Aruna
Bengal gram -H-208, C-214, C-235
Barley -RD-56, Jyoti, C-138
Mustard -RH-30, RL-18

Sub Mountain Soils

Debra Dun Region

Maize -Ganga -2, Ganga -5, Vikram
Rice -RP-79-5,DR-92, CR-142-3-2
Soybean -Bragg, Pb-l, Semmi
Arhar -Prabhat, T-2l, Pant A-3
Wheat -.HD-198l, HD-2009, HD -2021
Barley -PL-56, PL-142, PL-133

Hoshiarpur Region

Wheat -WL-4l0, WL-7ll, C-306
Bengal gram -C-235 Rai -RL-18

Rakh Dhinsar Region

Maize -GS-2
Bajra -BJ-l04

Green gram -R-286-8
Mash -Pant U-26
Wheat -WL-410, IWP-72
Gram -C-235
Mustard -RLM -198,':. Lentil -T-36,";;' Pea -PG-2:i,'-

AGRONOMIC APPROACHES

The major objective of dry farnlingprogramme is to conserve the soil and moisture and to achieve maximum production from the dry farnling areas. In the past two decades, we have been able to' solve many hurdles in the aforesaid areas but there had been no break through as in case of irrigated crop production. Now we have the promising crop varieties and technology available with us about the maximum soil and water conservation.

The agronomic approaches can be dealt with under the following four heads based on land types.

Agronomic Approaches for Highly Undulating Lands

These lands are confined to the hills of the locations which have suffered serious soil erosion problems and have been divided into various gullies. The soils of these areas are more prone to further erosion if they are not properly managed. Therefore, in this category, the crop management practices are entirely different from other areas.

The object of soil and crop management under such situation should be:

- To stabilize the soil by forestry and pasture management with a regulated grazing or no grazing at all.
- To level the land gradually through contour bunding, terracing, etc.
- To practise strip cropping and pitcher farming.

Agronomical Approaches for Marginal Lands

Generally, marginal lands are very poor in fertility. The crop management in these lands is carried out in lines of crop management for leveled lands or flat lands which will be discussed later in this chapter.

Agronomical Approaches for Diara Lands

Diara lands are located on either side of rivers or between two rivers and are often flooded by these rivers. These diara lands are formed due to flood and may have deposition of fine to coarse sands.

These areas often lack irrigation and need a careful crop management. Since the land of this areas is highly susceptible to floods, kharif cropping is practically impossible. But certain fodder crops can easily be grown soon after the onset of monsoon and harvested depending upon position of floods. The harvesting or cutting of crops is started from close to the river beds and as the water spreads the harvesting is also advanced. The life saving irrigations can be given by lifting water from the river or by drilling cavity wells or bam boo borings. However, in most of the cases these wells go out of order after a flood occurs. Therefore, the cavity wells or bamboo borings are made at a distant location from river stream.

Agronomical Approaches for Plain Lands

Plain lands form the main dry land tracts of the country. There has been major emphasis on finding out ways and means through which the total soil productivity could be increased. Following recommendations should be followed on plain lands for an improved crop productivity and an efficient soil and water conservation.

Tillage Requirements of the Crops

Tillage starts with the seed red preparation and ends with mulching and control of weeds. Deep ploughing during summer helps in destroying weeds and suppressing insect pests and diseases. It also helps in an efficient root penetration very deep into soil Placement of seed at 5 cm and fertilizers at 7.5 cm in the same furrow followed by soil compaction have resulted in better germination, plant vigour, extensive root development and higher crop yields.

Selection or Crops and Varieties

There are a number of improved varieties of different crops which are drought tolerant or resistant to water stress. The most commonly grown crops in dry lands are rice, maize, sorghum, pearl millet. finger millet, wheat, barley, pulses, oilseeds, etc. The improved varieties of these crops have already been described area-wise.

Sowing or Crops

Sowing of crops deals with several associated factors namely sowing time, method of sowing, depth of sowing etc. It is important in the sense that once the ideal plant population is achieved. the crop is bound to give yield.

Sowing time can markedly influence the production and productivity of dry land crops. Early sowing of kharif crops results in early crop maturity and thereby it facilitates early sowing of succeeding rabi crops. Early sowing of rabi crops helps in overcoming the moisture stress at later stages of plant growth, particularly at grain filling stage.

Broadcasting of seeds should be avoided as it involves several losses and seed does not properly come in contact with moisture. Placing the seeds at about 5 cm depth through pora or seed drill is desirable.

To get an ideal plant population it is necessary that about 25 per cent higher than required seed rate should be applied. Care must be taken to reduce plant competition for moisture by removing excess plant population about 2-3 weeks after the sowing depending upon the crops.

Fertilizor Management

Use of fertilizers in dry lands is limited as compared to irrigated areas. Today we use on 'an average only 60kg/ha fertilizers in dry fanning areas as against 60 kg/ha national average.

Reasons for application of fertilizers in dry fanning are as follows:

- Poor response because of faulty method of application;
- Poor financial condition of fanners to purchase fertilizer;
- Wrong concept of the fanners that fertilizers will burn the seedlings, and harm to the soil; and
- Application of organic manure only, which can not meet the total nutrient requirement of the crop.

There are different Schools of thoughts about the application of fertilizers in the dry lands. Some people think that application of fertilizers in dry lands results in a better crop yield than that in irrigated areas because in the latter case the soil becomes very poor in residual fertility due to high intensity of cropping, whereas, the dry lands still preserve nutrients as they are not depleted badly due to low cropping intensity. Some people think that fertilizer application in dry lands aggravates the moisture problem, but truly speaking deep placement of fertilizers followed by foliar application results in extensive rooting up to deeper soil layers where the plants extract moisture to meet their demands.

Spreading of fertilizers at the surface or applying them at the seed layer is not so beneficial. Therefore, a careful and judicious fertilizer scheduling is a must frr achieving higher and better crop productivity in dry lands.

Use of organic manures is always desirable but they alone are not enough as—they can not supply nutrients at the required speed and dose. Therefore, atleast half of the nutrient requirement of the crop must be met by readily available source of nutrient *i.e.* fertilizers. This also improves water use efficiency.

Following points should be considered to improve the fertility status of dry lands.

- Green manuring should be practised in kharif season.
- Inclusion of a legume crop in rotation adds about 20-25 kg of nitrogen per hectare, reduces cost of fertilization and increases crop productivity.
- Inoculation of legumes through Rhizobium culture and nonlegumes with Azotobacter adds about 30-35 kg of nitrogen per hectare.
- Foliar application of urea having lowest biuret content along with micro-nutrient fertilizers like zinc sulphate will increase grain yields in dry farming.
- Growing forage legumes in rotation with pearl millet in kharif season will provide a better condition for rabi crop.

Therefore, proper fertilizer scheduling will help the farmers to induce drought tolerance/resistance in the crops and provide higher yields.

Cropping Systems

Cropping system refers to an arrangement in which various crops are grown together in the same field. The cropping systems followed in dry lands differ from those followed under normal conditions. Only those crops can be grown under dry land conditions which require less water to complete their life cycle or which can stand or yield under drought conditions. This can include both drought resistant and drought tolerant plants. In addition, plants can be grown only where some water is available to sustain the growth of plants.

Following are a few intercropping systems for dryland areas:

- Moong + Bajra
- Guar + Bajra
- Til + Guar/moth/mung

Mixed cropping is also followed to minimize the effect of unpredictability of rain. Mixed cropping may have low yield potential but it works as a buffer against failure under possible unfavourable conditions. Mixed cropping may be defined as sowing of two or more crops simultaneously on the same piece of land in separate rows. Examples: Guar + Arhar + Moong, Bajra + Arhar + Moong and Maize + Urd etc.

Cropping Pattern

Cropping pattern is defined as sequence of growing crops in a particular field at a particular period. The most common cropping pattern for dry land farming are discussed below:

For North Indian Conditions

- Sorghum -Safflower/mustard
- Sorghum –Mung/urd/cowpea -Gram/wheat -Gram
- Rice -Gram (for low lying areas)
- Bajra -Gram + Linseed
- Bajra + Urd/Mung/soyabean -Wheat/barley +
- Gram/m ustard
- Maize-Gram/safflower

For Central Indian Condition

- Green gram -Rabi sorghum
- Green gram -Safflower

For Bhubaneswar Region

- Rice -Horse gram
- Ragi -Red gram
- Groundnut -Niger
- Maize-Niger

Weed Control

Presence of weeds in the crop field, especially in case of dry lands, cause a severe crop weed competition for water, nutrients and light The reduction in yield due to weeds varies from 30-75 per cent depending upon the crop and nature and extent of weed infestation. Weeds may be controlled by hand weeding, intercultural operations and herbicidal application or by adopting an integrated approach.

Plant Protection Measures

In light textured soils of arid and semi arid regions termites and white grubs cause extensive damage to emerging seedlings and also to grown up plants. Use of BHC 10 per cent dust@ 25-30 kg or Aldrin 5 per cent dust@ 10-15 k/ha, in the soil and incorporating it well into the soil at the time of the last ploughing will control termites. The white grubs may be controlled by drilling of Thimet 200 granules @ 15 k/ha along with seeds. Aphids in mustard are very destructive, therefore, they are controlled by spraying 0.2 per cent Metasystox or Dimecron. Similarly, the pod borers in pulses are controlled by spraying 0.05 per cent Endosulfon.

The viral diseases of pulses should be controlled by seed treatment and spray of some fungicides to kill the insect vectors.

AGRO-FORESTRY AND DRYLAND AGRICULTURE

Agroforestry is the cultivation of trees in association with crops. It has assumed a great importance in order to solve a number of problems of dryland farmers. The twin objectives of Agroforestry are to increase the farmers income and sustain the ecological! Environmental balance. Agroforestry, as it provides fuel wood to the fanners, enables them to save the animal dung and use it as manure.

The following points should be considered while choosing trees for cultivation in association with crops:

- The tree should grow fast and stand repeated prunings.
- Its roots should explore soil layers not tapped by agricultural crops.
- The crown should not be too large to prevent sun light from reaching the crop.
- The peak period of flush and leaf faII should not be detrimental to the crop grown in association.
- As far as possible, the tree species should be a legume, the root nodules of which accommodate nitrogen manufacturing bacteria.
- The branching should be sparse and light.
- The tree should meet the socio-economic and ecological needs of the region.

Some agro-forestry combinations are given for the main dry fanning areas of the country.

Trees suitable for growing in association with crops in different dry land regions are given below:

- *For north western arid and semi arid zones*: Prosopis cineraria (khejri), Zizyphus maurlliana (jujube), Acacia IOrlilis(israely babool),Leucaena leucocephala (su-babool), Acacia auriculiformis.
- *For Central arid Vindhyan zone*: Acacia nilolica var. cuprissiformis, Punica granalwn (anar).Kinnow (citrus), Psydiwn guajava (guava).
- *South eastern regions*: Acacia albida, Acacia ferruginea, Prosopis cineraria, Leucaena leucocephala.
- *Himalayan regions*: Alnus neplensis (utis), Sehima wallichianum, Citrus species, Sesbania sesban, Prosopsis juliflora

RECOMMENDATIONS FOR DRY FARMING AREAS

The research programmes of all India coordinated research projects for dry land agriculture have concluded into certain recommendations to the farmers of dry land areas which are described below:

- Bunding across the slope and levelling the land should be done before onset of monsoon.
- Deep summer ploughing should be followed by surface tillage during monsoon months and also rest of the year.
- Application of organic manures like FYM compost. etc. @ 15-20 tonnes/ha or green manuring should be done. These manures should be applied about 20-25 days before sowing and should be well mixed in the soil.
- Fertilizers should be basal placed at a depth of 7.5 to 10cm in the soil and the seeds should be sown in the same furrows about 3 cm. above the fertilizers. This is important especially during winter season. The nitrogen (20-50% of total) should be top dressed by side or band placement method at about 10- 15 cm apart. The crop rows should be done soon after the rains but if there is not sufficient moisture in the soil, the nitrogen should betrayed over the foliage with urea solution containing 3-5 per cent nitrogen. Zinc and sulphur should be applied as basal if needed.
- Soil application of BHC (10%) dust @ 25-30 kg/ha for termites and Thimet 20 G @ 15 kg/ha for white grub should be done. These chemicals must be mixed with soil properly while ploughing or at the time of sowing.
- Selection of suitable crops and their varieties should be done according to their suitability to a particular region/micro climate.
- Seeds must be treated with a suitable fungicide and that of legume with Rhizobium culture before sowing. Soaking seeds in plain water for rabi sowing helps in getting higher germination, better seedling vigour and an early maturity within weeks time.
- Proper crop rotation should be followed which should preferably have at least one legume every year.

- For better seed soil moisture contact through soil compaction should be done by running a plank or roller especially for rabi crop.
- At the event of total crop failure during kharif season a suitable catch crop like urd (T-9) or toria etc should be sown.
- Intercropping of oil seeds and pulses should be done with jowar, bajra and maize crops for the purpose of making best use of soil and inter row moisture harvesting.
- Line sowing by drilling the seed at a depth of 7.5 to 10cm or even more depending upon the situation should be practiced because it helps in better seed germination. This also helps in stabilizing the required plant population and thereby in getting better yield.
- Proper weed management practices should be followed by adopting integrated weed control measures.
- Mulching should be done by providing frequent interculture and pulverizing the soil. If intercultural operations are not possible then use of artificial mulches like covering the surface with tree leaves, uprooted weeds, sugarcane leaves, saw dust or polythene sheets are used to check the evaporation of water from the soil.
- Water harvesting between the rows should be done by growing some pulse crops and run off water should be collected in some nearby located ponds and used as life saving irrigation.
- An efficient plant protection measure should be adopted to protect the crop from insect pests and disease damage.
- The crop should be harvested at proper physiological maturity so that the following or succeeding crop may be sown slightly earlier than the scheduled time and best use of rain water or residual moisture may be made for crop production.
- Crops like cotton, chilies, etc. should be sprayed with CCC or cycocel and groundnut should be sprayed with planofix for modified growth, higher drought resistance and better yield.

2

Risk Management

BACKGROUND

The vulnerability of Indian agriculture to risk and uncertainty has increased rapidly due to changes in farming conditions, pressure on natural resources and climate variability, as also the changes in policy environment due to global market integration.

The climatic aberrations such as incessant rains, temperature swings, droughts, cyclone and degradation of natural resources have exposed the farmers to risk at all stages of the production chain. Unfortunately, the existing responses to mitigate risks are inadequate to provide safety net for the poor and vulnerable farmers. Hence, there is need for ensuring livelihood safety and income insurance to the farmers through using innovative insurance products including weather based derivatives.

Agricultural insurance is an important instrument for management of production risks. But the available options and insurance products are limited to mitigate risks that farmers are likely to be exposed to. The situation becomes worse because of the currently limited coverage and inadequate access to information to the farmers and other stakeholders.

The designing and developing demand-driven agricultural insurance products requires evolution of efficient tools and refinement in methodology of accurate risk profiling. The novelty of linking quantitative risk to agricultural insurance products is that it takes care of variety of risk regimes protecting millions of small farmers against risks. This is a major challenge to agricultural R&D system and policy makers. The implications of climate change for the agriculture sector are incorporated in the National Policy for Farmers, 2007 which was approved by Government of India basing on the reports of the National Commission on Farmers.

Apart from conservation and development of bio-resources required for sustainable development of agriculture sector, the Policy provides for preparation of contingency plans, alternative land use and water use strategies, training of experienced farmers as 'climate managers' in the art of managing drought, floods and aberrant monsoons. The policy also provides for preparation of Drought Code, Flood Code and Good weather Code for drought prone, flood prone and arid areas respectively, so that the required corrective/mitigation measures can be taken well in time.

PRIORITY AREAS FOR ACTION

For improving the risk management in agriculture sector, the following priority areas have been identified in the National Action Plan for Climate Change (NAPCC):

- Strengthening of current agricultural and weather insurance mechanisms.
- Development and validation of weather derivative models (by insurance providers ensuring their access to archival and current weather data).
- Creation of web-enabled, regional language based services for facilitation of weather-based insurance.
- Development of GIS and remote-sensing methodologies for detailed soil resource mapping and land use planning at the level of watershed or a river basin.
- Mapping vulnerable eco-regions and pest and disease hotspots.
- Developing and implementing region-specific contingency plans based on vulnerability and risk scenarios.

STRATEGY

RESEARCH AND DEVELOPMENT

Following are the strategies to implement the priority areas of action:

- Development of the models of risk assessment under various risk regimes:
  - Magnitude of risk exposure and the availability of the supportive infrastructure including resources and relevant data depending on risk measures vary differently depending on the risk mitigation measures. While the impact of risk increases from national to individual farmers' level, the resources, on the contrary diminishes at the farmer level. Therefore, Developing differentiated strategies for risk management and mitigation, particularly for the small and marginal farmers is important.
  - Development of dynamic models and methods for risk assessment considering multiplicity of risks.
  - Availability of appropriate technologies and their back-stopping support system that has long term effect on reduction of risk mitigation.
- Linking the model parameters to develop innovative insurance products and address the issues of existing calamity mitigation measures:
  - Weather index based insurance measures are new generation agricultural insurance products, which need effective promotional strategies and validation at the grass root level. This has the advantage of speed and accuracy of loss assessment.
  - There is also need to evolve strategies to design, develop, disseminate the products to ensure farmers' acceptance. The products need to be designed to suit the different risk regimes and to capture cross sectional variability. This will include development of blended and integrated farming system insurance for different agro-ecological zones as well as for different Farmers' Groups.

- Gravity of emergence of newer sources of risk due to climate change:
  - Strategies are also required to deal with the emerging newer types of risk due to climate change These include high intensity rain, depletion of ground water and water contamination, increasing global warming, hailstorm, frost etc.
- Developing good governance and risk mitigation strategies:
  - The challenge for evolving governance structure and institutional framework for sustainability of risk mitigation measures requires more in-depth attention in order to make the insurance products more farmer-friendly.
- User-friendly decision support systems (DSS) for risk assessment and alternative insurance products:
  - Appropriate decision support system (DSS) is needed, which require more synergistic development of scientific information for assessing risk and risk profiling at farm level, regional level as well as at national level including appropriate advisories for risk mitigation. Relevant information need to be converted to knowledge before it is transferred to the grass-root for wider impact and dissemination.

STRENGTHENING THE CURRENT AGRICULTURAL AND WEATHER INSURANCE

The following strategies would be adopted for strengthening the existing agricultural and weather insurance mechanisms.

- It is important that the financial support from the Government is available for the agricultural insurance since it is difficult to make these insurance schemes financially self-sustaining. The existing arrangement is to share the financial burden on the government between the Central and State Government in the ratio of 50:50. Hence continued financial support from the Government would be necessary for modifying or strengthening agricultural insurance to make it more effective and farmer friendly.

- The emphasis would be on preventing the risk in addition to mitigation. Capacity building of the farmers to manage risks more effectively would be a necessary element of the strategy.
- The climate change along with other factors impinge significantly on the agricultural bio-security of the country. Threat of new pests and diseases apart from preventing and controlling the existing pests would be a priority. As provided in National Policy for Farmers, the National Agricultural Bio-security system would be put in place to effectively deal with this problem.
- The plan of action to strengthen the existing agricultural insurance products should focus on increasing the coverage of farmers from the existing level and reducing the response time between detection and mitigation measures.

PLAN OF ACTION FOR STRENGTHENING INSURANCE SYSTEM

Taking into account the current state of development in the crop insurance sector, following plan of action for strengthening the current agricultural insurance mechanism would be undertaken:

Strengthening Area Yield Crop Insurance (NAIS)

Though a number of operational limitations have been observed in area yield insurance, however its conceptual strengths hold substantial relevance for Indian agriculture based on its dependence on actual yields for insurance payout. Due to the large diversity in agro climatic parameters (soil profiles, terrains, microclimates etc) and intra-farm differences (nature of inputs used, staggered sowing, irrigation facilities, intercropping, susceptibility to environmental risks), area yield crop insurance that factors in such variability should continue to be promoted both independently and also in conjunction with other emerging crop insurance product types. Area yield crop insurance should continue to be the mainstay of the Indian crop insurance programme.

The following improvements in traditional crop insurance have to be pursued vigorously for enabling it to meet the expectations and requirements of Indian farmers:

- *Scaling down of insurance unit to the village/village Panchayat level for major crops*: For area yield insurance to be effective, the yield variability within the area (insurance unit) should ideally be very low if not zero. However, considering that the present insurance units are largely administrative and political boundaries, yields within the unit are hardly uniform. It is desirable that the insurance unit should be as small as possible.
- *Improvements in computation of threshold yield (Guaranteed Yield)*: Presently Guaranteed Yield, based on which indemnities are calculated, is the moving average yield of the preceding three years for rice and wheat, and five years for other crops, multiplied by the level of indemnity. The present method does not provide adequate protection to farmers, especially in areas with a perpetual high risk regime which pulls down the average yield. Such average guaranteed yields may represent only a segment of the overall farmer population in an insurance unit. Use of long period average with appropriate de-trending method would be effective particularly in the context of climate change.
- *On-account payment of claims*: To offset the delays in claim settlement, it would be of great value to introduce on-account payment of claims based on indices like weather, satellite imagery based crop health, etc. The on-account payment could be adjusted against the final payment based on yield estimates.
- *Individual assessment of losses in case of localized risks*: NAIS presently provides for individual assessment of losses in case of localized disaster events *viz.* hailstorm,

landslide and flooding, on an experimental basis. It is felt that the experiment is not adequate, and it should be implemented on a full scale, covering all areas. Earlier reviews have supported the view that the localized calamities should be assessed on an 'individual' basis in all the areas. Action in this direction needs to be expedited.

- *Coverage of pre-sowing and post harvest losses*: In some states, crops like rice, wheat etc. is left in the field for drying after harvest. Quite often, this 'cut and spread' crop is damaged, by rain, cyclones and floods. Since, the yields are estimated on the basis of crop cutting experiments, post-harvest risks are outside the purview of the present programme. There is a scope to pay indemnity for such losses on a re-sampling basis, or on 'individual' plot basis. Similarly, pre-sowing risks could be covered based on weather index.
- *Review and improvement of yield estimation methods*: On account of the procedural limitations and perceptual biases associated with the existing method of yield estimation based on Crop Cutting Experiment, there is a need to identify administratively robust and more reliable alternatives for yield estimation. With rapid improvements in computation of production estimates for major crops through remote sensing technologies, it is quite possible to provide solution in the long term not only as a substitute for the expensive method of crop cutting experiments, but also in minimizing the moral hazard (of under reporting of yield estimates). Therefore, greater use of remote sensing technology needs to be promoted and used such assessments.
- *Actuarial Regime*: An actuarial premium rate supported by up-front subsidy in premium is most likely to inject the much needed professionalism and financial discipline to the programme, besides minimizing the delays in settlement of claims. However, keeping in mind the catastrophic nature of claims, it would be appropriate if in the initial years, the government acts

as the 'reinsurer of last resort' or integrating relief administration with insurance in order to encourage smooth transition to an actuarial regime for agricultural crop insurance.

- *Risk due to Pests/diseases*: Potential threat due to altered biotic stress out of the novel organisms, mutants or variants of the existing pest-species as well as those that come up due to ecosystem and population displacements is perceived under the influence of climate change in agriculture. The quick response shall be towards mobilization of mitigation measures like activated and dynamic surveillance (through ground-truth surveys with digitization and e-reporting system), remote sensing-based database as well as by futuristic reconnaissance research on anticipated risky organisms in agricultural pestilence, mobilization of pest suppression measures including adequate expertise, appliances and pesticide for destruction of primary inoculums source and reconnaissance efforts to suppress multiplication of the organism. In order to anticipate and prevent the spread of pests/diseases, it is necessary to develop a system for reducing response time between detection and actionable decisions to manage/contain pests/ plant diseases. The National Agricultural Bio-Security System that is proposed to be established by the Ministry of Agriculture would initiate appropriate action in this regard.
- *Application of Information Technology*: Information and Communication Technology (ICT) would be utilized for collating information relating various weather, soil, water and pest related risks. Converting the information to knowledge and transforming into action required to prevent/manage the risk would be ensured through application of technology. Synergy in the existing efforts of various Ministries/Agencies to create a data base with advisory for farmers to effectively manage the risks would be emphasized.

Strengthening Weather Index-based Insurance

Weather insurance has emerged as a potent instrument for managing risks of farmers arising from weather vagaries. Its strengths of objectivity, transparency and faster settlement have been well-established during the five years of its usage in India. It also can virtually obviate the possibilities of moral hazard making it an attractive proposition for insurers. However, the two biggest limitations of the present weather-based crop insurance programme are: designing a proxy weather index with predictive capability to realistically measure crop losses taking into account the inter-farm variability; and the large basis risk inherent in the rainfall index which is the most preferred and widely-adopted weather index in India.

However, it can substantially contribute to improve the risk management in agriculture through following action points:

- *Weather index insurance products for crops where no historical yield estimates exist*: There are still crops in India which do not have adequate historical yield data or where the yield data is unviable/infeasible to collect. Many of these crops do not lend themselves to 'traditional insurance' due to either low value or high complexity. Weather insurance could be the answer for these crops and areas.
- *Use of weather index to design double trigger insurance products*: For major crops of India grown on a large scale, it can complement traditional crop insurance by acting as the basis for indemnifying catastrophic losses on account of weather events. This provides a scope to base a portion of the total crop insurance coverage of the farmer on weather index. The insurance product can be developed on two independent parameters (triggers)—1st trigger being weather index and would operate early; and 2nd trigger being area yield estimate and operate after harvesting of the crop.
- *Design of macro level insurance products using weather index*: Weather index based insurance could be an ideal tool for limiting state liability at District/Regional/State level against drought or floods. The macro level

weather index could be constructed using the network of weather stations at District/ Regional/ State level.

- *Infrastructure for collating weather data*: Weather data are critical for weather insurance to generate credible results in terms of payouts. The higher the quality of the data, the stronger would be the forecasting capability of the weather insurance models. There are about six lakh villages, about 2.7 lakh gram Panchayat and about 5000 blocks in the country. It would be difficult to set up weather stations/rain gauge stations at the level of gram Panchayat/village level. Assuming that a weather station can be representative in about 5 km radius, the country needs about 20000 automatic weather stations (AWS). If one automatic rain gauge (ARG) can be installed in a radius of about 2.5 km, then about 80000 ARGs would be required. This infrastructure can effectively cover the data at Panchayat level. At present, there are 550 weather stations and 3500 rain gauges functional in the country. One AWS can be set up in each block by IMD for crosschecking and validating the data. Hence about 5000 AWS cab be installed by IMD with an investment of about ₹ 50 crore, which can be shared equally by Central and State Governments. Rest of the AWSs and ARGs can be installed by private sector for which an appropriate revenue model would be worked out.

Blended Crop Insurance Products

During the recent years, the agriculture risk management sector has witnessed the introduction of a number of products which blend the features of the three major basis of indemnification namely area yield, weather index, and remote-sensing based indicators (like Normalized Difference Vegetative Index, Leaf Area Index, etc). Blended products, by their very nature, would be introduced as these products incorporate the respective strengths of indemnification parameters while limiting the undue dependence on any one of them.

Catastrophe Protection

Non-loanee farmers account for more than 50 per cent of the total farmer base in the context of institutional/formal sources of credit. Such a huge segment of farmers comprises mostly the non-loanee farmers, who are already devoid of cheaper institutional credit; virtually pay the penalty as they are largely left out of a majority of governmental programmes including the crop insurance programme. At present, there are provisions to provide relief to such farmers in case of catastrophic weather events or natural disasters, but the quantum of such relief is limited. In order to protect the non-borrowing farmers from extreme financial distress and provide basic economic security, 'Catastrophe Protection' for farmers as a safety net needs to be examined. This protection would operate in circumstances that manifest into large scale crop losses on account of extreme weather conditions.

Linking with Agricultural Relief Measures

Operation of Calamity Relief funds with objective of assisting the farmers affected by natural calamity needs further strengthening. Crop insurance can be used as a conduit for channelizing calamity and disaster relief funds from central and state governments. By linking relief funds to Crop Insurance or Catastrophe Insurance, the benefit of such relief can be passed on to the targeted groups with greater efficiency and transparency.

Integrated Farming System Insurance

Despite huge subsidy on the current crop insurance, its penetration has not been growing at desired pace. Steps would be taken for developing insurance products to address the needs of different farming systems, transition towards insurance of mixed crops and integrated farming systems with crop, livestock and fisheries having much lower risk perception compared to mono crop systems and with lower risk premium as a consequence.

Crop Insurance Under Contract Farming

With an increasing focus and participation of private sector entities across the entire agricultural value chain, the role of quality-oriented agricultural production is also gaining impetus through an increasing number of contract farming initiatives. It is a known fact that the economic exposure to uncontrollable risks is significantly higher for a farmer participating in contract farming initiative than his peers on account of the higher investments by the former for crop inputs, technology and quality control. In order to safeguard the interest of farmers participating in contract farming and to promote trials/adoption by other farmers through demonstration effect, crop insurance needs to be given the status of a mandatory input under contract farming initiatives. The responsibility of arranging crop insurance from suitable insurers may be with the contract farming sponsor or aggregator. Taking into account the diverse nature of crops covered under contract farming, it is essential to give thrust to new product development by insurers to cater to the demand by contract farming sponsors.

SHGs and other Farmers' Group-based Models of Crop Insurance

Self-help groups (SHGs) for rural women and farmers are one of those few programmes that have endured and given good results in terms of improving income and improving access to credit and marketing institutions. Their achievements have been impressive in mobilising the potential for savings and thrift even among the poorest of the poor. They have helped in delivering bank credit to the poor and in inculcating the habit of timely repayment of bank loans. With the outreach and penetration of self-help groups (SHGs) and other Farmers' Groups spreading deep into the rural hinterlands of India, there are enormous opportunities to leverage these SHGs for increasing the patronage and reach of crop insurance in India. In stead of covering individual farmers, farmers as a group can be covered under insurance products. SHGs and Farmers' Groups can also be utilized as a vehicle for change. Distribution and post-sales service delivery which is going to be a win-win proposition as it can reduce the typical insurance problems of moral hazard, high administrative and transaction costs, and lack of customer feedback and poor post sales service delivery.

Public-Private Partnerships in Agricultural Risk Management

The agricultural risk management sector in India can take cues from successful models of public-private partnership (PPP) in other countries. PPP would be encouraged under Area Yield Insurance in a phased manner. To begin with a 'co-insurance pool' would be created with scope for participation of private sector.

Capacity Building and Training

Self Help Groups (SHG) is found to be effective in empowering the farmers. SHGs will be strengthened for delivering bank credit and insurance facility. Capacity building and training of farmers through SHGs will be given high priority. SHGs would be provided with revolving funds. Farmers and elected Panchayat members would be trained to advise farmers for better management of floods, drought and aberrant monsoons would be accorded high priority.

PLAN OF ACTION

Priority Areas of Action	Further Action to beTaken
(i) Strengthening existing agricultural and weather insurance mechanisms	(i) Testing the efficacy of the severalexisting products under different production environments (ii) Develop models and methods of risk assessment under different risk regimes (iii) Strengthening and enforcement of insurance system and develop innovative products (iv) Strengthen SHGs and capacity building of farmers about risk prevention and mitigation (v) Implement proposed modified NAIS and widen scope of weather index based insurance
(ii) Development and validation of weather derivative models (by insurance providers ensuring their access to	(i) Derive demand-driven innovative products suitable for heterogeneous production systems (ii) Validation and piloting of different products

(*Contd...*)

archival and current weather data)	(iii) Develop business models for insurance products (iv) Develop insurance pricing mechanisms including actuarial methodology
(iii) Creation of web-enabled, regional language based services for facilitation of weather-based insurance	(i) Development of regional and sub-regional hub for identifying and assessing location specific requirement of insurance products to mitigate specific risk
(iv) Development of GIS and remotesensing methodologies for detailed soil resource mapping and land use planning at the level of a watershed or a river basis	(i) Creation of on-line data base and analysis using state of art tools.
(v) Mapping vulnerable eco-regions and pest and disease hotspots	(i) Identify the sources of risk (conventional and newer sources) (ii) Map the risk hotspots
(vi) Developing and implementation of region-specific contingency plans based on vulnerability and risk scenario	(i) Develop user-friendly decision support system to help assessing risk and develop region specific contingency plans.

COLLABORATING AGENCIES

Following are the collaborating agencies for above plan of action for strengthening agriculture risk management:

- *Research and Policy: National*: NCAP, NDRI, ICAR, IARI, IMD, CAZRI, CRIDA, SAUs, IFPRI, ICRISAT and India based CGIAR centres as well as the Insurance Companies in the public and private sector would be associated in the research and development for risk management.
- *Development and dissemination*: AIC, private insurance companies, SAUs. State Agriculture Departments, NGOs, civil society organizations and Farmers' groups.
- Develop location and situation specific insurance

products, which require real time data on disaggregated level and be orchestrated in collaboration with the Insurance Companies and the Economic Statistics wing of the Ministry of Agriculture as well as States, NIC and IMD.

FINANCIAL OUTLAY

DEVELOPMENT COMPONENT

It has been assumed that the proposed Modified NAIS is to be implemented on pilot basis in 100 districts during the remaining three years (2009 to 2012) of the 11th Five Year Plan. The penetration of the scheme has also been assumed at 25 per cent. The estimated financial implications to the Government would be about ₹.1, 839 crore (₹.613 crore per year). In case the Modified NAIS is to be implemented in all the 500 districts of the country at 25 per cent penetration the financial implications works out to ₹.3,065 crore approximately per annum. With penetration level of 50 per cent likely by start of the XII Plan, financial implication would be about ₹. 5,000 crore per annum for entire country and financial implication may be higher by about ₹.10, 000 crore for XII plan period. With increase in the risk pooling because of greater penetration the liability is not likely increase proportionately because of law large numbers and better risk management.

The outlay for strengthening of existing insurance products under development component is as per details in Annexure—V for total of about ₹. 17,214 crore (to be shared between Central Government and State Government at the ratio of 50:50) for XI and XII Plan period, assuming a penetration level (coverage) of 25 per cent. For higher level of penetration the financial implication would be about ₹. 5000 crore per annum assuming extension of Modified NAIS to the entire country and accordingly the financial implication would be higher. Above estimate of ₹. 17214 crore includes the cost of infrastructure required for expanding weather index based insurance products and most of the infrastructure is envisaged through private sector with an appropriate revenue model that will be worked out by Agricultural Insurance Corporation.

RESEARCH COMPONENT

	Groups	Coverage	Budget (₹. in Crore)
A	Risk and Insurance modelling. At least four groups will be identified covering the critical ecosystems to develop ecosystem based risk assessment methods and models to create appropriate insurance products including blended products farming system approach.	Strategic institutions/organizations	32.18 (details as in Annexure - VI)
B	Requirement analysis, Constraints Analysis, village survey and Pilot testing. A representative set of selected blocks will be studied.	Selected sampling of desirable size with proper representation	Included in A
C	Capacity building, training, advocacy and Dissemination	Implementation and dissemination	10.00
	Total		₹. 42.18 Say 42.00 Crore

GENERAL SYSTEMS CLASSIFICATION

Discussion and analysis of systems can be of them as *actual systems* (*e.g.*, of constituent physical processes in the case of natural physical systems) or as *representational systems.* Common representations or models of actual systems take such forms as written descriptions, physical models, mathematical models, flowcharts, tables of data and computer programmes. In the following discussion, reference is to representational systems.

NATURAL, SOCIAL AND ARTIFICIAL SYSTEMS

Systems can be classified into three broad families or divisions as either natural, social or artificial systems (See Figure on page 71).

- *Natural systems*: Those that exist in Nature - consist of all the materials (both physical and biological) and interrelated processes occurring to these materials which constitute the world and, *inter alia,* provide the physical basis for life. They exist independent of mankind. Our role in relation to natural systems is to try to understand them and, as need be, make use of them. We also (increasingly) attempt to duplicate them, in part or whole; but at this point they become, by definition, man-made or artificial systems. These fundamental natural systems remain unaffected by attempts at imitation. Those natural physical and biological systems (shown in their totality as the division of natural systems in Figure) which are relevant to agriculture will be self-apparent: rock weathering to form soil; plants sustained by such soil; animals sustained by such plants... are examples of the outward forms of agriculturally relevant natural systems in operation.

- *Social systems* are more difficult to define. Essentially they consist of the entities forming animate populations, the institutions or social mechanisms created by such entities, and the interrelationships among/between individuals, groups, communities, expressed directly or through the medium of institutions. Social systems involve relationships between animate populations (individuals, groups, communities), not between things. Concern here is with human social systems as they relate to or impinge upon farming, and the term social system is used broadly to include institutions and relationships of an economic, social, religious or political nature. There is a certain degree of ambiguity in defining social systems. As an example, the law of property is in its essence a social system. Insofar as it is viewed as consisting of concepts, principles and rules, it is a pure social system, independent of natural systems. But its existence also presupposes the existence of property, including natural physical things, some of which exist as systems. To this extent, as a social system the law of property is dependent on or subordinate to natural systems.
- *Artificial systems* do not exist in Nature. They are of human creation to serve human purposes. All artificial systems, including agricultural systems, are constructed from either or both of two kinds of elements:

– Elements taken from either or both of the other two higher-level orders of systems at division level, *i.e.*, from natural and social systems, and

– From elements which are constructed or Proposed for specific use by each respective artificial system as the need for this arises.

The upper part of Figure depicts the dependence relationship between natural and social systems on the one hand and between these and artificial systems on the other.

The relevant relationships are:

- Natural systems are independent of systems of the other divisions;
- Social systems could also be viewed as being independent, but generally a more legitimate view would be that they depend immediately or eventually on natural systems for the essentials of their material existence; and
- Artificial systems are directly dependent on either or both natural and social systems, or indirectly on natural systems (through the dependence of social systems themselves on natural systems).

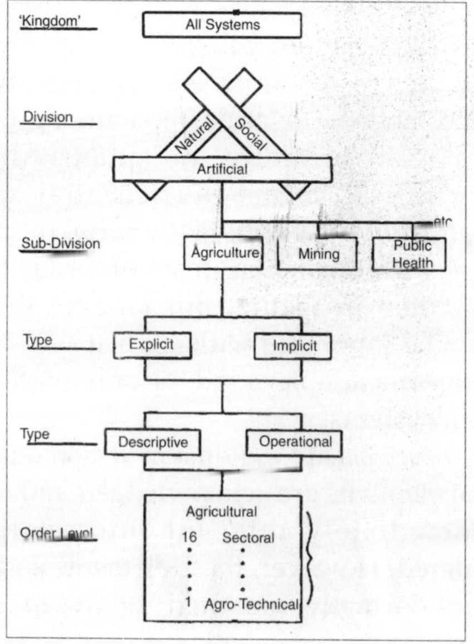

In the Figure, agriculture is shown as comprising one of a very large number of actual or potential artificial systems at the sub-division level. Others are those relating to mining, transport, public health, education etc. What such systems at this sub-divisional level have in common is that each is artificial: each is based upon or draws elements from higher-level natural and social systems; and each also contains elements which are purposefully created by some human agency in order to meet its needs.

FURTHER SUB-CLASSIFICATION OF SYSTEMS

As shown in Figure, systems within the three broad divisions or their multitudinous subdivisions can be further classified according to system 'type', a loose term but one which might be used to differentiate among agricultural systems according to a number of factors of which only two are shown in the sketch. As outlined below, first, the system might be either an explicit or implicit one; second, its purpose might be either descriptive or operational.

Other 'type' designations could be added; e.g., operational systems could be further classified according to whether or not they are amenable to optimization:

- *Explicit systems* are those in which the constituent elements are more or less closely identified and defined, and the relationships among these elements are stated formally in quantitative, usually mathematical, terms. Agricultural scientists and economists who work with farmers are concerned mainly with explicit systems of Order Levels 1 to 10 as specified in Figure. But farmers themselves will seldom be concerned with explicit systems - only with systems of a simpler kind, or only with selected parts of such systems.
- *Implicit systems* are systems in which only the main or critical elements are acknowledged and only the major or immediately relevant interrelationships are considered. However, these elements and relationships are not formally recorded, analysed or evaluated.

Farmers themselves deal primarily with implicit systems. In both traditional and more modem societies particular agricultural systems of Order Levels 1 to 10 are implied in what farmers do, or deliberately do not do. In more 'advanced' societies, farmers might formalize and work with a few explicit systems or parts of systems (farm record books, simple crop budgets, household expenditure accounts) but here also most agro-management systems will exist by implication.

The purpose in here distinguishing between explicit and implicit systems is to discourage the view that, because farmers (especially small traditional farmers) do not deal with explicit formal systems, these farmers are backward, ignorant, unsophisticated and generally inferior as resource managers. If anything, the facts generally point to a contrary conclusion. While bad farmers can be found anywhere, any close study of small traditional farmers and farming villages in the developing world will, with patience, identify implicit systems at agro-technical, enterprise, farm, farm-household and village levels which are far more complex, sophisticated, sustainable and socially efficient than most agricultural systems found in developed countries.

- *Descriptive systems* are usually intended to facilitate an understanding of the organization, structure or operation of a productive process. This might be their sole purpose; *e.g.*, a farmer might construct a simple input-output budget table in order to learn the structural configurations of some potential new crop. Depending on the results of this, he or she might then proceed to construct a more detailed budget (an operational system) to find how best to fit this new crop into his or her farm plan. At higher Order Levels an organogram describing the administrative structure of a ministry of agriculture or of an extension service might be constructed or the flowchart of a commodity from farm to consumer might be drawn—these also are descriptive systems.

- *Operational systems* are constructed (by an analyst or manager or research worker) as a basis for taking or recommending action aimed at improving the performance of the system. Such systems are often elaborate (as exemplified in Chapters). However, increased precision is not infrequently achieved at the cost of decreased practical usefulness. Thus farm managers themselves work primarily with simple operational systems, although the actual physical systems which these represent may be very complex.

As outlined by Dillon (1992), it is also sometimes useful to recognize that, like other systems, agricultural systems may be categorized as:

- *Purposeful* or *non-purposeful* depending on whether or not they can select goals and the means by which to achieve them.
- *Static* or *dynamic* depending on whether or not they change over time in response to internal or external influences.
- *Open* or *closed* depending on whether or not they interact with their environment.
- *Abstract* or *concrete* depending on whether or not they are conceptual or physical in nature.
- *Deterministic* or *stochastic* depending on whether or not their behaviour exhibits randomness over time, *i.e.*, their future behaviour is uncertain.

AGRICULTURAL SYSTEMS CLASSIFICATION AND ORDER HIERARCHY

Agricultural and particularly farming systems exhibit great diversity as shown by, *e.g.*, Duckham and Masefield, Grigg, Kostrowicki and Ruthenberg. They have been classified in various ways as reviewed by Fresco and Westphal who also present an ecologically-based classification and typology of farm systems. The hierarchical classification of farm systems presented here is distinctly different.

It is specifically oriented

- To a farm management and farm-household perspective; and

- To use as a framework for analysis of what are proposed as the six basic types of farms found in Asia (and elsewhere in the developing world).

Figure 2.1 is an elaboration of the lower part of figure and relates specifically to agricultural systems. These are listed in largely hierarchical order encompassing 16 Order Levels. Alternatively, with a few minor exceptions, the Order Levels 1 to 16 could have been depicted, reflecting their nested character, as a set of concentric circles with Order Level 1 as the innermost and Order Level 16 as the outermost circle. In Figure 2.1, the sectoral system, 'all agriculture', is specified as being of the highest order rank, *i.e.*, Order Level 16. Any national or regional agricultural sector, however, consists of such subordinate sub-sectors or subsystems as agricultural credit, education, research, production, transport etc. Each of these constitutes and would be analysed, administered and managed as a system of Order Level 15.

Each such (sub)system may then be further disaggregated into commodity-based industry systems of Order Level 14 such as for coconuts, rubber, wheat, coffee, fish etc. If that flow-path relating to production is being followed, as depicted in Figure, this would then lead to villages or other community units where such production occurs (systems of Order Level 13); these would in turn consist of and could be disaggregated into the individual farm-household systems of Order Level 12 which comprise such villages. Further lower Order Level systems relate to the agro-economic structure of individual farms and, in turn, their component crop and livestock enterprises and to the activities and individual agro-technical processes which underlie such enterprises.

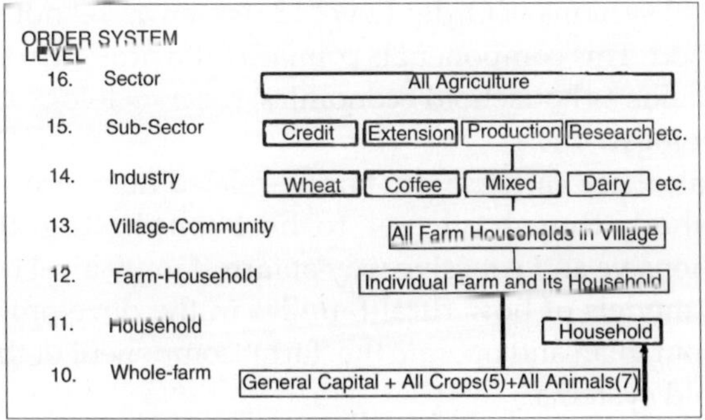

(Contd...)

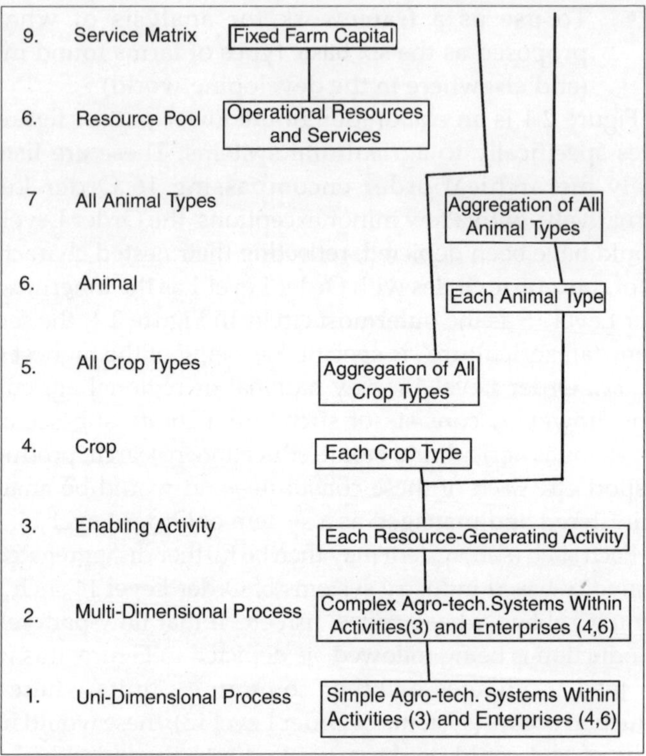

Fig 2.1 The Hierarchy of Agricultural Systems

Systems of Order Levels 1 to 12 comprise the field of farm management. But systems of Order Level 1 and 2 are also, indeed primarily, the domain of the applied agricultural sciences. A further proviso is that the 'household' components of farm-household systems of Order Level 12 remain as yet not very well understood. This component is primarily the province of workers in such fields as household economics, rural sociology and social anthropology.

While these various farm family-related fields are fairly well established, they have yet to be brought together in a comprehensive and cohesive way at farm-family level to provide verified models of how rural families in the developing world think about, plan and operate the 'farm' component of their farm-household systems.

Figure 2.1 depicts the direction of hierarchical status as proceeding downward from sector to industry to village to farm to crop etc. But whether this direction of subordination is valid will depend on circumstances and analytical purpose. Agricultural scientists would probably reverse the order-ranking shown for the systems on the grounds that, unless the basic agro-technical processes (Order Level 1 and 2 systems) are well developed, the production of individual crops will be inefficient, total farm production will be low and the agricultural sector itself will in consequence be an impoverished one. Similarly extension workers might be inclined to place household systems at the top of the systems hierarchy on the basis that good farming practices (Order Level 1 and 2 systems) will not be adopted unless the household systems are working well, nor consequently will the 'higher'-order systems at industry and sector level operate at their full potential.

NATURE OF FARM-LEVEL SYSTEMS

The nature of each farm-level system (i.e., Order Levels 1 to 12) of the hierarchy presented in Figure 2.1 may be specified from a management point of view as follows:

- *Order Level 1: Uni-dimensional process systems.* Systems of this lowest order are of an agro-technical nature. They involve an issue or problem which for purposes of analysis or management is abstracted from the context in which it naturally or normally occurs. One example is the application of a single fertilizer element, say nitrogen (N), to a crop and consequent plant response to N in terms of crop yield Y. As noted previously, systems of this order are primarily the domain of physical scientists, but those systems which have practical relevance for farmers thereby also have an economic dimension and so fall within the scope of farm economics. Such simple single-dimensional systems are later examined as processes and as input-output response relationships.
- *Order Level 2: Multi-dimensional process systems.* Systems of this second order are also concerned with limited

agro-technical relationships and again they are primarily the domain of physical scientists. They differ from Order Level 1 systems in that they take - or are defined to take—a wider and more realistic view of a subject or problem. To use the same example of fertilizer response: at Order Level 2 an agro-technical system might involve the response of plant growth or yield *Y* to not one but to several or a large number of input factors such as nitrogen, phosphorous, irrigation water, crop hygiene, soil tilth etc. These multi-dimensional systems also are later examined as processes and as response relationships. Order Level 2 systems can be viewed as aggregations (often interactive) of constituent Order Level 1 systems.

- *Order Level 3: Enabling-activity systems.* Systems of this order are certain enabling activities which generate an intermediate product intended for use as an input/ resource by enterprises which do produce a final product. An example is offered by a legume crop turned under to provide fertility for a following (final product-generating) paddy crop. There will often be alternative ways of obtaining this resource: *e.g.*, stripping leaves off leguminous trees, keeping cattle for their manure, or buying a bag of fertilizer. These are all enabling, resource-generating activities but only some of them, the complex ones, warrant designation as systems. They are intended to supply resources to systems of Order Levels 4 and 6.
- *Order Level 4: Crop systems.* Systems of this order relate to the production of individual crops; but if these are primarily intended to produce inputs for other crops or livestock, they are regarded as systems of Order Level 3. On many small farms, crop and livestock enterprises produce both final products and resources.
- *Order Level 5: All crop systems.* Systems of this order, known also as *cropping systems,* refer to the combined

system of all the individual crops on a farm. On a farm with a single mono-crop, this Order Level 5 system will obviously be equivalent to an Order Level 3 system; but on small mixed farms there will usually be four, five, six or more different crops (of Order Levels 3 and 4) grown in some degree of combination and as many as 20 or more on the highly diversified forest-garden farms of South Asia.

- *Order Level 6: Animal systems.* These systems relate to single-species animal enterprises or activities - *e.g.*, dairy cows, camels, fish, ducks. They are the animal equivalent of Order Level 4 (*i.e.*, individual crop) systems.
- *Order Level 7: All animal systems.* These systems are the aggregation of all Order Level 6 (sub)systems on a farm. Known as *livestock systems*, they are the animal equivalent of Order Level 5 (*i.e.*, all crop) systems.
- *Order Level 8: Resource pool.* This subsystem is a conceptual device for farm-system planning in which resources and fixed-capital services required by other subsystems are 'stored' in a 'resource pool' from which they are allocated to the other subsystems (of Order Levels 1, 2, 3, 4 and 6). The resource pool is central to operation of the whole farm-household system. It is discussed in Chapter 3.
- *Order Level 9: Farm service matrix.* A system of this Order Level consists of all the fixed capital resources of a farm which are pertinent to the operation of the farm as a whole but are not assigned to the exclusive use of any particular enterprise or activity: land, fences, barns, irrigation channels and work oxen are common examples. Some of these capital items are true (sub)systems, having interdependence among their component parts (as in an irrigation storage/ delivery/distribution network, a grain drying facility, an integrated network of soil conservation structures etc.). Some are only things (*e.g.*, fences, a plough, a barn). But, in its totality, such capital is managed and

manipulated as a system for the purpose of providing general services which, while not specific to them, enable the functioning of lower Order Level systems of the farm.

- *Order Level 10: Whole-farm systems.* Systems of this Order Level consist of all the lower Order Level (sub)systems which go to make up a farm. They consolidate in a single entity all the farm fixed capital, all the operating capital, all the final-product enterprises, all the activities and all the agro-technical processes which underlie such enterprises and activities. Structuring and managing systems of this Order Level are the main tasks or focus of farm management as carried out, on the one hand, by farmers and as investigated, on the other hand, by farm management economists in their professional capacity of providing advice to farm managers, development agencies and governments.

  The terms farm *system* and *farming system* are often used interchangeably. Here the practice is to use farm system to refer to the structure of an individual farm, and farming system to refer to broadly similar farm types in specific geographical areas or recommendation domains, *e.g.*, the wet paddy farming system of West Java or the grain-livestock fanning systems of Sind.

- *Order Level 11: Household systems.* On small farms the household itself is the most dynamic and complex of all farm-level systems, although it is a social system not an agricultural one. It dominates the agricultural systems which comprise the farm component. It has two functions: as *household* it provides purpose and management to the farm component, and as major system *beneficiary* it receives and allocates system outputs to itself and other beneficiaries.
- *Order Level 12: Farm-household Systems.* These consist of two components or (sub)systems of Order Levels

10 and 11, *i.e.*, the whole-farm system and its associated household system, respectively. The term is a very useful if not mandatory one when used to refer to the small farms of Asia. It carries an insistence that the technical analysis discussed in following chapters will amount to nothing at all unless it is applied to achieving the real needs and aspirations of the household—which, as discussed in Chapter 6, might be quite a different thing from evaluating the performance of a farm system according to the subjective or preconceived ideas of agricultural technicians and economists. As the peak farm-level system, the farm-household system may be described in system terms as a goal-setting (*i.e.*, purposeful) open stochastic dynamic system with a major aim of production from agricultural resources. These attributes are sufficient to make it also a complex system. The purposefulness of a farm-household system is ensured by its human and social involvement which enables the system to vary its goals and their means of achievement under a given environment. The openness of the farm-household system is obvious from its physical, economic and social interaction with its environment. The non-deterministic or stochastic nature of the farm-household system is guaranteed both by the free-choice capacity of its human (and, if present, animal) elements and by the stochastic nature of the environment with which it (and all its subsystems) interacts. Necessarily, a farm-household system is also dynamic by virtue of its purposefulness, openness and stochasticity which ensure that the system changes over time. Too, any farm-household system is a mixture of abstract and concrete elements or subsystems. The concrete elements are associated with the physical activities and processes that occur in the system. The abstract elements relate to the managerial and social aspects of the system.

VILLAGE-LEVEL FARMING SYSTEMS

Not infrequently in parts of Asia, as also elsewhere in the developing world, the village may replace the farm-household in whole or part as the focal entity for agricultural production.

Systems of Order Level 13, i.e., village or community systems, are thus often relevant to the performance of farming systems.

- *Order Level 13: Village-community Systems.* Village-level systems or community systems in some situations replace all or part of individual farm-household systems. Three situations are common. *First,* some production activity in its entirety, including the operation of whole farms as production units, may be on a formal cooperative or group basis. *Second,* only part of an activity might be carried on by individual farmers while critical parts of it (such as land preparation, the supply of inputs, harvesting and/or marketing) are the responsibility of a formal farmers' club or cooperative. *Third,* and most difficult to analyse, is the situation found in many Indonesian villages where informal and temporary groups form to perform certain production tasks in common (such as land preparation, irrigation and/or harvesting) then disband and re-form to do different tasks on different crops, with membership continuously changing as individuals drop in and out of groups according to their interests, needs and mutual obligations. In a village there might be 10, 20 or 30 such 'cooperatives', though none might exist officially. Other examples are offered by the semi-nomadic livestock farmers of West Asia who sometimes operate as individual households and sometimes as members of a collective. In all these situations the boundaries of individual units are often so fluid and obscure that the focus for productive analysis has to be the group or village community. (Nevertheless, much externally sponsored farm-development planning remains locked into the mythology of agricultural individualism; perhaps that is why on the small farms of Asia it has borne so little and often poisonous fruit.)

Before proceeding, however, it will be useful to examine those constituent structural elements of a farm-household system which are relevant to its organization and management.

STRUCTURAL ELEMENTS OF THE FARM-HOUSEHOLD SYSTEM

The definition of an agricultural system given in Section 1.1 is a general one and applies broadly to systems of all the Order Levels.

When applied specifically to a farm-household system of Order Level 12 it implies the system involves ten structural elements or components:

- Boundaries
- Household
- Operating plan
- Production-enabling resources: the resource pool
- Final product-generating enterprises
- Resource-generating activities
- Agro-technical processes
- Whole-farm service matrix
- Structural (interdependence) coefficients
- Time dimension.

Those elements marked by an asterisk have been considered above as subsystems of the farm-household system. The ten elements are briefly discussed below and, except for structural coefficients and the time dimension, their interrelationships as components of a farm-household system of Order Level 12 are sketched in the example of Figure where they are denoted E1, E2... E8.

- *Boundaries:* This first element, the boundaries of the farm-household system, set it apart from other systems and from the world at large. These boundaries are provided partly by the structural characteristics of the particular type of farm, and partly by the purpose of analysis, *i.e.*, to some extent they are subjective and relate to more than the simple physical boundary of the farm. Boundaries are discussed in Chapter.

- *Household:* As previously noted, the household plays two roles: first, it provides purpose and management to its associated farm system and, second, it is the major beneficiary of its associated farm system. Its role as beneficiary is discussed. In its first role it provides purpose, operating objectives and management to the farm component of the farm-household system according to its broad domestic and social goals. Obviously these goals vary widely with culture, tradition and the degree of commercialisation and external influences to which the household is exposed. However, one would probably be not too far wrong in offering a generalization that the primary economic goal on most small farms is security and the primary non-economic goal is social acceptance. If this is correct, the primary objectives for the farm are, first, production of a low-risk sustainable subsistence for primary system beneficiaries; second, generation of a cash income to meet needs not directly met in the form of food and other farm-produced materials; and third, pursuit of both of these in ways which are not in conflict with local culture and tradition. Goals, objectives and planning criteria are discussed.
- *Operating plan:* The above objectives are pursued through preparation and execution of a farm operating plan. The core of this may be taken as selection of the best possible mix of agro-technical processes, activities, enterprises and fixed capital (systems of Order Levels 1, 2, 3, 4, 6 and 8). Formulation of operating plans is discussed.
- *Resource pool:* This element was noted above as a system of Order Level 8 central to the management of other subsystems within the farm system. It is discussed in Chapter.
- *Final product-generating enterprises:* These were noted as systems of Order Levels 5 and 7 in the previous section and are discussed.

- *Resource-generating activities:* These also were previously discussed as systems of Order Level 3. They are intended to supplement or entirely supply the resource pool as discussed.
- *Agro-technical processes:* These were defined above as systems of Order Levels 1 and 2. Processes may be of a biological or mechanical kind. They are a shorthand designation of all the potentially complex and interrelated physical and biological factors underlying production from crop or livestock species, only some of which may be economically relevant.
- *Whole-farm service matrix:* This was discussed previously as a system of Order Level 9. It is further examined.
- *System structural coefficients:* These coefficients identify and quantify linkage relationships
  — Among the various parts or elements within each sub-system; and
  — Between subsystems. From the general system definition, an essential property of any system is that there be interrelatedness between its parts. In farm-household systems (and in subordinate subsystems of lesser Order Level, particularly Order Levels 4 and 6) such interrelatedness is specified by these coefficients.
- *Time dimension:* Unlike mechanical systems which stamp out buttons or TV sets, agricultural systems rest on biological processes which occur over considerable periods of time from, *e.g.*, a few days in the case of quick-response agricides to 70 or more years in the case of growth and decline of a coconut palm. Agricultural systems are thus inherently stochastic: being dependent on the passage of time, *ex ante,* their outcomes are uncertain. Moreover, because agriculture is also a set of economic activities, the old adage applies: time is money. Other things being equal, a system which yields its product or ties up resources over a short time is better than one

which yields its output or occupies resources over a long time. Strictly speaking, time is not a system component; rather it is a dimension in which the system operates. The time dimension in relation to resource use is discussed. The evaluation of activities which occur over long time periods is examined. The latter chapter also considers uncertainty as it occurs in farm planning and decision making. Also important from a time perspective are the sustainability and environmental compatibility of the farm system being used. If, over time, the farm system is not biologically and economically sustainable or causes resource degradation, as discussed, this is to the disadvantage of both the farm household and society at large.

STRUCTURAL MODEL OF A FARM-HOUSEHOLD SYSTEM

Before examining the elements of a farm-household system in more detail in later chapters it is useful to consider where they lie in relation to each other in the structure of a small mixed farm as exemplified in Figure 2.2.

Element 1, system boundaries: Depending on the purpose of analysis, the farm-household system may be specified with different boundaries. In Figure, these are suggested by the shaded circle around the system which sets it apart from other neighbouring systems and from the larger community or environment in which it is imbedded.

Element 2, household: As noted at the top of Figure, the household provides objectives and management of the farm-household system and, at the bottom, it exists as the primary internal beneficiary of the system, while distributing some of the system output to external beneficiaries.

Element 3, Operating Plan: As shown in Figure, this is determined largely by the household but it might also be influenced by the requirements of external individuals, agencies or other influences, some of whom might be (external) beneficiaries of the system as outlined below.

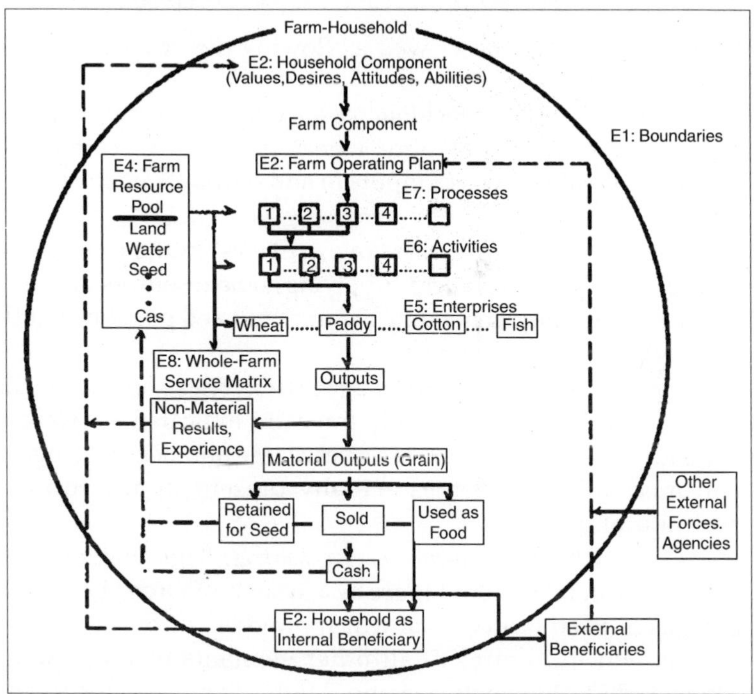

Fig 2.2 Interrelationships of Elements in a Simple Farm-household System

Element 4, Resource Pool: This element consists of resources which are initially present at the time of planning or commencing operation of the system—some pool or stock of land, water, seed, cash etc. which the other elements of the farm system may draw upon. Once the system begins operating, certain components of it (the resource-generating activities and by-products of the enterprises) will replenish the pool.

In the schematic sketch of Figure, the arrows from the farm resource pool indicate that items from the resource pool flow to processes as well as to activities and to enterprises (as well as possibly to maintenance of the whole-farm service matrix). Strictly speaking, resources should be shown as flowing directly only to processes, since this is the level (subsystems of Order Levels 1 and 2) at which they are actually used. But from a practical viewpoint and because most of the potential processes are actually ignored in planning the operation of a farm system, resources may also be viewed as flowing directly to activities and enterprises as indicated.

Element 5, final-product Enterprises: Only four enterprises are shown in the system of Figure: wheat, paddy (rice), cotton and fish. Only the flow lines of inputs to and output from the paddy crop are shown.

Element 6, Resource-generating Activities: In the example of Figure, there are two of these supplying some resources to paddy (*e.g.*, a prior fertility-generating legume crop and possibly a cattle activity providing oxpower).

Element 7, Agro-technical Processes: These underlie the activities and enterprises. Only three are indicated as relevant to paddy in Figure but there are a very large number of biological and mechanical processes actually present in any form of agricultural production.

Element 8, Whole-farm Service Matrix: This was defined previously in relation to Figure as a system of Order Level 9. It consists of fixed farm capital which provides a flow of services (not shown in Figure) to all other elements of the system, particularly to Elements 5, 6 and 7 but it is not specific to any one of them.

Element 9, Structural Coefficients: These are not depicted in Figure.

Element 10, Time: In the schematic example of Figure, the time dimension is not specified explicitly but the model would probably refer to a single operating phase with a duration equal to the life of the longest-term enterprise subsystem, here cotton with a term of six to seven months, or, if climatic seasons are constraining, to a full seasonal cycle of one year. If the system proves to be a 'good' system in terms of household objectives, it might be reactivated in successive phases and continue indefinitely; if a 'very good' system it might permit further farm intensification and development; if a 'bad' system it might be restructured; if a 'very bad' system it will, in the absence of restructuring, prove to be non-sustainable and eventually collapse.

Figure 2.2 is intended only as a schematic example to indicate the broad relationships which the elements of a farm-household and its associated whole-farm system bear to each other. Real small-farm systems are much more complex than Figure suggests, particularly in their internal cycling of resources. The following chapters are essentially an elaboration of Figure 2.2 in terms of managerial considerations.

Outputs of the farm component of the farm-household system depicted in Figure are, as an example, shown as flowing from the paddy enterprise. They do not comprise a separate element but are part of Element 5 (final-product enterprises). Outputs are allocated to the farm component and to system beneficiaries. Thus, to enable continuation of the system in subsequent phases (seasons or years), some paddy grain output is cycled back to the resource pool to replenish the seed stock. Similarly, to replenish the cash resource which was used up in this phase, some rice grain is sold.

Whatever grain is left might also be sold to generate cash income or be used as food. These latter outputs will be distributed among system beneficiaries who might be internal to the system, *i.e.*, the household, or external to it. External primary beneficiaries may consist of needy relatives and friends, landless neighbours, a landlord receiving cash or part of the crop as rent etc. External secondary beneficiaries, as discussed, might also be present - usually the tax collector. External beneficiaries often also play another role: they can exercise a direct influence on how the system is planned, constructed and operated. This influence is indicated in Figure by the broken line indicating feedback from external beneficiaries to Element 3, formulation of the farm plan. Returning to the paddy flow column of Figure, the system will also generate a second type of output apart from the material one of grain, namely *non-material output.*

This consists of the knowledge and experience gained from operating the system over any phase. Farm-household systems are dynamic: the results of one operating phase flow back not only as products giving sustenance and cash income to the household but also as knowledge and experience to influence the formulation of plans for future phases.

3

Farm Management

INTRODUCTION

SCOPE

To a layman 'farm management' probably means just that—a body of activities and procedures carried out by a farmer in the ongoing management of his or her farm and for which advice may be available from professional specialists in farm management. To an extent this is correct (as per farm management in Field A) but, more broadly, farm management as considered here is a professional discipline which relates to the description, construction, analysis and evaluation of farm systems of Order Level 10 (Figure). In this wider sense, farm management is the discipline within whose ambit farm-level systems analysis most clearly falls. (This does not exclude from farm systems analysis other disciplines of a technical or special-purpose nature.) Farm management system analysis can have several operating *objectives*; there are several alternative *bases* on which analysis can proceed; and it can operate in four *fields* and in four *modes* within these fields. These several aspects of farm management as a systems-related discipline are now briefly discussed in turn.

DEFINITION

Except when it serves a descriptive purpose, farm management is the science (and art) of optimizing the use of resources in the farm component of farm-households, *i.e.*, in systems of Order Level 10, and of achieving the optimal functioning of these systems in relation to household-specified objectives; and since Order Level 10 systems consist structurally of subsystems, farm management is also concerned with the operation of subservient subsystems of Order Levels 1 to 9 in such fashion as to optimize the whole-farm system. However, for reasons discussed in Chapter, it is often essential, especially when dealing with small farms, that farm management extends also to the family or household component, thus its true scope extends to Order Level 12 systems. A second consideration is that the village is sometimes a more relevant unit for analysis than the farm, and where this is so the scope of 'farm' management extends to systems of Order Levels 1 to 13.

OPTIMIZATION

Optimization of the planning objective is defined as achieving the farm household's goals as efficiently as possible in the face of whatever constraints of a physical, environ-mental, legal or socio-cultural nature may be relevant. This implies obtaining maximum possible net benefit over time from the operation of the farm system. Net benefit is measured, as appropriate, in terms of output or profit or, more broadly, as satisfaction or utility. Maximization of net benefit implies efficient use of available resources and opportunities. For the achievement of a given level of net benefit, it implies the minimization of costs.

This reflects a theoretical view. In the real world, as discussed in Chapter, the general objective is often constrained by household and social factors other than availability of physical inputs and their costs. Thus many small-farm households place a high value on the long-term sustainability of their farm system. Also, in the real world, uncertainty will generally prevail about yields, prices and other relevant influences so that the farmer's choice will lie not between sure alternatives but between alternative (subjective) probability distributions of net benefits..

Optimization can occur at two levels: local or global. When operating in Field A, farm management will seek optimization at the global level of the Order Level 12 farm-household system. This sets it apart from other farm-related agricultural sciences which are usually (though not always) concerned primarily with optimization of lower order subsystems, *i.e.*, local optimization. Two examples will clarify this point. First, a farm might involve only two irrigated crops, cotton and sugarcane. If only the cotton is considered, the local optimum might be to use all of the water supply on cotton, but if the farm as a whole is considered, *i.e.*, a global optimum sought, this might well require that the water be shared between both crops.

Second, a farm-household system itself might be only a subsystem within some larger system. For example, the optimal irrigation water supply to a farm might, from the viewpoint of the farm, be 1 000 m^3, but if such water is to be provided only as a minor by-product by a large multipurpose dam project (the chief purposes of which are power generation and flood control), these purposes will determine what discharge rate/farm supply is optimal from an overall project or global viewpoint and this would override whatever supply rate might be optimal from a farm perspective.

OBJECTIVES

Optimization of farm-household systems takes the form of conditional maximization over time of the socioeconomic welfare of farm families. The term 'welfare' is used broadly to include money income, sustenance food, farm-produced consumption goods and factors of production, non-material benefits such as those enabling the attainment of education and health standards, and satisfactions derived from work well done as well as from cultural and religious sources. Whichever of these system outputs/ family benefits are relevant in a particular farm situation will depend on the farm type and on the values held by the particular family-values which will normally reflect the society and cultural context in which the farm-household exists. Welfare maximization is conditional because it is constrained by resource availability and, as relevant, legal constraints and socio-cultural mores.

Typically the farm plays only an enabling role towards achieving broad family goals. Thus farm management is concerned with conditional optimization of only part of a farm-household system—but usually the most important material part. The specific objective might be to maximize money profit or, recognizing the presence of uncertainty, to maximize the expected utility of risky profit (farms of Type 4, 5 and 6 and possibly Type 3), or such money profit might be only incidental to other objectives (Type 2 farms), or hardly relevant at all (Type 1 farms).

ECONOMICS AS THE FRAMEWORK FOR FARM-SYSTEM ANALYSIS

Economics or *economic analysis* is the science of making choices so as to best achieve desired objectives given that only limited (physical and other) resources and opportunities are available and that the future is uncertain. There are no choices to which the science of economics cannot be applied. It is just as pertinent, *e.g.*, to the choice of a spouse as to the choice of which crops to grow or to the choice between using an insecticide or using environmentally friendly integrated pest management. In contrast to this wide applicability of economic analysis, *financial analysis* is restricted to matters that are naturally of a financial or monetary nature.

Financial analysis is thus a subset of economic analysis and, in circumstances where everything is valued in money terms, may be the natural way in which to conduct economic analysis. In other cases, it may be feasible to facilitate economic analysis of possible choices by imputing money values to possible gains and losses. And in yet other cases, such as assessing the resource sustainability and environmental compatibility of alternative farm systems, it may often be infeasible to impute money values to the gains and losses of alternative choices. Decisions must then be made using economic analysis based on non-money values, intuition and judgement.

Farm management economics (*i.e.*, economic analysis applied to the choices confronting farmers) provides the general disciplinary basis for farm-level systems analysis. Obviously other farm and family-related disciplines will be involved in systems' construction: agronomy, animal husbandry, soil and water conservation/management, human nutrition etc. However, except in the case of special-purpose technical systems (*e.g.*, when the farm-household unit is analysed in terms of nutritional or energy flows among components as discussed below), these other disciplines should play subordinate contributing roles coordinated by farm management economics as the lead discipline. That in fact this often does not happen and the lead is taken instead by workers in other disciplines is really not important. It might just reflect the fact that many agriculturists are aware of the necessity for a systems approach if application of their expertise is to be effective; or that many agricultural economists are content in the more modest role of economics apparachnik.

Nevertheless, the disciplinary basis of farm management remains economics - but economics of a special wide-ranging kind, the core of which is production economics supported by other branches of economics of which marketing, resource economics, agricultural credit and data analysis (including operations research, econometrics and risk analysis) are probably the most important. When working with the household component, especially of small traditional farms, the most important supporting disciplines are sociology and social anthropology.

ALTERNATIVE BASES FOR FARM-SYSTEM ANALYSIS

There are several reasons why farm economics provides a good conceptual framework for most farm-household systems analysis. The most important of these is the necessity to bring the many relationships of a system and between systems to some common unit or basis of comparison. Unless this is done, systems analysis and the comparison of alternatives will not be possible. The base usually most convenient—and in the case of commercial farm systems most relevant and which has the highest degree of universality—is money or financial value. But several other bases for systems analysis are possible and in certain circumstances they might well be more relevant than money value.

The four most important bases of comparison are as follows:

- *Money Value:* The convenience of using money or financial values as the basis of commercial farm systems analysis will be obvious: it permits the various system inputs (*e.g.*, seed, fertilizer, power, labour etc.) to be standardized as money costs and the various system outputs to be standardized as money returns so that net revenue, *i.e.*, money returns minus money costs, can be used as the basis of comparison between alternatives. In commercial farming, all or most of these inputs/costs and outputs/revenues can be stated in explicit quantitative terms. On the other hand, when dealing with less commercialized systems where there are no actual price-setting markets for farm inputs and/ or outputs, one is often obliged to base the analysis on imputed values. However, this is possible only up to a point; beyond this point, as one moves further from a commercial environment towards a traditional one, the attempted use of money value as the basis or numéraire for analysis becomes too abstract to be useful and one has to search for some other base.

- *Family Labour Effort:* Probably the best alternative to money value on small family farms of a subsistence or semi-subsistence nature is labour input, both as a measure of inputs and as a yardstick to judge the worth of outputs. At least this is so in the eyes of the majority of Asian (and African) small-farm families for two reasons. First, on these farms most production activities involve few if any commercial inputs and most outputs are also not disposed of through commercial channels. Money hardly enters into the matter at all. What such activities do have as their common factor is family labour—often very hard labour—from hand-preparation of fields, to carrying all inputs/outputs perhaps long distances, to hand-pounding the harvested grain. Not unnaturally then, these families plan, compare and evaluate their several different farming activities and alternatives (*i.e.*, analyse their systems) in terms of labour content. To conduct such analysis on any other basis such as money value would be an incomprehensible abstraction. However, 'labour' is not a simple quantity. It can have several dimensions: quantity when labour is measured in terms of standardized units (*e.g.*, labour-days or task-days on estates); quality where the relevant factor is the actual effort required or the degree of skill or unpleasantness associated with separate tasks; and agency where the labour measurement reflects the social position or status of the person performing the task. Thus, in different societies, patriarchal or matriarchal, women's labour will be valued less or more highly than the labour of men regardless of the actual effort expended, while the labour performed by children might also be valued according to their (usually inferior) social status rather than to the actual work they perform. These dimensions of labour and the implied difficulties of measurement often limit the use of this factor as an alternative to money value. Nevertheless labour often provides a more relevant basis for systems analysis of a very large number of small traditional farms than does money.

- *Bio-mechanical Energy:* A factor which all farm-household systems and their subsystems have in common is their explicit or implicit energy content. Farm-system models have sometimes been structured on the basis of such energy content and inter-component energy flows—see, *e.g.*, Axinn and Axinn. Use of energy-based farm systems analysis rests on the view that, in a world of declining energy resources and materials that can be represented by their energy content, the energy generation and consumption of farm-household systems is a more valid basis for systems analysis than is money profit, and usually also that energy flows which are directly or indirectly involved in all economic activities (including agriculture) are not properly represented—indeed they are often severely distorted—by commercial pricing mechanisms. However, these views involve issues and require solutions at much higher than farm level. Farm systems analysis based on energy flow is more appropriate for some aspects of macro/industry/sector strategic planning than for farm-level operational planning where the immediate interest of farm families is in income (in whatever form it takes) and the effort required to achieve it.

- *Water Consumption:* A fourth possible basis for analysis of farm systems is offered by water with systems analysis conducted in terms of the relative water consumption of different crops and animal populations and the implicit water content of products and by-products. Water is obviously the critical common factor in all the farming systems of that great belt of lands stretching from North Africa to India, so much so that even the very wealthy Gulf States, while they have been able to import or create all other agricultural resources, including soils, micro-environments and farmers, remain constrained by water. Moreover, in the 'wet' tropics, the critical nature of this input common to all parts of all farming systems is not yet widely recognized; *e.g.*, even 'well-watered' Java will probably exhaust its water supplies before its soils. However, as important as water is, like bio-mechanical energy it is more appropriate as a basis for some aspects of macro-level systems analysis than for operational-oriented systems analysis at farm level.

In summary, except when used in connection with special-purpose systems, such bases of analysis as energy, water, ecological balance etc. lack the universality and the value orientation required of a general systems base. Money value and labour will probably continue to be used as such a base, either separately in the case of commercial and near-subsistence farms respectively, or jointly in the case of the bulk of small traditional partly commercialized farms.

FARM MANAGEMENT FIELDS

Farm management analysis and advisory activities can be categorized in terms of four fields defined in terms of the purpose of the analysis as follows:

Field A consists of those problems and analyses which are only or primarily of direct interest to the farmer subjects of the analysis and where solutions to problems are offered on the basis of their beneficial effect on the welfare of these farmers and their families. The great bulk of farm management systems analysis occurs within this field. Field A is the conventional area in which farm management operates, directed to solving the on-farm problems of individuals and groups. Except where otherwise noted, this book is concerned with farm management within Field A; it needs no further discussion at this point except to note that such analysis should, whenever possible, involve farmer participation so as to ensure that the farmer's felt needs are considered.

Field B consists of those problems and analyses which should not really fall within Field A (*i.e.*, they do not properly constitute farm-level problems) but which for convenience or purposes of analysis can be defined, regarded and treated as if they do. Examples of the scope of Field B farm management analysis are offered by the agricultural industries and sectors of some of the mini-states. For example, the agricultural sector of the island nation Kiribati is equivalent to not much more than a single good-sized coconut estate with a few supplementary enterprises added. This sector (a system of Order Level 16) could easily and probably most effectively be analysed, of course with the necessary modifications, as if it were a system of Order Level 10 or 12. An example at industry level is offered by the banana industry of Western Samoa which, although it consists of a large number of individual farms, has been centralized (through the government) in fruit collection/inspection/transport/export and other important aspects. The industry could justifiably be analysed as a single large 'farm system' even though in fact (and in respect of banana-growing activities) it really consists of many farm-household systems.

Obviously, since this type of higher-than-farm-level analysis will be concerned with a range of subject matter in addition to farm economics—processing, marketing, transport, research, extension etc.—farm management can operate successfully in Field B only if the analyst can ignore artificial divisions which are conventionally imposed between the various disciplines. Another condition is that the analysis could not be better performed by a systems analyst working within the conceptual framework of some other discipline. (If this is the case then farm management analysis would operate in a subservient role in Field C.)

Field C consists of problems or issues arising within or in relation to higher systems of Order Levels 13 to 16, towards the resolution of which farm management plays only a secondary contributing or partial role, *e.g.*, the lead discipline might be water resource engineering if the problem is planning of a public irrigation project, or agronomy if it consists of planning for the introduction of new crops, or agricultural credit if it is to plan the establishment of a farmers' bank. In this type of supporting role, farm management can operate in any or successively all of Modes 2, 3 and 4, *i.e.*, description, diagnosis and prescription, respectively, as defined below. However, any 'prescription' that is offered will be of a limited kind and fall short of being a plan for the overall project or programme. Analysis will be directed towards the achievement of some global optimum which is not defined in terms of farm management itself.

A few of the very large number of situations in which farm management operates in Field C are:

- *Descriptive* studies of farm-household systems to provide background for local or multi/bilateral investment programmes in agriculture and/or agricultural infrastructure (*e.g.*, the Country Background Reports of the World Bank). This type of analysis is in Mode 2.
- *Diagnostic* studies of farm-households to determine just what developmental or investment assistance is needed (*e.g.*, roads, health, transport, extension, credit etc.), and the priority ordering of specific projects to provide such assistance (Mode 3).
- *Prescriptive* analysis (*i.e.*, Mode 4) aimed at providing the farm-related part of some uni- or multi-purpose project or plan: *e.g.*, farm-level demand schedules for irrigation water in a multi-purpose water storage

project (where irrigation is only one planned activity in addition to power generation, flood control, fish production etc.); scheduling of produce supply as part of a feasibility study for the establishment of a cannery.

Field D consists of farm management in the role of generating data for the guidance or support of agricultural policy making. Provision of such data might not require special studies or systems analysis for this particular purpose; often such data will be an incidental output of analysis undertaken for some other purpose, *e.g.*, in Field A. Field D analysis is also of a supportive kind and operates in Modes 2 and 3. The aim is usually to generate knowledge about farm-households or their component subsystems which is to be used by governments, public agencies etc. as a basis for structuring agricultural or broader economic policies—setting farm-input prices or consumer food prices, establishing transport services or credit programmes etc.These policies might imply either enhancing farmer welfare or reducing it (*e.g.*, if their thrust is to minimize urban living costs). This is a very important and wide-ranging field: it is difficult to think of any policy which is to affect farmers which should not be based at least in part on farm-level analysis, despite the fact that such farm-level analysis is in fact frequently not carried out, much to the detriment of sound policy making.

FARM MANAGEMENT MODES

Farm management operates in four modes within the above fields.

Mode 1 encompasses *routine operational and control* activities. It is concerned with the day-to-day operation and management of an actual farm, estate, cooperative or other farm-based producing/marketing entity. This may be thought of as practical or 'muddy-boots' farm management. Management in this mode is largely outside the scope of the present discussion, except that the systems concepts discussed here will, it is hoped, provide principles to guide practical (*i.e.*, Mode 1) management.

Mode 2 refers to *descriptive* activities whereby farm management provides a conceptual framework for the study, understanding and description of farm systems or farm-related problems. This might be an end in itself; or more likely it will be a necessary stage in the logical-event sequence towards action, as suggested in Figure. The chief function of descriptive farm management studies is to provide a basis of understanding before problem diagnosis is attempted. There are still many societies in the world with farm-household systems of which we are in nearly complete ignorance; understanding and description of these systems must precede problem diagnosis and, if need be, prescription of solutions.

Mode 3 refers to *diagnostic* activities concerned with the identification of problems and weaknesses in farm-level systems of all Order Levels 1 to 10 and those parts of Order Level 11 household systems relating to the farm. Such problem diagnosis includes the identification of potential opportunities. Problem diagnosis is usually carried out as a separate mode, but on some commercial farms it might be built into their routine monitoring and management mechanisms (as also on more sophisticated estates).

Mode 4 refers to *prescriptive* activities in which farm management is aimed at the prescription of action plans for both (*a*) the overcoming of problems or weaknesses and (*b*) the seizing of opportunities uncovered in Mode 3 (diagnostic) analysis.

Analytical Situations Within Modes

In Modes 3 and 4, three analytical situations will arise, viz.:

- *Diagnose and Prescribe:* First, the problem might require that a diagnostic analysis be made of a system of Order Level from 1 to 10 (or 1 to 12) leading to the identification of some specific weakness or opportunity to be investigated by research on the farm or experiment station - see Norman *et al.* If the problem falls within the competence of the investigator, the analysis would at this point go into prescriptive Mode 4 to develop and offer solutions.
- *Diagnose and Refer:* This second situation arises when the diagnosed problem lies beyond the competence of the analyst: *e.g.*, low milk production on a dairy farm

might be due to animal disease or a genetic factor or to the household itself (such as a low educational level leading to product adulteration). In such situations the role of the farm analyst is - or should be - to refer the problem to some relevant agency or specialist, *i.e.*, to diagnose but not to prescribe.

- *Prescribe Only:* Often only a prescriptive analysis is called for: *e.g.*, if the problem is to generate land-use plans intended to serve as the agro-economic basis of new settlement projects or transmigration schemes.

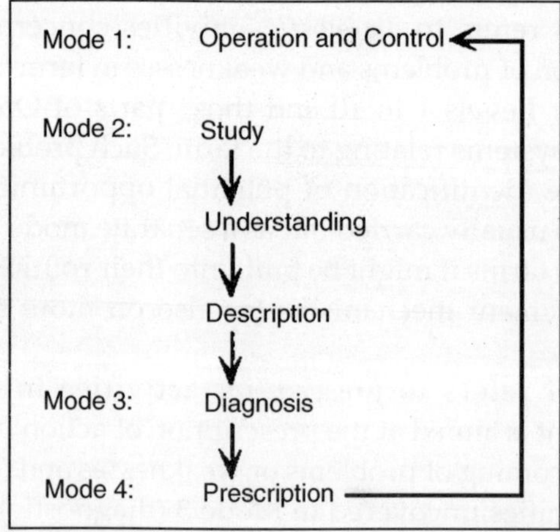

Fig 3.1 Relationship between the Four Modes of Farm Management Activity

FARM TYPES AND STRUCTURE

To date, farms have most often been classified on the basis of agro-ecological factors (such as climate, soil, slope, altitude and, not unrelated to these factors, the crop and livestock systems used) overlaid, to a lesser extent, with socio-economic criteria (Fresco and Westphal). Inevitably such an approach leads to a plethora of farm types. A different approach is taken here.

Emphasis is on farm-system structure from a farm management and farm-household perspective with classification based on:

- The main purpose of the farm;
- Its degree of independence; and

- Its 'size'. From such a structural viewpoint there are basically six major types of farm system to be found in Asia and elsewhere around the developing world with dozens of subtypes constituting a continuum of farm types between the extremes of a totally subsistence to a totally commercial orientation.

FARM TYPES

The six basic farm types are:

- *Type 1: Small subsistence-oriented family farms.*
- *Type 2: Small semi-subsistence or part-commercial family farms,* usually of one half to two hectares, but area is not a good criterion: the same basic structure can be found on much larger 20- to 30-hectare farms as in the Punjab, Sind, and North West Frontier Provinces of Pakistan.
- *Type 3: Small independent specialized family farms.*
- *Type 4: Small dependent specialized family farms,* often with the family as tenants.
- *Type 5: Large commercial family farms,* usually specialized and operated along modified estate lines.
- *Type 6: Commercial estates,* usually mono-crop and with hired management and absentee ownership.

Each of the six farm types is now discussed in turn.

Type 1 Small Subsistence-oriented Family Farms

There are two main subtypes. First, and of lesser numerical importance, are those based on only one or two crops or livestock types (*e.g.*, on maize or cassava or coconuts; or on yaks or camels). Some farms of this subtype are based more on exploitation or management of a local natural resource—in the extreme case, by use of shifting cultivation or by nomadism—than on deliberate choice of their main farm enterprise (*e.g.*, on indigenous sago palm, palmyrah, coconut or nipah). However, the main group of Asian subsistence-oriented farms is based on a wide range of crops and animal types. This second subtype is of necessity more highly mixed than are Type 2 part-commercial farms. Farms which are completely self-sufficient are rare, but self-sufficiency remains the operating objective and, if forced by circumstances, farms of this type could exist in isolation from the outside world. The structure of a Type 1 farm is exemplified in Figure. The focus for evaluation and analysis of Type 1 farms is the household rather than the farm component of the system. However, Type 1 farms have most of the characteristics of Type 2 farms and these are discussed below in relation to this latter type.

Type 2 Small Semi-subsistence or Part-commercial Family Farms

This type is predominant throughout South and South East Asia in terms of the number of such units, the large number of people supported by them and the total volume of their production—especially of basic foodstuffs.

- *Operating Objective:* The general operating objective of this farm type is family sustenance, pursued first by production of foodstuffs for consumption and of produce/materials for use on the farm, and second by generation of some cash income for the purchase of
  - Non-farm produced food essentials (salt, tea etc.);
  - Other essentials such as clothing, medicines, transistor radio, batteries etc.; and
  - Some farm inputs (such as agricides and fertilizer).

  Such cash is obtained primarily by sale of commodities which are surplus to family requirements, and secondarily—where this is possible - by production and sale of some cash crop raised specifically for this purpose.
- *Production Activities:* Type 2 farms can be further classified according to geographical occurrence (*e.g.*, wet tropics; sub-tropics of India/Pakistan; temperate zone of North India, Nepal, Bhutan), and by whether these farms are dryland (as most are) or part irrigated. However, they are all basically similar in their crop activities which consist essentially of one or more staple food crops plus a leguminous protein source plus an oil crop. Some examples of geographically typical crop mixes are:

— *Himalayan Hills*: Barley or buckwheat; beans or peas; mustard.
— *Sub-tropics*: Wheat; Soybeans; Sesame.
— *Wet tropics*: Cassava or rice; groundnuts; coconut or sesame.

In general, land is cropped to its maximum intensity, but the number of crop species grown in each of the energy/protein/ oil crop subgroups, as well as the area of each, is limited by length of growing season (dependent upon temperature), rainfall occurrence and/or irrigation water supply.

Livestock, whether fish, poultry or larger animals, are typically important on Type 2 farms. They are closely integrated with the crop activities, and here—unlike the situation on farms in developed countries—they are kept for a range of purposes: direct production, draught power (except on the smallest farms), transport, manure production to sustain field and pond fertility levels, and as a store of wealth. The combination of livestock with crops results in a large number of activities, and an even larger number of different farm products.

A special subtype of this highly-mixed farm type consists of the forest-garden farms of the wet tropics as found in Kerala, Sri Lanka, Malaysia and Indonesia. These consist of both whole farms, *e.g.*, the forest-garden farms of Kandy in Sri Lanka—see McConnell—or the house-yard parts of farms forested with a more or less dense mix of economic species as in the Pekarangan lands of Java. Except for poultry, livestock are relatively unimportant on this subtype.

Farm System Boundaries: Discussion of system boundaries in Chapter mainly relates to farms of this type. Briefly, boundaries of Type 2 farm systems (and of Types 1, 3 and 4) segregate them distinctly from the external world, but the boundaries between individual farms are relatively weak. In contrast with farms in developed countries, they often have much stronger links to and interdependence with other farms in the local community than they do with the outside world, *i.e.*, with commercial input suppliers and markets for their outputs. Through such practices as exchange of labour and animal services among farms, group farming, community work ('gotong royong' in Indonesia) to develop irrigation channels, village roads etc., barter of food grains for animal products, and village-level savings' mobilization ('arisan' in Indonesia), each farm-household unit is a link in an often highly developed agro-socioeconomic network within the local community. Whatever the basis for such informal integration - culture, religion, isolation—its effect is to provide strong structural boundaries around groups of farms, hamlets and villages rather than around individual farms. Each Type 2 farm is very much a part of the community and often could not function effectively if divorced from it. It might well be said that 'No such farm is an Island, entire unto itself.'

Activity and Product Diversity: Diversity, or the degree to which farm income (however measured) is derived from a range of activities and products rather than from a single. Type 2 farms are typically the most diverse of all farms. Diversity has three elements: the number of crop/livestock activities present; the number of products obtained from those activities; and the number of ways in which each product can be used or disposed of.

The mixed farms of the Punjab commonly consist of four to six crop activities and three to six livestock activities; those of Bhutan somewhat fewer. In Sri Lanka the forest-garden farms commonly grow up to 16 or so tree and vine species producing 20 to 30 different products; and since each can be disposed of in up to four different ways (sold/bartered, consumed, processed, stored), such a system will possibly generate some 60 or so end products. This contrasts sharply with the situation on farms of Type 6, the estates producing a single product (tea, rubber etc.) with a single end use (sale).

Even a common field crop such as maize may be managed so as to yield four or five primary products (green pick, dry grain, fodder leaves and stalks, fuel, live stripped stalks as supports for a companion bean crop), and two or three subsequent processed products (maize cakes - an important kitchen industry in parts of Bhutan, alcohol etc.).

Diversification of Type 1 and 2 farms has several bases. Broadly it follows from their sustenance orientation. In remote tracts of Nepal and Bhutan it is a necessity. In the Punjab it results largely from the possibility of growing a wide range of summer and winter crops and combining these with livestock. On the closely integrated vegetable-poultry-pig-fish farms of West Malaysia and Sarawak it results from a business-like approach to profit maximization. On the forest-garden farms of Kandy in Sri Lanka it results partly from historical circumstance (the wide botanical base provided by Indian, Arab, Portuguese, Dutch and British immigrants and colonizers) and partly from a tendency of the Kandyans to plant a tree/vine/shrub in any vacant space. (If they did not, the space would soon be filled anyway through natural seed fall and germination.)

Sources and Uses of farm Resources: An important characteristic of Type 2 farms (and of farms of Type 1) is the high proportion of farm and household resources generated on the farm and, correspondingly, the low level of dependence on purchased inputs. Further, where purchased resources are used, it is common practice to restrict their use to cash crops (cotton, sugarcane, tobacco etc.) with non-cash crops receiving no purchased inputs or being grown on the residual fertilizer (and often soil tilth and soil moisture) from some previous commercial crop. Those farms which do use purchased inputs often operate at dual levels of technology—'advanced' for some main crop, 'traditional' for the rest.

Farm-generated resources including food supply (as distinct from purchased resources) are obtained in a wide variety of ways as follows:

- By operating separate specific-purpose resource-generating activities. These, as distinct from cash-generating activities, are relatively important on farms of Types 1, 2 and 3. The most common example is livestock kept primarily for manure production (as well as for other purposes). Growing a green manure crop serves a similar purpose. Growing and lopping the leaves from leguminous trees for paddy fertilizer is still common in Java. Such activities need not be elaborate: in Bali and Sri Lanka the most common 'resource-generating' activity is simply growing a clump of bamboo in the house-yard (for construction material, produce containers, fences, water pipes).

- Through simple apportionment of part of a commercial crop for household use as food or livestock feed.
- By carrying on parallel crop activities by growing one variety/type for the market and another for the family's own use. The first, typically a high-yielding improved variety, might be deficient in taste and storability but will generate cash. The second might be capable of long storage and possess other qualities valuable in rural but not in sophisticated urban markets.
- Through extensive use of all by-products: stalks of maize, tobacco, pigeon pea, cotton etc. as household fuel; wheat straw for mud brick making; etc. With some crops—especially tree crops—the 'by-products' may take on such relative importance in the range of their uses as to make unclear just what the 'main' crop is.
- By growing/keeping generally low-yielding but multi-purpose types of crops and livestock rather than high-yielding specific-purpose types. Maize, wheat etc. might be grown nearly as much for green/dry animal fodder as for grain, or—in the case of maize—as a standing trellis for some following climbing crop, *e.g.*, beans or cucumbers. (Thus the not uncommon observation that farmers are 'backward' because they do not adopt 'improved' varieties is often based on ignorance as to the real reasons why the 'old' varieties are grown.)
- Finally, resources are also generated by the multiple use of farm capital. A common example is provided by farm boundary and roadside fences. In the Matale district of Sri Lanka most of the fences consist of kapok trees planted at very close spacing. They also support pepper vines and thus yield four 'products': kapok floss and seed (for oil) and black pepper, as well as field security. Farm fences in the Yogyakarta-Boyolali area of Central Java are used to generate a wider range

of resources (or to directly produce a marketable commodity). There are four main types:

i Bamboo-lattice fences, invariably used also as supports for long-beans;

ii Napier grass fences consisting of a single row of grass, laced together into an upright position by a strip of bamboo about a metre above ground level which permits the growing top of the fence to be regularly cut for cattle feed;

iii Live leguminous trees whose leaves are harvested periodically for cattle feed or seasonally as field green manure; and

iv Cassava fences, formed by planting cassava very close (15 to 20 cm) and weaving one or two bamboo strips through the line of cassava stems at about one metre from ground level. The cassava stems are then used also as a bean trellis.

Following is a partial list of the farm and household resources/inputs/capital equipment commonly generated on farms of Types 1 and 2.

The list suggests the high level of self-sufficiency that characterizes these farm-system types, especially in isolated areas.

- *Labour and power:* All labour (except at peak periods, then by labour exchange or mutual help); all ox/ buffalo/camel draught power, grain grinding power and transport; ox/buffalo treading power for grain threshing (mainly of paddy).
- *Crop inputs:* Most seed, animal manure (with a chemical fertilizer supplement on some cash crops); lopped high-nitrogen tree leaves for paddy fields (wet tropics); packing materials for market (woven bamboo baskets, teak and plantain leaf wrappers).
- *Capital equipment:* All ploughs, harrows, rakes and levellers from farm or village timber; all animal harness and repairs; fences (live kapok, areca palm, napier grass, cassava, woven bamboo); sugarcane roller crushers; oil extractors; irrigation water delivery systems (bamboo pipes in parts of Bali and the Madiun Valley of Indonesia).

- *Buildings and household:* Building panels/roofing/flooring (woven bamboo and sago/nipah/coconut leaves); buckets, containers (areca palm spathe and woven bamboo); cordage, twine, ropes; granary containers (woven, wood, packed earth); stoves and jaggery sugar boilers (packed earth); household fuel (crop residues, tree prunings); domestic light (coconut oil, butter lamps).

Type 3 Small Independent Specialized Family Farms

The key characteristics of Type 3 farms are:

- Their specialization in some particular crop or livestock activity which distinguishes them from the mixed farms of Types 1 and 2; and
- Their management independence which distinguis-hes them from Type 4 farms.

Type 3 farms fall into three subgroups according to their management orientation/purpose and type of income:

- Commercially-oriented farms, and family sustenance-oriented farms which achieve this objective through either
- Sale of part of their production (which makes them of necessity part-commercial farms) or
- Multiple-use of produce from their single specialized activity and/or barter of some of this produce for necessary commodities/goods which cannot be produced or purchased. In this latter situation such farms are also a subtype of subsistence farms (Type 1), but differ from the main body of near-subsistence farms in that only one main production activity is pursued. A sub-classification of Type 3 farms is shown in Figure. Some examples of these Type 3 farm subtypes are noted below. Probably the most important are the Subtype B near-continuous paddy farms of the wet tropics.

Subtype A (commercial):

- Small farms specializing in poultry, pig, dairy or vegetable production around metropolitan areas.

- Orchid and horticulture farms.
- Vegetable farms in upland areas throughout Malaysia, North Sumatra and Java.
- Smallholder rubber, oil palm or pepper holdings in Malaysia and Indonesia.
- Citronella and cinnamon farms in southern Sri Lanka.

Subtype B (part-commercial):

- Continuous and near-continuous paddy farms of the monsoon lands.
- Upland/dryland maize and cassava farms.
- Smallholder coffee or cacao farms.

Subtype C (near-subsistence):

- Near-subsistence maize farms of East Bhutan, Nepalese hills and Sarawak.
- Cassava-based farms on poor soil in South Java.
- Sago farms of South East Asia and New Guinea.
- Yak/sheep migratory farms of the high Himalayan valleys.

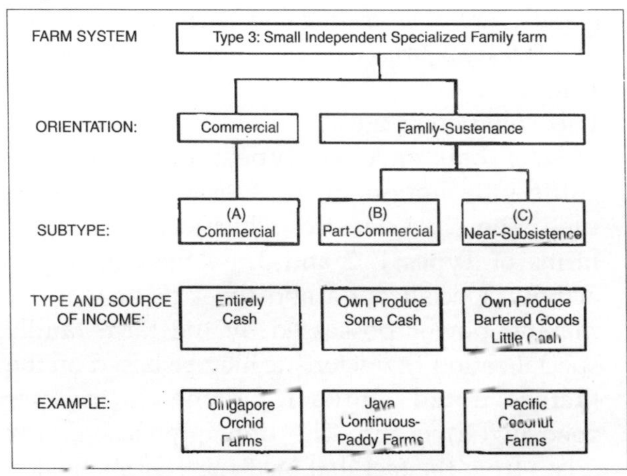

Fig 3.2 Sub-classification of Type 3 Fanning Systems

The specialization of Type 3 farming systems is based on a wide range of factors as follows:

- *Subtype A farms*: On commercial/profit opportunity and proximity to urban markets (poultry, pig, dairy and vegetable farms). The development of such profit-oriented peri-urban farm activities is a reflection of economic growth with its demands for intensively produced products with a high income elasticity of demand.

- *Subtype B farms*: On the presence of specific physical/ geographical factors (water and good soils for continuous paddy farms; favourable temperature and rainfall regimes for coffee or cacao farms).
- *Subtype C farms*: On necessity (cassava on the poor soils of South Java; yaks and sheep in the high valleys of Nepal and Bhutan).

Yet other bases for specialization are historical accident (*e.g.*, smallholder tea in Sri Lanka on lands acquired from previous tea estates); or prior presence of some natural resource (*e.g.*, the sago and nipah farms in the coastal swamps of the Philippines and New Guinea).

Type 4 Small Dependent Specialized Family Farms

Structurally, except for their lack of independence, Type 4 farms are quite akin to Type 3 farms and contain the same three:

- Commercial
- Part-commercial and
- Near-subsistence subtypes; however, they are sufficiently important to be examined as a separate type. The characteristics which set them apart from farms of Types 1, 2 and 3 are their high degree of activity specialization and the lack of real decision-making power possessed by the farm family. The specialization characteristic may be based on the same factors noted above for Type 3 (independent specialized) farms. The dependence characteristic arises from the fact that on Type 4 farms the family is not free to decide what to produce, nor frequently the conditions under which some obligatory activity is to be carried on. This lack of independence can be due to several factors, *viz.*:
- *Terms of Tenancy:* Tenant farmers are often obliged to produce one or more specific crop or livestock

products, as dictated in a landlord-tenant agreement. The tenant-operated vegetable farms of Qatar are an example.

- *Structural Integration:* In this situation small family farms are integrated more or less closely as the production arm of some larger farming cum processing system. Small tenant-operated farms supplying sugarcane to a mill or leaf to a tobacco-processing factory are common examples of such vertically integrated farms. Not only is the crop which is to be grown specified, but the conditions of production—timing of planting and harvesting, amounts of fertilizers to be used, spraying programmes etc.—are also dictated by the controlling authority.
- *Debt:* Some agro-industrial units (such as milk processing plants) often provide farmers with input factors (such as cattle, feed and technical assistance) in order to achieve a regular or higher quality supply of their needed raw material (*e.g.*, milk). These advances are usually made in the form of a loan at attractive terms, but often the only way farmers can liquidate this loan (and perhaps eventually regain their independence) is to continue to produce the particular commodity—usually under conditions set by and to the relative advantage of the lender.
- A second kind of debt, that entered into for consumption rather than production purposes, can also provide the basis for farmer dependence. Thus for generations the small cardamom farmers of the southern Bhutan hills have been indebted to the cardamom traders/money lenders of the towns along the West Bengal border. The only hope these farmers have of liquidating such debt—usually used for food, clothing and household items—is to continue to grow this specialist crop and sell it at whatever terms may be offered by the traders.

- *Government Policy Directives:* In some countries, farmers' lack of independence in production decision making is the result of government power to issue production directives. In Indonesia, *e.g.*, the Government has the broad power to direct that some percentage of those village lands which lie within the command area of each sugar factory be planted to sugarcane. Typically each hectare of land, owned by individuals of the village, might be under sugar for one year during which time it is farmed by the company as part of a larger estate. It then reverts to its owner for three years during which period he or she will operate it as a complete and independent farm, until it is again taken for sugar. During this three-year period the farmer has all normal decision-making powers (crop selection and how each is grown). During the one-year cane phase, for which the farmer receives payment as a 'landlord', he or she has no decision-making power whatsoever. This system thus involves the alternating of two distinctly different farming systems (as shown diagrammatically in Figure).
- *Lack of Alternative Market Outlets:* Absence of any real independence in management can also be due to lack of alternative market outlets, especially when the product is too bulky or fragile to be transported far from the farm. For example, most of the small cassava farms of Perak in West Malaysia are located on poor soils which would grow little else except cassava (many are located on tailings or spoil from tin mines). This accounts for their specialization. The second factor, their lack of management independence, is due to the high bulk/low value of their product which must be disposed of to chipping factories in the immediate vicinity. There is little practical possibility of seeking higher prices by transporting the raw cassava further afield. Similar situations face the citronella grass and cinnamon leaf farmers of the Galle-Matara district in

southern Sri Lanka. Here again the high bulk/low value of these farm outputs deny the growers any real choice in disposing of their crops to other than the local oil mills under price/quality conditions set by the mills.

- *Source of farm Resources:* Farms of Type 4 (and Type 3) are usually not self-sufficient in resource-generation; *e.g.*, the continuous cropping of specialized paddy farms (Subtype B) is usually possible only because it is based on some purchased package of 'high technology' inputs-HYV seed, artificial fertilizer and agricides. Dependence on commercial inputs is even greater on farms of Subtype A, *e.g.*, purchased feed and veterinary supplies for specialist poultry and pig farms. However, Subtype C farms might exist with only minimal purchased inputs; *e.g.*, the upland near-subsistence maize farms of Nepal, Bhutan and Sarawak are based on use of retained 'local' seed, no artificial fertilizer and no agricides.
- *System Boundaries:* The boundaries of the specialized farms also vary with subtype. Those of the commercially-oriented farms of Subtype A will interface more to the outside world (*i.e.*, to suppliers of inputs and product markets) than to other farms; however, the boundaries of farm-system Subtypes B and C will tend to be stronger around groups of contiguous farms or all the farms of a hamlet or village in much the same way as the communal boundaries of Type 1 and 2 farming systems set these apart from the outside world.

Type 5 Large Commercial Family Farms

Type 5 farms are similar in most respects to estates except that usually the primary beneficiaries are members of an (often extended) family rather than absentee owners or shareholders. They fall into two subtypes. The first consists of mono-crop farms which are at the fringe of the estate sector proper and which are usually dependent on this estate sector for research, availability of new crop varieties and often for processing and marketing facilities. The 10- to 20-hectare coconut farms of Sri Lanka which exist side-by-side with the large (now nationalized) coconut estates are examples.

The second subtype consists of either mono-product or mixed farms which are not part of any estate sector but are organized along commercial lines, *e.g.*, using hired labour, being dependent on purchased rather than farm-produced inputs and, except in the case of tree-crop farms, adjusting the activity or activity mix according to commercial opportunity. The larger cinnamon farms of Galle-Matara and the mixed coconut-dairy farms of Sri Lanka are examples of this subtype. So also are the large 30- to 50-hectare mixed grain-livestock farms of Sind and Punjab.

The operating objective of Type 5 farms is profit or utility maximization through market sales. As a group and in pursuit of that objective, they are the most dynamic of the six farm types discussed here.

Type 6 Commercial Estates

Commercial estates are generally mono-crop in nature. They are largely a colonial legacy, first established to provide cheap raw materials (and later some food and beverage products) to the industries of Europe and North America. This role continues except that they now also serve national industrialization.

The Chief Characteristics of this farm Type are as Follows:

- *Crops:* The main crops on which Type 6 farms were initially based are rubber, sugar, cinchona, cacao, tea, coffee, cinnamon, cloves, nutmeg, coconut and the coarse fibres. Some of the old traditional crops have become uneconomic (sisal and to some extent cinchona); some have become primarily smallholder crops (the spices and coffee); and new estate crops (such as flowers, oil palm and citronella) or improved varieties of old crops have emerged. Recent years have also seen the emergence (usually close to metropolitan areas) of livestock-based estates, particularly for pork and broiler production.

- *On-estate Processing:* Primary processing is an integral part of the operation of most estates (*e.g.*, tea manufacture, sheet and crepe rubber production, copra curing). This requires a high level of capital investment which, to be fully utilized, requires a flow-type of operation rather than a batch-type. This has two effects. On the one hand it tends to restrict estate production to those crops which yield a fairly uniform year-round flow of produce (tea, rubber, coconut, cocoa etc.). On the other hand it gives estates certain advantages, *e.g.*, quality control, relative to smallholders producing these same products. Some crops which naturally give an intermittent or irregular product flow are also made amenable to continuous estate-type production by relay-planting or chemical control of growth time-patterns (*e.g.*, sugar, sisal and pineapple).
- *Size:* Estate size is commonly from 200 to 2 000 hectares but area itself is not an important criterion: a 40-hectare orchid estate will generate about as much income and employment as will a 200-hectare tea estate or a 400-hectare coconut estate.
- *Marketing:* Marketing plays a very important role in estate operations. Most estates are jealous of their product reputation or 'mark' and make deliberate attempts at product differentiation. They also maintain close contact with buyers and monitor demand trends. Thus the larger cacao estates of Malaysia might be in daily telex or e-mail contact with buyers in Hamburg and Amsterdam. This contrasts sharply with the situation on smallholder farms growing the same crops: most smallholders have little interest in their product once it leaves the farm gate and, not infrequently, have no knowledge of its use after export.
- *System Beneficiaries and Operating Objectives:* Previously, the primary beneficiaries of estates were usually absentee shareholders who employed professional expatriate management and often also a docile expatriate labour force (as was the case in Malaysia,

Sri Lanka, Fiji and Mauritius). Thus, before their nationalization, the estates of Sri Lanka were referred to accurately, if somewhat emotively, as 'islands of privilege and prosperity in a sea of poverty'. With exceptions, this situation has changed markedly; consideration of the interests of secondary beneficiaries now receives far greater attention than formerly and these are more widely defined to include the host government, the estate labour force and their dependants, local communities and councils. Profit remains the main operating objective but this is increasingly tempered by the condition that worker retirement schemes, schools, clinics, roads, village welfare centres etc. be provided at estate cost. In short, increasing proportions of operating profit are being diverted from the primary to the secondary beneficiaries of this system type.

- *Management:* A mono-product estate system is at once more simple and more complex than the systems found on mixed family farms. Since only one product is usually involved, only one production activity exists, and there is no need to allocate resources among five, six, seven or more competing production enterprises, as on a typical mixed family farm. Also, very little if any of an estate's resources have to be generated within the system's boundaries. (On a typical tea estate usually only fuelwood and hydro power might be produced as inputs to tea production, and even the use of these is declining.) Thus, again in contrast with family farms, there are no resource-generating activities to divert attention from the main production task. However, although only one production enterprise subsystem rather than a multiplicity exists, it is carried on at a sophisticated level. Volume production usually means that per unit profit margins are thin; the wrong decision at some critical time, especially with long-term tree crops, can have serious and long-lasting consequences.

Specialization means that the advantages of crop diversification are not available; there is no possibility of making up on the swings what might be lost on the roundabouts. If a Bhutanese farm with one pig suffers an outbreak of swine fever the farmer would probably shrug his shoulders and go off to the paddy field or do something else. If it happened on a 500-sow estate it could spell disaster. Moreover, insofar as most estates are based on one or other of the tree crops, the effects of some sub-optimal decisions (*e.g.*, regarding variety/strain of crop to be planted, spacing, initial fertilizer etc.) might well have long-lasting if not permanent adverse effects, possibly over the 30-year life of a rubber stand, the 65-year life of a coconut stand, or even longer in the case of tea.

While not requiring the allocation of resources among enterprises, planning and management of a mono-product estate system requires the explicit recognition, organization and optimization of a large number of agro-technical processes. An example is given in Figure which shows the sequential steps in establishing and operating a tea crop. For each step, several alternatives are possible.

If this were only one of several crops to be grown (*e.g.*, as on a mixed smallholding), most of the questions listed in Figure would not be asked; each operation would proceed on the basis of village tradition, farmer experience or local lore. But on an estate they have to be explicitly asked and answered if the optimal level of long-term sustainable production and profit is to be achieved. In the management planning of estates,

Three kinds of management analysis can be particularly important:

- Evaluation of some single production enterprise (crop or livestock) over a long time period;
- The optimization of processes because even small marginal reductions in inputs/costs will become important when spread over many hundreds of hectares or thousands of tonnes of produce; and
- Simulation of estate operations as a whole system under uncertainty.

Having defined the six main farm types and outlined their chief structural characteristics, it is now possible to turn in following chapters to a consideration of the field of farm management analysis as this would be applied to these farm types, especially the small farms, *i.e.*, Types 1 to 4. First, however, two contrasting examples of small-farm systems are presented in the following section.

Table 3.1 Alternative Processes in Producing Tea on an Estate

Sequential operations		Alternative processes for each operation	
(1)	Clear land	Method:	Labour? elephants? tractor?
		Level:	What season? depth? tilth?
(2)	Establish cover crop	Method:	Which crop?
		Level:	for how long? 15,18 or 24 months?
(3)	Plant tea	Method:	What kind? seedling or vegetatively propagated?
		Level:	What population density? 3-4-5 000 plants/acre?
(4)	Weed	Method:	How? hand? chemical? men? women?
		Level:	Every 4, 6, 8... weeks?
(5)	Fertilize	Method:	What type(s)?
		Level:	What levels of application? frequency? timing
(6)	Pick	Method:	How? machine? hand? male or female?
		Level:	Frequency? every 25, 30, 35... days?
(7)	Cure/pack	Method:	How? for which of many markets?
		Level:	Mix grades? in what proportions?
(8)	Etc.		

STRUCTURE OF SMALL-FARM SYSTEMS

A useful way of introducing the discussion of following chapters is to look briefly via examples at the structure of two of the small-farm types, the partly commercialized farms (Type 2) and the near-subsistence farms (Type 1).

Model of a Type 2 Farm

Based on McConnell, Figure presents a model of the annual operation of a 'representative' Pathan farm in the Peshawar district of North West Frontier Province, Pakistan (the data are actually means of a group of 11 similar farms). The central core of the farm system consists of two livestock, seven crop and two on-farm processing activities: dairy and draught cattle, berseem (clover), a mixed orchard, sugar beet, sugarcane, maize, millet and wheat. The processing activities consist of converting some of the milk to ghee for sale or consumption (in this particular year it was all consumed), and crushing/ boiling some of the sugarcane to make gur (unrefined 'country' sugar), some of which is consumed, some sold. These 11 activities are represented by bar columns in the middle part of Figure. Input and output values are in rupee (Rs) terms. The levels of the various activities, livestock population and other relevant structural data are summarized below.

Crops	Level
Berseem (cattle feed)	0.6 Acres
Orchard (use + sale)	1.1 Acres
Sugar beet (sale)	0.7 Acres
Sugarcane (sale + gur)	1.3 Acres
Maize (use)	1.3 Acres
Millet (use)	0.2 Acres
Wheat (use)	2.0 Acres
Sugarcane:	
Produced	542.0 Maunds[2] plus 15.5 Maunds of gur
Sold as cane	542.0 Maunds
Livestock	
Bullocks	2.0 Head
Milk animals:	1.7 Head
Producing	1.1 Head
Dry	0.6 Head
Young Stock (Dairy + Draught)	1.2 Head
ox traction available (pair)	365 Days
Actually used	74 Days
Milk produced:	22.0 Maunds
Used/sold as milk	18.4 Maunds
Converted to ghee	3.6 Maunds

Note: [2] Maund (abbreviated to mds in Figure 2.4) is a volumetric measure corresponding to about 90 pounds (40 kg) of sugarcane; ghee is measured by the seer (about 14 pounds or 6 kg).

Figure consists of two sections: the *household component,*

circumscribed by a boundary line in the top right section of the diagram, and the *farm component* of the farm-household system which constitutes the remainder of the diagram.

Referring to the *household component* of Figure, the farm family consists of seven members of all ages. Together these members are capable of supplying 1 053 labour days annually. In fact there is only enough work on the farm to occupy 443 labour days, and only 21 days of off-farm work can be found, thus 589 days are either occupied in farm maintenance or development work not connected with any particular crop, or are occupied in social/religious activities, or are idle. (Here they are shown as 'idle'.)

The second general input by the family into the farm component is cash for meeting the direct costs of each of the production activities. This cash is obtained by the household as ₹ 2 848 from sale of farm produce plus ₹ 65 from 21 days of off-farm work. (Of course the family component also supplies other vital inputs to the system—management, direction and purpose —but these cannot be measured.) These family-provided inputs into each of the activities, cash and labour days, are shown in Figure in the two top rows of the farm component.

Consider now the *farm component* as depicted in Figure. *Activities:* Referring to the activity columns in the body of Figure, each of these is an abbreviated activity budget showing first the inputs to and then the outputs from the activity. For example, the inputs to 0.7 acres of sugar beet are cash ₹ 79, labour 48 days, bullocks 8.5 days, manure 66.5 maunds; and the outputs are 32 maunds of leaves (by-product) and 175 maunds of beets.

Similarly, the inputs to sugarcane are cash ₹ 250, labour 82 days, bullocks 14.4 days, manure 80.6 maunds; and the outputs are 185 maunds of cane tops (for bullock feed) and 542 maunds of sale cane, plus a small but unknown amount of cane diverted to home processing for gur which as a separate activity uses ₹ 77 cash, 25 labour days and 2.2 bullock days, and yields 15.5 maunds of such 'country' sugar of which 6.8 maunds is consumed and 8.7 maunds is sold.

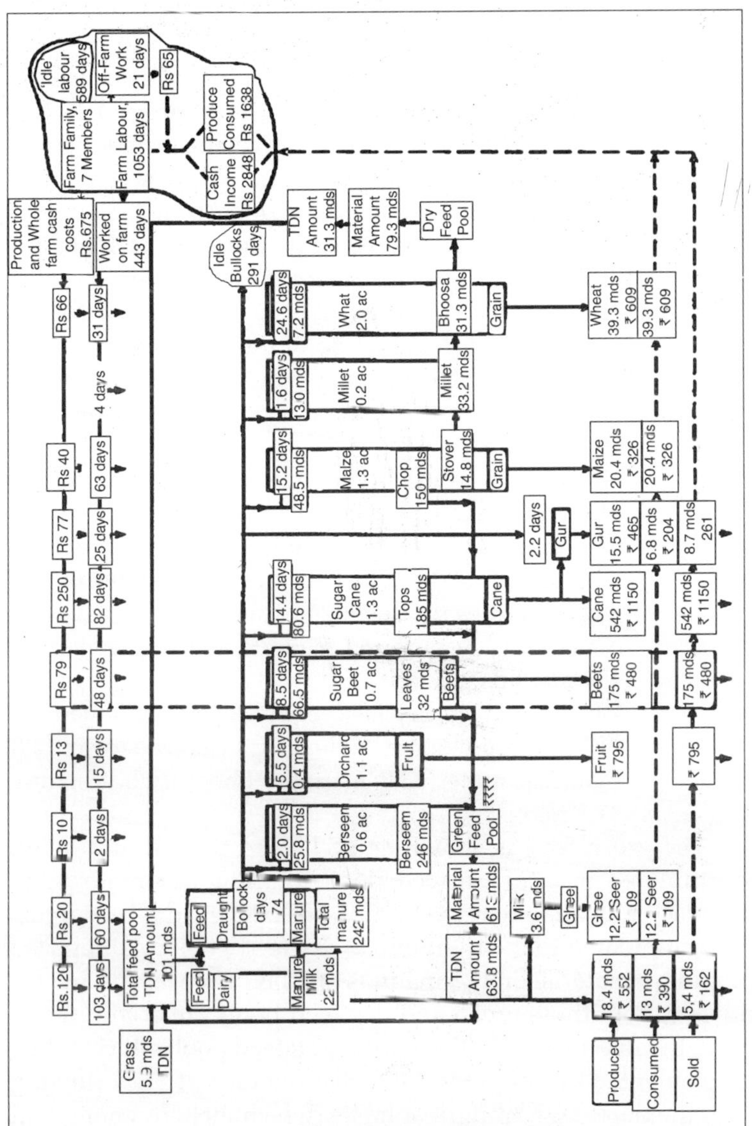

Fig 3.3 Structural Model of a Pathan Farm Exemplifying a Type 2 Farm

The two livestock activities—dairy and draught oxen—are shown at the left side of the model. Inputs are cash costs, labour and livestock feed.

This latter is somewhat complex.

- *Livestock Feed:* Feed is shown in two units of measurement: amount (*i.e.*, maunds of around 40 kg) of actual material, and the equivalent in maunds of total digestible nutrients (TDN). This conversion is desirable in order to standardize each of the several different feedstuffs produced on the farm, each having a different nutritional value, into a common basis of units of TDN. The total amount of feed fed to the livestock is shown at the top of the livestock columns, 101 maunds of TDN, coming from the 'total feed pool'. All feed entering this common pool comes from one of three sources:
  - Grass (cut from the orchard) equivalent to 5.9 maunds of TDN;
  - 613 maunds of green feed, equivalent to 63.8 maunds of TDN, which comes from some of the crop activities (berseem 246 maunds, beet leaves 32 maunds, cane tops 185 maunds, maize green chop 150 maunds) and
  - 79.3 maunds of dry feed, equivalent to 31.3 maunds of TDN, from some of the crops (maize stover 14.8 maunds, millet 33.2 maunds, bhoosa/wheat straw 31.3 maunds).

The green feed is shown as cycling to the left and being accumulated in a 'green feed pool' totalling 613 maunds of material, equivalent to 63.8 maunds of TDN; the dry feed items are accumulated to the right into a 'dry feed pool' totalling 79.3 maunds of material or 31.3 maunds of TDN. Then, as the arrows indicate, both these green and dry feed pools are accumulated above the livestock activities into a 'total feed pool' which, when supplemented by cut grass, totals 101 maunds of TDN flowing to all the dairy and draught animals (which include young and dry stock as previously listed).

These feed flows refer only to feed produced on the farm. In addition, stock are grazed on village common lands when grass is available there (the amounts of such grazing could not be recorded).

In summary, the following widely diversified feedstuffs are obtained on this type of farm: grass from the orchard, some rough common-lands' and roadside grazing, berseem clover, beet tops, sugarcane tops, green maize chop, dry maize stalks, millet and wheat bhoosa (straw).

Only two of these items are specially grown for the cattle, namely berseem and millet.

- *Livestock Outputs:* The cattle activities generate three outputs: bullock power, manure for the crops, and milk. The number of bullock days flowing to each of the crops are shown, being 2.0 for the clover, 5.5 for the orchard, 8.5 for the sugar beet etc. Crushing of sugarcane for gur also uses 2.2 days of bullock power. Bullock power not used is shown as 291 'idle' bullock days. Below the livestock activities, a total of 242 maunds of manure are accumulated from all the livestock. This also is shown flowing to the crops: 25.8 maunds to berseem. 0.4 for the orchard, 66.5 for the sugar beet etc.
- *Final Activity Outputs:* The lower section of the model shows the final products flowing from each activity and the amount of each product consumed by the household or sold, each in quantity and value terms.
- *Household Income:* Farm income consists first of the value of produce consumed. This is accumulated to the right in Figure and enters the household component of the system as a total value of ₹ 1,638. Second, cash from farm sales is similarly accumulated and has a total value of ₹ 2,848. Total income, real plus imputed, is ₹ 4,551 which includes the small income from non-farm work. Thus, for this year, income in kind from home-consumed production constitutes 1,638/4,551 or 36 per cent of total gross family income. On this basis, it might be said that the farm is about one third subsistence oriented and two-thirds commercially oriented.

As shown, total cash inputs into all the activities amount to ₹ 675. Thus, in this particular year, the household would have a cash 'surplus' of ₹ 2 848 + 65 - 675 or ₹ 2 238. This amount would be available to meet any cash costs in farm maintenance (which were not considered as a cost in the model), and to meet cash living expenses for purchased clothing, food, medical expenses etc. Any final surplus after meeting these latter expenses would be available as savings.

In summary, this Pathan fanning system from the North West Frontier Province of Pakistan is a highly diversified one. It has 11 major production and processing activities and it produces 15 separate products and by-products (excluding bullock power, young livestock and manure for the fields). Cash inputs are low, mainly for fertilizer for some of the crops and a minimal amount of agricides; most seed is retained. Although a significant degree of self-sufficiency is present, it is not a true subsistence farm.

Model of a Type 1 Farm

Most farms of Type 1 (*i.e.*, small subsistence-oriented family farms) in Asia now have at least some element of commercialisation and generate at least some small amount of cash for the purchase of essential items. At the top end of the structural scale this type merges into the small mixed Type 2 farms; at the bottom end it includes the locally-shifting cultivators of Sarawak-Kalimantan (and these merge into the hunter-gatherers and forest dwellers of New Guinea, Kalimantan, Sarawak and Sumatra).

Subsistence or near-subsistence is a condition more often imposed than voluntary: one sub-classification could be on the basis of external causal factors; *e.g.*, the near-subsistence farms of India, the hills of Nepal and parts of Java exist because of shortage of land; those of Bhutan (where land is seldom limiting) because of isolation and the lack of roads and markets; and those of the new settlement areas of Sri Lanka because of the lack of family labour and oxpower to till more than a minimal subsistence area.

When examined from the viewpoint of their range of activity, variation of this farm type ranges all the way from being highly mixed to almost mono-crop. In the first of these conditions, this type merges into Type 2 farms. In the second extreme condition these farms are structured around production of a single bulk staple - usually maize, dry paddy, cassava, palm sago or coconut. Secondary foodstuffs and non-food subsistence items are obtained by supplementary activities: fishing; hunting or collecting in nearby forest areas for food or items for sale (birds, monkeys, butterflies, orchids, beeswax, rattan etc.); or by sending a family member off to work somewhere outside the subsistence environment.

Although they can generally be described as resource-poor, poverty is not necessarily a characteristic of Type 1 farm families. At one end of the scale the economic condition might be poverty verging on destitution, even starvation. At the other extreme it might be prosperity when that condition is judged by an availability of resources in excess of those needed to maintain a reasonable physical existence.

Again the best way of illustrating systems of this subsistence type is with the aid of a model. Such a model is shown in Figure which describes the structure and operation of a near-subsistence farm located at about 1 700 m (5 500 feet) above the town of Wangdiprdan in Central Bhutan. The chief features of this farm are its highly diversified activities and its very high level of self-sufficiency. In this example the farm is a prosperous one (as that term was defined above) and its subsistence nature is based on isolation, poor roads, lack of markets and therefore of incentive—indeed opportunity—to enter the commercial world.

The model refers to an operating period of one year:

- Data from a 1985 farm survey by Nim Dorji and the senior author. The monetary unit is Ngultrum (Nu) = US 8.7 cents in 1985.

The farm's land resources consist of 1.75 langdo[4] (0.25 hectares) of dry paddy fields, 1.25 langdo (0.18 hectares) of dry fields, and 4.00 langdo (0.4 hectares) of wetland rented from a local monastery. However, the effective size of this farm is only 5.75 langdo: the 1.25 langdo of dryland is too far away to be easily worked and, since more accessible land can be rented from the local monastery, the dryland portion is not used.

(If it were cultivated there would be no market for the extra produce, which would also be surplus to family requirements.)

- [4]A langdo is the area a pair of oxen can plough in a day: a dry langdo is about one seventh of a hectare and a wet paddy-field langdo is about one tenth of a hectare.

The farm family consists of five adults, all able to work full-time if necessary, *i.e.*, a population density and potential workforce of six persons per hectare. It is assumed that this family could provide a potential supply of 1 200 labour-days annually. Livestock resources are also high relative to farm size: two oxen, two milkcows, three young cattle, three pigs, three hens. Cattle are grazed off the farm on common lands for more than half the year.

The farm structural model of Figure consists of six parts as indicated by the circled numbers 1 to 6 in the diagram. Part 1 shows human, livestock and land resources, as noted above. Part 3 shows the farm resource pool. All resources except rented land are owned or are generated by the system itself (all seed, manure, bran, labour etc.). There are no purchased inputs; even the rented land is paid for by barter with the monks. In Part 2 of the structural model, all productive activities (subsystems) are listed in separate activity columns. There are nine of these (plus one external resource-generating activity): tending cattle, pigs and poultry; growing paddy, wheat, buckwheat, mustard, vegetables/chillies and fruit. The external resource-generating activity consists of one family member working part-time off the farm (for local government, clearing paths and roads after landslides).

The coefficients within each upper column of Part 2 are the resources used by the respective subsystems: *e.g.*, the paddy crop uses 5.25 langdo of land, 115 labour days, 29 kg of seed, 14 tonnes of manure and 23 draught ox days. Of the used total area of 5.75 langdo, two langdo are doublecropped. Part 4 shows all intermediate products (bran, grain, straw, draught days, manure and seed) which are produced by the nine farm activities. These are generated in the activity columns, accumulated to the left in the 'intermediate outputs' section (Part 4), then cycled back to the resources pool of Part 3 and from there to the activities which use each such resource/input. As shown by the left-side arrows from Part 4 to Part 3 and thence to Part 2 of Figure, resources used up by the activities (Part 2) in any year are replenished by the activities producing intermediate products, but these need not exactly balance because some resources may be held over in storage: *e.g.*, in this year 21.5 tonnes of manure are used on the crops but only 15 tonnes were produced; 6.5 tonnes came from storage not recorded in Part 3 of Figure.

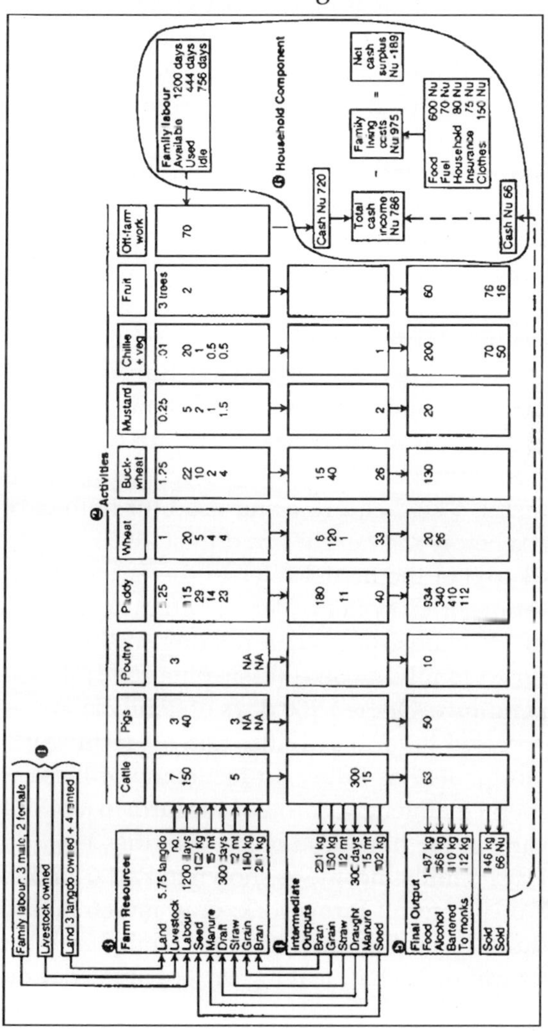

Fig 3.4 Structural Model of a Bhutanese Farm Exemplifying a Type 1 Farm

Part 5 of Figure lists and aggregates final outputs from the nine activities: *e.g.*, for the paddy activity the intermediate products from paddy (bran, straw, seed) cycle to the left in Part 4 and then up to the resource pool. But the final paddy products consist of 934 kg of grain used for family food, 340 kg converted to alcohol (consumed not sold), 410 kg bartered to other families for other types of food not produced on this farm and 112 kg of paddy paid as rent to the monks for the four langdo of wetland.

The various food items produced and consumed on the farm are shown in the 'food' line of Part 5: 13 kg of butter and 50 kg cheese from the cattle, a 50 kg pig, 10 kg eggs, 934 kg of paddy, 20 kg of wheat etc. Alcohol was made from a total of 366 kg of grain (paddy and wheat).

The bottom of Part 5 shows those outputs which were sold. In this particular year the only marketed items were some citrus fruit (76 kg) and vegetables (70 kg) which were sold for Nu 16 and Nu 50 respectively at the Wangdiprdan weekly 'hat' (street market).

Clearly this farm system is one very close to complete subsistence. There are no purchased inputs into the crop/livestock activities and all farm capital items such as ploughs, harrows and ox gear are home-made, as are the woven storage bins for grain storage. The mustard seed oil for home use is extracted using a kitchen press and used for both cooking and in the lamps before the family's Buddhist altar.

Parts 1 to 5 of the model refer to the farm components of the farm-household system. Part 6 refers to the household component: this consists of data relating to the use of family labour, and to family income (cash plus food) and non-farm family expenditure. Of the 1 200 days of family labour available, 444 days are used in farm activities and off-farm work, leaving 756 days designated as 'idle'. (In fact some of these would be used in general maintenance around the farm in jobs not directly related to any of the nine production activities.)

Total cash family income as shown in Part 6 amounts to Nu 786: Nu 720 is from off-farm work; only Nu 66 is from sale of farm produce. From this cash income, family cash (non-farm) living costs are deducted, leaving an apparent net deficit this particular operating year of Nu 189. The items comprising family cash expenditure are shown: Nu 600 for purchased food, Nu 70 for purchased fuel (kerosene), Nu 80 for household items, Nu 75 for insurance and Nu 150 for clothing. The apparent negative cash balance of Nu 189 would be made up from savings or by obtaining credit for purchases.

Due to off-farm work and cash expenditures for the items shown, the farm-household system at this point has ceased to be a purely subsistence one. However, if the family's economic conditions changed for the worse, the expenditure pattern could be easily adjusted to reduce or eliminate some of the cash expenditure items (especially food which consists mainly of 'luxury' items), and the remaining needs for cash could be met by sale of a pig or a little mustard oil.

It is now possible to turn in following chapters to an examination of the individual structural elements of this and other types of farm systems.

4

Boundaries, Household and Resources

BACKGROUND

This Sub-Mission addresses problems related to Access to Information among different stakeholders in agriculture including farmers, development agent's researchers, and policy makers. The objective of this Sub-Mission is to fill the knowledge gap providing valuable information to all the stakeholders in time. The collaboration, partnerships and strategic alliances between, Department of Agriculture and Cooperation, research organizations and other related organizations can provide useful information.

It is well recognized that dissemination would generate recommendations for better decision-making. The knowledge warehouse for sustainable agriculture developed under this Sub-Mission will not only provide strong capabilities to the stakeholders *i.e.* farmers, researchers, decision makers to understand the impact of climatic changes but also help to build models for providing timely forecast of status of agricultural situation well in advance.

AREAS OF PRIORITY

The priority areas are:

- Development of regional database of soil, weather, genotypes, land-use patterns and water resources.

- Monitoring of glacier and ice-mass, impacts on water resources, soil erosion and associated impacts on agricultural production in mountainous regions;
- Providing information on off-season crops, aromatic and medicinal plants, greenhouse crops, pasture development, agro-forestry, livestock and agro-processing;
- Collation and dissemination of block-level data on agro-climatic variables, land use and socio-economic features and preparation of state-level agro-climatic atlases.

Since monitoring of glaciers and ice mass is being dealt with by another Mission for Sustaining the Himalayan Ecosystem, the same has not been covered in this Sub-Mission.

STRATEGY

DEVELOPMENT

Access to information shall be ensured in time to the farmers and other stakeholders. Experience has shown that small changes in climate parametres can be managed reasonably well, and the losses minimized, by changing the planting schedules, spacing of the crop plants and input management, etc. Development of alternate cultivars and farming systems (such as mixed cropping, crop-livestock) that are more adapted to changed environment can further ease the pressure. In this regard, the National Agricultural Research Project (NARP) was launched by ICAR for initiating agricultural research in the agro-climatic zones of the country. The objective was to set up or upgrade a zonal research station in each agro-climatic zone for generating location specific, need-based research, targeted for specific agro-ecological situations.

The focus was on analysing agro-ecological conditions and cropping patterns and come out with a programme directly targeted to solve the major bottle necks of agricultural growth in a zone based on natural resources, major crops, farming systems, production constraints and socio-economic conditions prevalent in that zone. Stress was on technology generation. Under NARP, the country is divided into 131 agro-climatic zones. Detailed information about Physical feature, soil, climate, temperature, land use pattern and cropping pattern up to district level is already available. Similarly the information about genotypes and other production technologies developed by research system in the country for various states/agro climatic zones/districts is also available in the form of data warehouse with IASRI. Such information is also compiled in the Strategic Research Extension Plans (SREPs) developed by many districts.

However, the following is required to be done:

- The available information needs to be put together for easy access by users;
- Block level data on agro-climate should be collected and disseminate the agro-climatic variables;
- In addition to above data, the crop advisories being developed by Ministry of Earth Sciences through IMD and National Centre for Medium Range Weather Forecasting (NCMRWF) will also be used for dissemination to the end users in general and farmers in particular.

RESEARCH

In the Indian Agricultural Statistical Research Institute (IASRI) New Delhi, the work related to design and development of the data warehouse was completed and repository of historical data covering important segments of agriculture has been created. This information base will be further expanded to provide a basic framework for the proposed knowledge warehouse for sustainable development of agriculture under various climatic situations. This warehouse will cater to the information needs of farmers, researchers and decision makers. It is proposed to develop number of decision systems and expert systems of important agricultural commodities for dissemination of this knowledge base to the stakeholders.

It is envisaged that the data mining would be initiated to churn out projections and forecasts of trends through incorporation of various climatic factors etc. in order to develop a decision support system for the research managers. Besides this, knowledge management would also involve extensive scanning and searching of the World Wide Web resources, documents, reports and articles available on public domains related to climate changes and its impact on agriculture. A centralized system for storing, indexing and searching will be developed under this knowledge warehouse.

To fill the research gap in this area, following research objective will be taken:

- To design and develop a system for scientific and technical knowledge management of agricultural research required for sustainable agricultural development in the context of climate change;
- To develop a prototype of ICT based information dissemination system for stakeholders for various agro-climate zones;
- Development of analytical tools, models and data mining techniques for agricultural systems to study the impact of various climatic factors;
- To build a prototype of early warning system models in agriculture under various climatic situations.

In order to achieve the above objectives, research projects will be initiated on different aspects of identified area/ commodity at collaborating institutions.

The selection of information nodes will be from two categories i.e.

- To provide information for development early warning system; and
- To provide scientific and technical knowledge at regional level. The information nodes established in the research system will collaborate with NIC through DAC to authenticate the information to be disseminated through the district level information nodes proposed to be established at district level which will in turn cater to the extension system at district level and below in the development component of this sub-mission.

PLAN OF ACTION

DEVELOPMENTAL ACTIVITIES

A revitalization strategy based on introduction of extension support at different levels *i.e.* the village; the sub-block; the block;

the District and the state level by providing the requisite specialist and functionary support and ICT at these levels has been conceived by the Ministry of Agriculture. The extensive use of ICT and its infrastructure is a critical component of the strategy to revitalize the National Agricultural Extension System (NAES). Under national e-Governance (NeGP) plan, infrastructure is being developed to link all the blocks by a wide area network and provide connectivity up to the village level through Common Service Centres (CSCs).

The infrastructure so created will be used to collect weather data like Temperature, Wind speed and direction, Rainfall, Soil Temperature, Sun Shine duration and humidity. The information from the available metrological laboratories under the IMD and NCMRWF will be used. Some Automatic Weather Stations (AWS) fabricated by IIT Chennai can also be installed at some selected locations where such infrastructure is not available. This location specific Meteorological information will be used/shared with various organizations developing Agro-Advisories for the farmers.

Under this Sub-Mission DAC proposes to collect data on agro climatic variables, land use and socio-economic and factors through NIC who in turn will use the database so developed as well the data warehouse developed by IASRI and other relevant sources such as IMD and National Centre for Medium Range weather forecasting (NCMRWF) etc of the Ministry of Earth Sciences for developing user friendly software tools and necessary hardware, integration into web based framework and development of decision support systems (DSS).

The activities under the present proposal envisage covering all aspects of agriculture and allied sectors including natural resources management to generate a number of deliverables. Agricultural Resources Information System (AgRIS) (http://agris.nic.in) of the Department of Agriculture and Cooperation is envisaged to see the convergence of data on soil, water and other natural resources available at various agencies at sub-district level (District, Block, Panchayat and village level). This project will further extend this convergence. Some of the important deliverables are to:

Developing a comprehensive spatial database on various parameters related to land use, input use (seed, fertilizer, agricultural technology and agricultural credit), water use, etc.

- Enable the extension workers and the farmers to access desired information for improving productivity;
- Capacity building, Farmers Training System and Extension activities;
- Plan for weather contingencies;
- Access research and technology database;
- Reporting model and knowledge processing framework with every level of Decision Support System (DSS);

Table 4.1 Components of the Sub-Mission will be as Follow

S.No	Name of component
1	Non-Spatial Component
2	Spatial Component (Thematic Layers)
3	Software Development (Including software tools and necessary hardware, integration into web based framework, development of DSS)
4	Infrastructure creation for Sub-Mission at DAC including capacity building (for Government officials as well as of the outsourced agencies
5	Sub-Mission Management
6	Documentation, M&E, Workshops etc.

Table 4.2 It is Proposed to Cover 600 Districts in a Phased Manner as Follow

	2009-10	2010-11	2011-12	2012-13	2013-14	2014-15	2015-16	2016 17
Number of Districts to be Covered	25	50	100	100	100	100	100	25
Total	600							

RESEARCH

The proposed plan is to utilize the data warehouse of INARIS project for providing basic analytical framework in this process and then further expand the scope of the project in other area. For drawing inferences, the integration of the output of the analysis with other basic information from other sources will be a key issue. Therefore, strong analytical and inferential tools will be developed for assessment of impact of climate change on agricultural productivity through integration of historical data with current information. Since agriculture is a vast subject, therefore, initially it is proposed to concentrate on some important areas/commodities of agriculture such as: Cereals, Oilseeds, Pulses, Fruits, Vegetable, Plantation Crops, Spices, Commercial Crops, Livestock Products and Fisheries:

Initially it is proposed to monitor the following important factors related to climate change for the above agricultural products,

Which are likely to have a major impact on our agriculture research:

- Agro - Meteorological Changes
- Status of Water Resources
- Infestations: Insects, Pests and Diseases
- Calamities: Floods, Drought
- Crop Production and Management Practices
- Availability of Inputs
- Global Technological Developments
- National/International Policies

It is expected that information requirement for this process will be coming very frequently and for the monitoring process of agricultural status in the country at least monthly information should flow from selected districts of the country on the following aspects:

* Status of Climatic Parameters
* Status of Inputs
* Status of Management Practices
* Status of Agricultural Infrastructural Support
* Expected Loss/Gain in Production

It is proposed to set up a central server at New Delhi in which required information from data bases designed and developed at various collaborating institutions related to the subject domain will be populated and integrated through existing network for development of above system. The number of data bases to be designed and implemented at various locations will be decided on the basis of requirement analysis of the respective domains which includes study of existing data bases, data gaps, information availability, use of information etc. The responsibility of designing of these data bases will be of IASRI. Apart from this IASRI will also be responsible for implementation of integrated knowledge warehouse at New Delhi.

The main responsibility of subject matter institution will be to collect, authenticate, populate the respective database. Apart from this, these institutions will also be responsible for development of models, DSS/ES etc. with the help of IASRI in their respective domains. The domain knowledge of these institutions will also be utilized for integrated model building at knowledge warehouse in New Delhi. The services of information nodes will be used for collection and dynamic information such as status of climatic parameters, status of inputs, infestations of insects, pests and diseases etc. periodically on the central server through public network system. This information will be integrated with the historical data to assess possible impact on agricultural productivity in respective region *i.e.* district. Attempt will be made to automate the whole data collection, modelling and information dissemination to various stakeholders.

The development of the integrated system at New Delhi will be in collaboration with NIC, which will be responsible for providing information nodes and regular updating of requisite data. The overall responsibility of coordination of the mission will be of DAC.

COLLABORATING AGENCIES

DEVELOPMENT

NIC and IASRI are the main agencies in developing this information data base. NIC through DAC will cooperate with following organization in this respect.

National Level:

- Department of Agriculture and Cooperation of Ministry of agriculture—Lead Organisation
- National Informatics Centre, Ministry of Communication and Information Technology
- Indian Agricultural Statistics Research Institute (IASRI)

- Indian Metrological Department, and National Centre for Medium Range Weather Forecasting (NCMRWF) of Ministry of Earth Sciences
- Ministry of Water Resources
- Ministry of Rural Development
- Ministry of Environment and Forests.
- Ministry of Information and Broadcasting (Radio and TV)
- Department of Space

State Level:

- State Departments of Agriculture, and other line departments like Animal husbandry, Horticulture, fisheries, Irrigation, Local Governments
- State Agricultural Universities and their research stations especially the Zonal Research Stations established at NARP Zones
- ICAR Institutes located in various states and their research stations including KVKs.
- Non-Governmental Organizations

At district and block level strong operational linkages are required to be established/ strengthened for all actors of ATMA.

RESEARCH

The creation of totally new infrastructure for the above purpose may be time consuming and costly, therefore, it is proposed to utilize the existing infrastructure available in the country especially in the NARS by supplementing it with some additional required resources. IASRI will establish collaboration with selected ICAR institutes as well as SAUs and KVKs.

FINANCIAL OUTLAY

DEVELOPMENT

The Cost Estimates for developing software tools including hardware, integration into web based framework and development of decision support systems (Recurring and non-recurring) for different activities proposed are given below:

(₹. in Crore)

Funds	2009-10	2010-11	2011-12	2012-13	2013-14	2014-15	2015-16	2016-17	Total
Non-Recurring	50	100	200	200	200	200	200	50	1200
Recurring	Nil	12	20	28	38	52	65	85	300
Total	**50**	**112**	**220**	**228**	**238**	**252**	**265**	**135**	**1500**

Since the dissemination is proposed to be taken up by the strengthened extension system (up to village level) through National e-Governance Plan, no budgetary provision is made.

RESEARCH

Table 4.3 The Total Financial Outlay Proposed for Different Programme of Research is ₹. 255.00 Crore as Given Below

S.No	Item/Institute	Budget (Rs. in crore)
1	IASRI	15.00
2	Individual Research Centers (40 Centres)	160.00
3	Establishment of Individual information nodes (100 nodes)	80.00
	Total	255.00

FARM SYSTEM BOUNDARY

In analysing any farm-household system or any other agricultural system, an obvious first step is to define the scope of such a system, *i.e.*, its boundary as relevant to the purpose of analysis. Sometimes this will present no problem, particularly if, as here, the focus of analysis is on farm production and its management. In this case, unless they relate significantly to production management, interfaces of a purely social, religious or political nature between the farm-household and its environment can be ignored. However, as the following examples illustrate, even if the focus of analysis is production and its management, the specification of the farm-system boundary (and likewise of the farm-household system boundary) may be quite complicated. Boundary definition may also vary with the purpose of analysis. Thus the relevant boundary for annual enterprise planning may simply correspond to the boundary of the physical farm entity. In contrast, for long-term development planning, the boundary may need to include off-farm income-generating activities and the interface with suppliers of long-term credit.

Modern Western and Asian farms in a highly commercial environment (*e.g.*, West Texas cotton farms and Malaysian rubber smallholdings and estates) have one or a limited number of farm production enterprises and clear sets of trading relationships between the farm and its input suppliers on the one hand and its output markets on the other. Relationships between a given farm and other farms will often be minimal, even non-existent. From a production management perspective, the boundary of this type of farm system will encompass the farm in its physical extent and its input suppliers and market outlets, but will typically exclude other farms.

In a second situation, as exemplified by many isolated near-subsistence farm-household systems of the Himalayan valleys, the boundary of the farm system also corresponds closely with the farm's physical boundary but in this case the system excludes the outside world.

More common is a third situation. It comprises the great bulk of small traditional farms of Types 1, 2 and 3 (*i.e.*, subsistence, semi-subsistence and specialized independent, respectively) which are moderately or heavily dependent on each other for supply of inputs - exchange or hired labour, oxpower, village transport etc. - and often also for the disposal of produce, *e.g.*, by barter or trading among friends and neighbouring families. In this situation the real boundary of a farm-household system, from an operational management viewpoint, might encompass all the farms of a hamlet or even of several mutually dependent villages.

This third situation in some of its variations can be quite complex. For example, the farms of the villages around Karanganyar in the Solo Valley of Java commonly consist of some area of household garden devoted to fruit trees and bamboo plus a larger area of fields. They are nominally 'owned' (in the Javanese sense, or held in trust in perpetuity) by the operating families who in fact do exercise full control over the garden or 'pekarangan' parts of their farms. In three years out of four the field area of a farm will usually be under paddy, grown either by the farmer himself or herself or more typically as a quasi-cooperative/mutual-help undertaking ('gotong royong') by the farmer and his or her neighbours. Thus in this first phase the boundary around each farm system encompasses its household garden and some area of paddy shared with other farm households. But in the fourth year the farm paddy fields, together with one fourth of all other village fields (which lie within the command area of a publicly owned sugar mill) are pooled, put under sugarcane, and the farmer becomes both a labourer (on his or her own land) for the mill and a landlord (receiving rent from the mill).

In short, the boundary of this farm system is fluid over time: it always encompasses the pekarangan (household garden) lands; it sometimes encompasses the rice field and other farm households which participate in the rice phase; and it sometimes exists only as one part of the boundary of a much larger sugar-estate system. The situation is depicted diagram-matically in the righthand side of Figure. The lefthand side of Figure refers to an isolated subsistence farm system. The central part of Figure depicts a commercial system in which the alternatives are to define the system as consisting only of the farm (implying boundary B') or as also including input suppliers and output markets (implying boundary B). The contrast in complexity between these three examples of farm-system boundaries is obvious.

IMPORTANCE OF BOUNDARY SPECIFICATION

At farm-household level, one obvious essential step in planning farm development programmes and investment projects is to accurately identify the relevant boundary of the subject system; yet it is a step sometimes not taken. In the 1970s a project in North East Africa was aimed at village economic development through introduction of modem rice-growing technology to Dinka tribespeople in the hope of supplementing and if possible replacing their traditional millet (as well as supplying rice to the urban population). Project planning overlooked the fact that, while millet was indeed important, the real boundary of the traditional farming system encompassed also keeping cattle and catching mudfish. Thus, while project planning management was directed at zealously maintaining field polder embankments to grow rice, Dinka management was directed even more zealously at breaking them down to get at the fish. (Planning that was less technically oriented would have aimed for the integration of all three components in a locally acceptable system.) This and similar mistakes in other farm projects also provide a caution that structuring or restructuring of a system must always start with an understanding of the farm-household system as discussed.

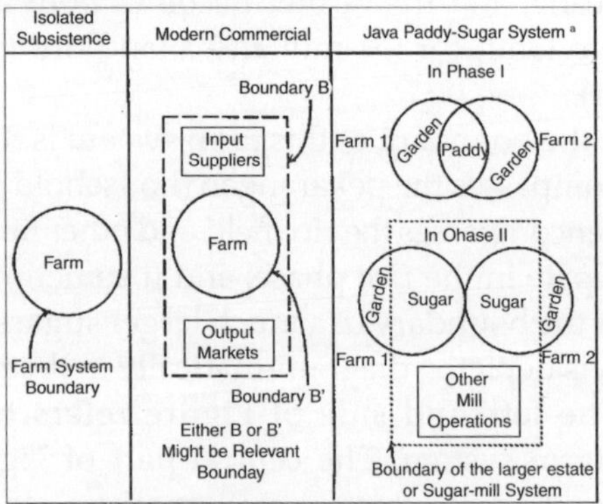

Fig 4.1 Boundaries of Three Contrasting Farm Systems

FARM HOUSEHOLD

The household component of a farm-household system is a somewhat flexible concept. It can consist only of the farm's nucleus family but more often includes extended-family members. It also commonly includes some number of more or less permanent domestic and farm workers and miscellaneous dependants. Most farm development projects are structured on the assumption that households are headed by males, but this is often not so. In a typical Javanese village anywhere from 10 to 25 per cent of households might consist only of women and children. Where poverty exists, here and elsewhere, it will generally be concentrated on such households.

FARM HOUSEHOLD AS RESOURCE MANAGER

The two roles of the household as resource manager and as

system beneficiary were noted. The household's role as resource manager is to provide purpose, direction, objectives and management to the whole-farm system and its subsystems. On farms of Type 5 (large commercial family farms) and especially Type 6 (estates) the place of the household might be taken by professional management.

However, on small farms and within limits set by the physical environment and available resources, the planning objectives are set by the household's broad social-value structure and local tradition (though the latter is increasingly being corroded by commercialisation and the influence of modem communications technology).

The farm economist is usually not well equipped to question these goals or the farm-planning objectives which result from them. His or her role is to attempt to optimize the farm component of the system in terms of whatever mix of socio-cultural, religious, traditional and material goals is relevant to the household.

He or she might also evaluate and convey the material consequences of alternative choices and management strategies within the farm component.

Decision Making Within the Household

It will often be necessary to enquire more deeply into who does what and who decides what within the household if sound farm planning is to be possible (in Field A) or sound farm development programmes are to formulated (Fields C and D). Real power and responsibility for the farm component might not always lie with the apparent or nominal household head.

Thus in the Wadi Hadramant of Yemen, as throughout most of Africa, although women might play an otherwise subservient role - or seem to - they are in fact the effective farmers, doing everything except the heaviest chores from planning the production system and executing most of it to preparing and allocating its output. Yet farm 'development' projects here and elsewhere—with few more than token exceptions and invariably conceived, planned, evaluated and managed by men—do not acknowledge this fact and remain directed at the mirage of some unspecified but assumed patriarchal 'farmer'. Without at least an insight into local culture, the conceptual models of how a system works which an analyst may have can be unproductive if not dangerous things.

Gender Analysis

As noted above, sound farm planning often necessitates an understanding of how resources, responsibilities, tasks and benefits are distributed between the men, women and children of the farm household. This is the subject of *gender analysis*as discussed and illustrated, Quisumbing *et al* and van Herpen and Ashby. The need for gender analysis, particularly in relation to the role of women in the farm-household system, is well illustrated by the following response by a small farmer when interviewed in a farm survey:

Q. 'Does your wife work?'
A. 'No, she stays at home.'
Q. 'I see. How does she spend her day?'
A. 'Well, she gets up at four in the morning, makes the fire and cooks breakfast. Then she goes to the river and washes clothes. After that she goes to town to get corn ground and buy what we need. Then she cooks the midday meal.'
Q. 'You come home at midday?'
A. 'No, no. She brings the meal to me in the fields - about three km from home.'
Q. 'And after that?'
A. 'Well, she takes care of the hens and pigs, and of course she looks after the children all day. Then she prepares supper so it is ready when I come home.'
Q. 'Does she go to bed after supper?'
A. 'No, I do. She has things to do around the house until about nine o'clock.'
Q. 'But you say your wife does not work?'
A. 'Of course she doesn't work. I told you, she stays at home.'

Tables provide an illustration of some aspects of gender analysis (labour and task allocation - but not the distribution of benefits) relative to a sample of small-farm households in Northern Mindanao, Philippines.

Table 4.4 Gender Analysis of Labour Use in Cassava Production in Northern Mindanao, Philippines[a]

Activity	Family				Exchange		Hired		Total		
	Adult Male	Adult Female	Sons[b]	Daughters[b]	Adult Male	Adult Female	Adult Male	Adult Female	Adult Male	Adult Female	Children
						(days/ha)					
Land Preparation	12.8	0.0	13.1	0.0	0.0	0.0	13.0	0.0	25.8	0.0	13.1
Furrowing	1.9	0.0	2.0	0.0	4.0	0.0	3.0	0.0	8.9	0.0	2.0
Putting up Sticks	2.6	2.2	10.9	0.0	0.0	0.0	7.0	3.9	9.6	6.1	10.9
Planting	5.5	5.0	9.5	8.0	6.0	2.0	3.3	2.8	14.8	9.8	17.5
Thinning	2.7	0.0	6.0	0.0	0.0	0.0	0.0	0.0	2.7	0.0	6.0
Weeding	8.7	6.0	9.9	9.4	22.0	0.0	18.3	23.0	49.0	29.0	19.2
Fertilizing	0.0	0.0	0.0	0.0	0.0	0.0	3.0	0.5	3.0	0.5	0.0
Hilling up	1.3	0.0	8.0	0.0	0.0	0.0	3.0	0.0	4.3	0.0	5.0
Clearing prior to harvesting	5.3	5.3	26.3	36.8	0.0	0.0	31.5	36.8	36.8	42.0	63.0
Harvesting	9.3	7.0	11.4	12.5	0.0	0.0	29.4	19.2	38.7	26.1	23.9
Drying	4.1	4.1	12.1	5.1	0.0	0.0	13.8	1.1	15.7	1.1	0.8
Hauling	2.0	0.0	0.8	0.0	0.0	0.0	13.8	1.1	15.7	1.1	0.8
Peeling/chopping	6.3	5.9	16.4	10.4	0.0	0.0	26.2	7.4	32.4	13.3	26.9
Sacking/packing	1.3	1.2	1.9	0.0	0.0	0.0	5.3	0.6	7.1	1.8	1.9
Storing	3.1	0.0	0.2	0.0	0.0	0.0	0.0	0.0	3.1	0.0	1.2
Marketing	1.2	0.4	0.0	0.0	0.0	0.0	0.0	0.0	1.2	0.4	0.0
Total	**68.1**	**37.1**	**128.5**	**82.2**	**32.0**	**2.0**	**174.0**	**97.9**	**273.9**	**136.8**	**208.6**

[a] Based on a sample survey of 75 small farms

Table 4.5 Gender Analysis of Participation of Farm-household Members in Household and Other Activities in Northern Mindanao, Philippines[a]

Activity	Participation (% of Respondents)				Time Spent[c] (Hours/week)			
	Husband	Wife	Daughters[b]	Sons[b]	Husband	Wife	Daughters	Sons
Go to market	40.5	81.3	35.9	19.0	3.5	3.8	1.0	0.7
Cook breakfast	23.0	89.3	38.5	11.9	1.5	4.1	2.7	0.9
Cook lunch	17.6	88.0	41.0	7.1	2.3	4.4	2.7	0.8
Cook supper	18.9	89.3	43/6	14.3	2.1	4.2	2.7	1.9
Wash dishes	17.6	80.0	66.7	23.8	0.7	1.7	1.7	1.0
Wash clothes	14.9	88.0	48.7	9.5	3.4	6.1	6.9	0.7
Iron clothes	1.3	30.7	7.7	0.0	1.0	2.1	2.4	0.0
Flech water	52.7	56.0	64.1	71.4	4.0	4.8	7.6	5.2
Clean house	17.6	86.7	61.5	16.7	1.6	5.1	4.3	1.1
Cut/collect firewood	68.9	24.0	15.4	50.0	4.2	2.8	2.7	3.9
Vegetable gardening	33.8	53.3	25.6	19.0	2.5	4.9	1.3	1.2
Fruit gardening	12.2	17.3	5.1	7.1	1.9	2.5	2.2	1.2
Look after children	32.4	66.7	33.3	9.5	4.2	18.4	12.7	4.8
Take children to school	0.0	8.0	0.0	0.0	0.0	1.8	0.0	0.0
Play with children	48.6	53.3	35.9	23.8	4.4	7.4	9.2	3.8
Farm production	85.1	61.3	28.2	59.5	36.0	19.9	8.4	27.8
Care of livestock	64.9	46.7	20.5	57.1	7.7	3.0	0.8	4.7
Care of poultry	32.4	32.0	23.1	21.4	2.3	1.4	1.1	0.8
Off-farm activities	64.9	36.0	20.5	40.5	20.0	18.6	20.5	20.8

[b]Over Six and Under 18 Years of Age.

[c]Average for those Respondents who Participated in the Activity

FARM HOUSEHOLD AS SYSTEM BENEFICIARY

On small farms the primary beneficiaries are usually the members of the household itself. However, external beneficiaries are also often important. In Bhutan it is common for farm family members long resident far from the farm and not dependent on its output to still retain important rights. They exercise these by returning at harvest time and taking their benefits in the form of pork and grain. In the villages of Central Java up to 30 per cent of households might be landless and subsist as farm labourers or—especially important in the case of households consisting of only poor women and children—by harvesting their neighbours' paddy in exchange for retaining one seventh or one tenth of the crop (the 'bawon' system).

This latter can be the only significant source of income for otherwise practically destitute people. They are perhaps proportionately more dependent on the farms of their more fortunate neighbours than are the farmers themselves, although they are from a formal viewpoint external to these systems. This is one common reason why some forms of Western-style farm 'development' do not occur. Javanese villagers have a strong sense of mutual economic and social responsibility. 'Advanced' technology which would prepare land more quickly (tractors) or give higher grain recovery rates (mechanical harvesters, grain dryers) or other technology whose first effect would be to increase the comparative wealth of the few would be frowned on because of its adverse effect upon the many.

Thus external beneficiaries can impose constraints on the household, in its first role as system manager and internal resource allocator, by exerting a collective moral influence on how crops are to be produced and even which crops are to be grown.

Other obvious groups of external beneficiaries consist of landlords, village traders, local governments as taxing authorities etc. and, at further remove, national governments deriving their foreign exchange from the export of farm produce. These can also influence how a farm-household functions in its first role as system manager, *e.g.*, through tenancy agreements, provision of credit, price policy etc.

FARM RESOURCES

The supply of resources in a whole-farm system can be examined from either an accounting or, more fruitfully, an operational perspective.

FARM RESOURCES FROM AN ACCOUNTING VIEW

From an accounting viewpoint with its ex post or backward looking emphasis, farm resources fall into two broad categories:

- *Fixed* resources provide services over a number of years or at least over a period longer than the production cycle of short-term (seasonal, annual) crop or livestock enterprises. Common examples are land, machinery, an irrigation system. These services may be used either by individual enterprises or to maintain the farm as a whole. In the very long run, of course, few resources are truly fixed in supply. Even land and climate in their productive dimension can be created (as in the controlled-environment greenhouses of Saudi Arabia, UAE and Qatar).

- *Short-term* or variable/operational resources are those that are usually entirely used up in the annual production cycle, *e.g.*, a supply of seed or fertilizer.

The essential difference between fixed and short-term resources is that the former provide a stream or flow of services over time while the latter consist primarily of quickly exhaustible material things or time-bound institutional sanctions.

From an accounting viewpoint, both fixed and short-term resources have two other relevant dimensions. In their economic dimension they become respectively fixed/long-term capital and operating/short-term capital; and in their financial dimension these generate, respectively, fixed costs and operating/variable/direct costs, *viz.*:

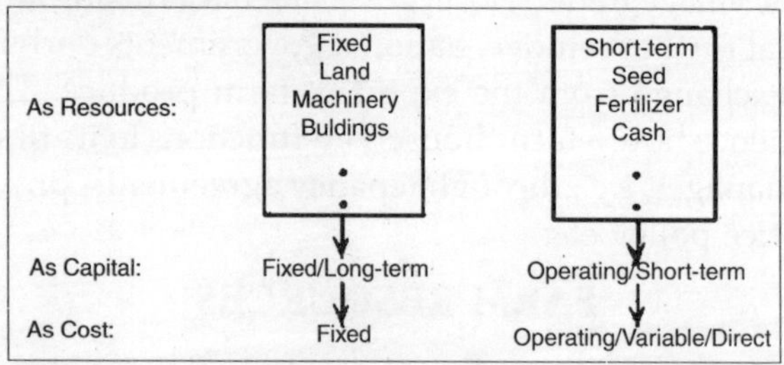

The distinction between these two cost categories of fixed and variable is discussed. Discussion so far has concerned resources when used at whole-farm level, *i.e.*, at Order Level 10. At lower Order Levels of farm systems (processes, activities and enterprises), the above classification of resources relative to capital and costs is parallel to that for the whole-farm: *e.g.*, the resources assigned to a paddy crop can be broken down and become fixed and operating paddy-crop capital, generating fixed and operating/variable/direct paddy costs.

FARM RESOURCES FROM AN OPERATIONAL VIEW

From an operational viewpoint the picture of farm resources is somewhat different. Here emphasis is on the *ex ante* potential or planned use of resources rather than the results of their past use. In this forward-looking context it is more fruitful to regard farm resources from a systems viewpoint. Distinction between fixed and short-term resources is now less relevant. As shown in Figure 4.2, more relevant are the flows of both short-term or operational resources and of services from fixed resources to the farm's subsystems.

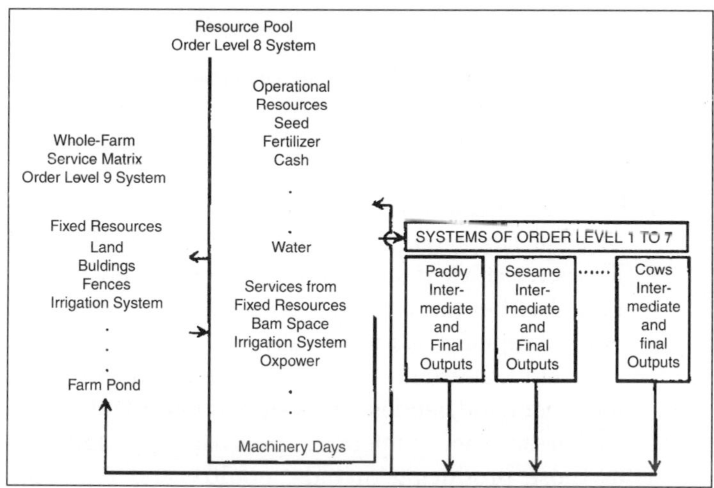

Fig 4.2 Direction of Resource Flows within a Whole-farm System

Central to these resource flows is the farm's resource pool (a system of Order Level 8, discussed from an operational perspective in Section 3.3.3 below). Short-term or operational resources flow from the pool primarily to lower Order Level production subsystems (processes, activities and enterprises) to generate the farm's intermediate and final outputs. Some also flow directly to the whole-farm service matrix to maintain the structure (repair of fences, buildings etc.) or permit the functioning of this subsystem (*e.g.*, payment of land, water and road taxes).

The services of long-term or fixed resources flow both to maintain the service matrix and to the resource pool from where they are assigned to the various production subsystems.

Any initial stock of both fixed and short-term resources must sooner or later be replenished from output of the productive enterprises/activities, either as materials purchased with income from the activities or as resources/intermediate products generated by these activities, *e.g.*, oxen produced as a by-product of the dairy activity. These resource return flows are indicated in Figure as flowing both to the resource pool and to maintain the stock of fixed resources or capital in the whole-farm service matrix.

OPERATIONAL RESOURCE CATEGORIES

From a planning and operational viewpoint, farm resources fall into five categories. Discussion from an operational viewpoint is focused on how specific resources might constrain or limit farm production.

The five resource categories are:

- *Material long-term:* This category consists of material things which yield their services over relatively long time periods. They were referred to above as fixed resources or fixed capital. Land is typically the most important such item and will usually provide its services indefinitely On the other hand, land is relatively less important on many capital- and labour-intensive specialist Type 3 farms such as those producing orchids, poultry and pigs. Other examples of resources in this category are irrigation systems and farm sheds generating their services over 20 to 30 years or an ox pair providing draught power over five or six years.
- *Material short-term:* This category, exemplified by such items as seed and other seasonal inputs, was also discussed above. In a commercial environment where these items are purchased, the production constraint is generally set by the amount of money available to buy them, not by the supply of these items in themselves.
- *Financial:* This category consists of cash, debts receivable, and access to credit from formal (banks, cooperatives) and informal (shops, traders, relatives) sources.
- *Institutional:* This category consists essentially of rights of access to materials, markets and services. In its financial dimension, this category takes the form of

land and road taxes, water-use license fees, payments for production-quota rights (as sometimes prevail for sugarcane, milk, tobacco etc.). They are termed 'institutional' because they consist of relationships between the farm family on the one hand and institutions/agencies/persons on the other. Note that where they are transferable and have financial value, these rights are assets as well as production resources.

- *Labour:* This consists of family labour available for general farm work or which might be available only for specific tasks. For example, specific-purpose labour might consist of the very old and young family members who can do only light work such as tending livestock; or a family member who prefers and is especially skilled in tapping toddy palms etc. (Management ability is an important attribute of family labour, sufficiently so as to sometimes warrant attempts at separate evaluation of its productivity, but it is usually not possible to measure management as an *ex ante* input, only in terms of what it actually achieves as discussed.

Resource Inventory for Planning

For planning *(ex ante)* purposes, specification of the farm resource pool simply amounts to making a list of the availability of those resource items which might limit production in the planning period, *e.g.*, for the coming year the resource pool may include the following resources.

Listing of the initial resources will depend partly on the resources actually available but also on the uses to which they are likely to be put, *i.e.*, the types of enterprises/activities which are likely to be operated. The procedure, therefore, is somewhat circular and subjective but in practice it poses no serious problems. The aim is to identify all the main farm resources, particularly those which are likely to be production-limiting and relatively costly, rather than to compile an exhaustive list of all resources which are present or which could conceivably act as constraints.

(1)	*Material long-term*	Land	0.25 Ha irrigated lowland
			0.60 Ha eroded upland
		Oxen	1 Pair
		Ploughs/harrows	3 Units
		Pump	1 Unit
		Buildings	1 House, 1 shed (100 m^2)
(2)	*Material short-term*	Fertilizer	6 Bags
		Cow feed	3 Tonnes
(3)	*Financial*	Cash	1 500 ₹
		Expected from crops	3 500 ₹
(4)	*Institutional*	Milk quota	20 Litres/day, sold in town
		Water license	0.25 Ha
(5)	*Labour*	Work-age adults	490 Labour days
		Children	180 Days (cattle only).

In almost all planning situations, the analyst will be able to form a general idea of the likely production possibilities and therefore the types or categories of resources needed to exploit such possibilities. If, as is often the case on many small farms, there exists two or three times the amount of labour likely to be needed to execute the production plan, one would not devote much attention to this resource. But, on the other hand, if the production system is likely, *e.g.*, to include strawberries, and this requires the deft fingers of children, then one would measure this particular category of available labour with some precision.

OTHER RELEVANT RESOURCE PROPERTIES

Resource Quality

For planning purposes it will often be necessary to quantify some resources according to the specific uses to which they can be put. These uses may have a quality as well as a quantity dimension. The example of child labour was noted above. If a farmer has 1.5 hectares of land and an asset statement is being prepared (below), it would be enough to describe this as simply 'Land.1.5 ha', but for planning purposes it would be necessary to list this in the resources pool as, *e.g.*:

Wet-land	(Necessary for paddy)	0.25	Ha
Upland	(Suited to maize)	0.75	Ha
Orchard	(Inter-cropping possible)	0.50	Ha

Similarly, if total crop-storage capacity is six tonnes, but only three tonnes of this is secure and rodent-proof, this fact will be specified in the resource pool statement. Likewise, while 'Pasture' might be an adequate description of a land parcel if all cattle/donkeys/buffalo/sheep are to run together as a combined herd, it would not be adequate if the producing dairy cows are to be given preferential treatment. The pasture might then be quantified as:

Good fresh pasture	(For cows only)	0.50	ha
Rough grazing	(All other stock)	0.70	ha

Resource-use Time Dimension

From the viewpoint of resource use in relation to time, resources fall into two groups: those which provide a *flow of services*over time, and those which consist of a *consumable store* or stock of materials or other farm resources. Land, family labour, oxpower, tractors and machinery, crop storage space, fences and livestock housing are examples of service-generating resources which provide their services as a flow over time. A store of seed or agricultural chemicals in a shed, a pond of irrigation water, a contract to produce sugarcane, or a shed of animal feed are examples of store-type resources, since once they have been consumed in the production process they cease to exist.

Flow resources have a time as well as a quantity dimension. Because agricultural production does not occur instantaneously but over some time period of months or years, the resources allocated to such production must be provided at discrete points in time or during specific time periods. Thus a one-hectare paddy crop to be grown from March to June might require the following resources: one hectare of irrigated land, 90 days of family labour, 21 days of ox work etc. This would be sufficient information if the purpose is to compare the economics (input costs versus output value) of paddy against other crops; but for planning purposes a more satisfactory statement concerning paddy-enterprise resource needs would be as follows:

	March	April	May	June
Land (ha)	1	1	1	1
Labour (days)	40	10	5	35
Oxen (days)	18	0	0	3

where 12 types of inputs are identified rather than just three, each having a quantity-time dimension. In short, in planning where the resource inputs of an enterprise have to be time-scheduled, *e.g.*, by months, then the farm resource pool also has to be specified in these same quantity-time units. Labour-days or ox-days in March are, respectively, different resources from labour-days or ox-days in June.

However, the more closely that the resource needs of a production activity are specified (as occurring in June, early June, first week of June etc.), the greater the degree of detail needed in quantifying the resource pool. Obviously this could result in the specification of an unmanageably large number of resource items. Some limits must be imposed on the procedure of adding a time-dimension to flow-type resources; but, on the other hand, a resource pool constructed without noting when resources are to be available would be of little use in planning.

The problem is largely removed by the fact that farm resource-using activities fall into four groups according to their relative needs for precision in time-specification, viz:

- *Highly time-specific:* These are farm production activities which must be operated according to some tight time schedule or calendar of operations. Examples are found in the production of vegetables/fruit/poultry/fish to be marketed on festival days such as Id or Chinese New Year. They must be ready on that day, not three days earlier or they would spoil, nor one week later or there would be no demand. All production operations leading up to final sale will be according to a close timetable. Thus, for the activities producing these commodities, the time dimension of inputs might be specified as closely as within a given week, perhaps even on a given day, rather than within, say, a looser one-month timeframe. In planning this type of enterprise it follows that the resource pool must also be specified in similar small quantity-time units: *e.g.*, so many labour days or so much transport in the first/second/third week of August etc. Note also that production on a continuous-flow basis throughout the year (as with orchids, pigs, coconuts etc. on some specialist farms of Types 3, 4, 5 and 6) implies ensuring adequate resource availability on a continuous basis throughout the year. Paradoxically, such production is thus highly time-specific on a continuing basis.

- *Moderately time-specific:* Typical of these activities is the planting/production of a crop under seasonal irrigation conditions. The appropriate time-unit for operation scheduling will usually be as broad as one month. In South India, the monsoon will probably arrive in late May and provide enough rain for paddy fields to be ploughed during June. The irrigation channels will start flowing in July to permit planting. July, August and September are the growing months, followed by harvesting some time in September. In this case, crop input requirements, and farm resource specification, need be on only a monthly basis (*e.g.*, June: oxpower and labour; July: planting labour; September: harvest labour etc.).
- *Low time-specific:* Activities in this category include some rain-fed crop production where the agricultural year typically consists of only two periods, the wet and dry seasons. If the farming system (in terms of the number of production activities) is not very complex, it may be sufficient to define farm resources only on the basis of season. The timing of operations will be quite flexible and if a wet-season crop is not

to be followed by a dry-season crop it will not matter much, within limits, how long some mature crops are left in the field (*e.g.*, for cassava this might be many months).

- *Not time-specific:* A few agricultural enterprises are not managed with respect to time or the seasons. A small two-cow dairy herd kept for household milk supply is one example. Commonly such stock are run on the common lands along with the other livestock of the village. They receive no special attention whether they are in milk or not, and inputs are the same throughout the year. The resource supply for this type of activity need not be specified as having a time dimension.

Family Labour Resources

Obviously family labour is a very important resource on small farms. In some areas of high population pressure, small farms might support nucleus and extended families of up to ten or more persons, all of whom except the very young and very old can supply some labour. But the actual available supply is often difficult to measure because family labour has *quantity, quality, time* and often *custom* dimensions. Difficulty in measurement arises from the fact that the different family age/ sex population classes often generate different amounts of labour service (*e.g.*, as differentially provided by young men, women, older children and grandparents), and that some farm operations/tasks are labour-type specific while others can use any class of labour. The custom dimension complicates things further by insisting that certain tasks which could well be done by men (or women) must in fact be done by women (or men).

Assuming that such activity-specific available labour has been identified, the procedure for quantifying the general family labour resource is to standardize all remaining labour according to some common quality unit, frequently adult male equivalents (AME).

In the following example, an extended family of 18 persons shown in column (2) is converted to a general farm labour force of 9.1 'adult male equivalents' in column (4). When dealing with these typically heterogeneous populations, this or a similar standardization procedure is necessary. But the limitations should be noted.

Col (1)	Col (2)		Col (3)		Col (4)
Age Group in Years	Family Members		Conversion Factor		Work Force in Adult Male Equivalents
	M	F	M	F	
0 to 8	2	3	0.0	0.0	0.0
9 to 15	2	1	0.5	0.5	1.5
16 to 55	3	4	1.0	0.8	6.2
56 and over	1	2	0.6	0.4	1.4
Total	**18**				**9.1**

First, the conversion coefficients of column (3) are necessarily subjective and thus somewhat arbitrary. Even if correct for one society, they might not be for another. In Nepal a man might be considered old at 50; but in parts of Iran he might be thought still capable of hard work at 70. Second, the male to female comparison suggested in column (3) is a generalization to which there will be many exceptions.

There are many field tasks which women can or do in fact do better than men (*e.g.*, planting seed, plucking tea, weeding, harvesting paddy). In these tasks the 1:0.8 comparison ratio of male to female labour is invalid (it possibly holds for heavy tasks). Finally, for some jobs children might in fact be equivalent in labour supply to only half an adult male, but for such jobs as herding livestock they are fully equivalent because one child can do as much as one adult.

Before leaving this topic, one further possible problem should be noted. The above procedure will result in a farm labour supply that is (it can be assumed) arithmetically valid but in some cultures this might still not be a measure of family labour actually available. Many families set a high value on what in developed countries would be called 'leisure' but which in South Asia would be regarded by even poor families as necessary participation in social and religious festivals, community affairs and village politics.

The labour supply standardization procedure might result, for example, in an apparent labour supply of, say, 750 AME labour days; but when this is adjusted for non-farm socio-cultural demands on the family's time, the actual supply might be only half this. The point could be of obvious practical importance in the planning of new farms (on irrigation or settlement projects etc.) where such planning should obviously be based on actual rather than apparent family labour resources.

Resources Vs. Assets

Quantifying a farm resource pool is roughly akin to constructing an asset statement for the farm family, but there are differences. An *asset statement* is a listing of all property owned and its value. Value might be based on the (imputed) productivity value of the assets, but is more commonly based on their current market value.

An asset statement might be prepared periodically as an instrument for measuring a family's economic progress over time (in terms of its changing 'net worth'), or occasionally as evidence of security in applying for a bank loan etc. A family's asset statement includes both farm and non-farm property and other items of financial value.

RESOURCE ACQUISITION AND GENERATION

As indicated the main structural characteristic of small farms of Types 1 and 2 is their orientation to internal generation of most of their needed resources. Farms of the other types must also generate their resources, at least in the long run, but do so through the medium of cash sales and external or off-farm purchase.

RELATIONSHIPS BETWEEN RESOURCES, CAPITAL AND COSTS

Perhaps the best way to conclude this discussion of resources is to summarize the relationships between resources, capital and costs,

As shown in Figure 4.3 on page 162, This shows

- How the five categories of resources discussed above become, in their economic dimension, either fixed or operating capital;
- The various types of costs which are generated by the use of capital; and

- How each resource/capital category (1) to (5) contributes to final total farm costs. Figure 4.3 serves as a useful introduction to discussion of the whole-farm service matrix and the evaluation of past whole-farm system *ex ante* operational planning. While Figure refers to a whole-farm system, the cost structure of an enterprise or activity subsystem would be analogous.

In Figure, starting with the first resource category of long-term fixed material resources in column 1, row:

- Shows this as becoming farm fixed capital. In row
- This type of capital gives rise to fixed capital costs. Then, going to row
- This group of fixed costs forms one component of total farm fixed costs (the other component of farm fixed costs being those fixed costs which might arise from institutional resources as discussed below).

Returning to column 1 and continuing down to row (v), this indicates the purposes for which total farm fixed costs are incurred: replacement of capital resources as these wear out or become obsolete, routine maintenance of these capital items, and (for some fixed capital or institutional items only) costs of operating them so long as these costs cannot be allocated to any specific farm activity or enterprise—if they could be so allocated, they would be included as a variable cost in column 3.

Continuing, row (vi) is a more precise description of each of the cost purposes of row (v): 'replacement' is achieved by setting up a depreciation fund (depreciation costs), 'maintenance' by incurring costs for repairs or periodic servicing of capital items, while 'operating' remains as 'operating'.

Column 2 refers to institutional resources. In row (ii) these do not become either fixed or working capital (although one could argue that such institutional resources as a licence to produce and sell milk to a town market is a sort of capital). In row (iii) the use of institutional resources could generate a type of farm fixed costs known as general charges, *e.g.*, the payment of a land or road or house tax which purchases the right to use or occupy these resources (as distinct from the physical resources themselves). In row (iv) such general charges or institutional fixed costs, if any, would combine with capital fixed costs from column 1 to give total farm fixed costs. In addition, in row (iii) some of the institutional resources might also incur variable costs (*e.g.*, payment of an output-based tobacco production tax), in which case they would combine with the variable costs of column 3 and (if relevant) column 4 to give total farm variable costs in row (iv) or total direct production costs for the system in row (v).

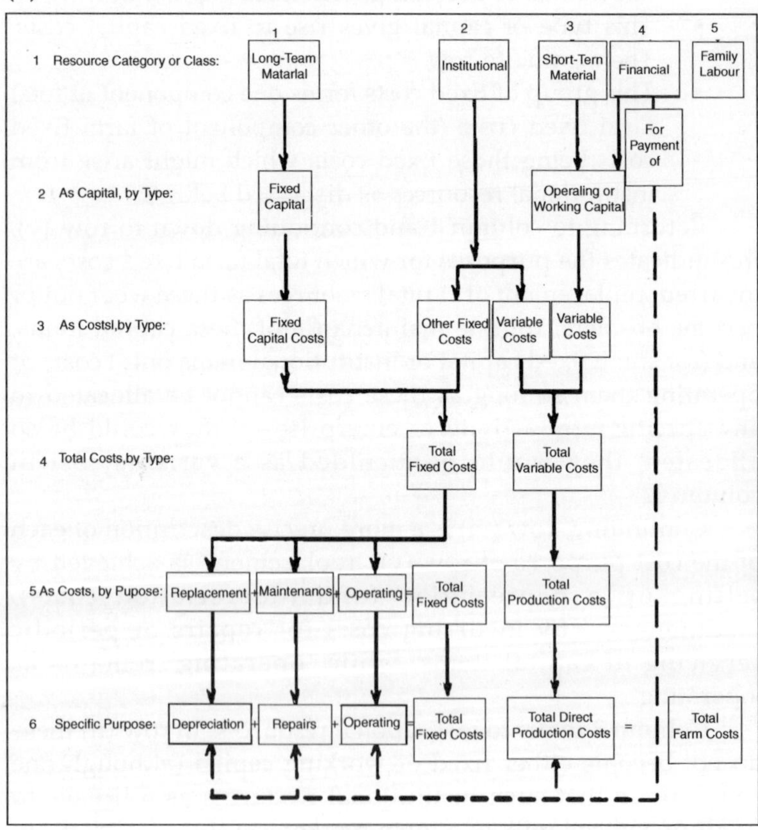

Fig 4.3 Relationships Among Categories of Resources, Capital and Costs in a Whole-farm System Context

Considering resource category columns 3 and 4 in Figure 4.3, these show short-term material and financial resources as operating or working capital in row:

- Which generates variable costs in row;
- These in turn are totalled in row;
- As total variable costs of the system. The specific purpose of these could be shown in rows; and
- Note that, as indicated in the diagram, while financial resources are used to pay for the fixed and direct farm costs, they may also incur variable costs through such items as bank fees and interest charges.

Family labour is shown as a resource in column 5 of Figure. In contrast to hired labour, it is usually not costed. Instead, family labour is taken as receiving income (for its services of labour and management) as a beneficiary of the farm system. However, as outlined and illustrated in Tables, family labour is costed on an opportunity cost basis in the calculation of such total productivity measures as total factor productivity and return on capital or equity. Row (vi) of Figure shows how all fixed and variable costs arising from the employment of the various categories of resources become total farm costs.

5

Farm Household System Budgeting

ENTERPRISES *VERSUS* ACTIVITIES

In everyday language, the terms 'enterprise' and 'activity' are often used interchangeably. In technical usage, however, these terms have quite distinct meanings. There are two reasons for this.

First, in systems analysis, many 'enterprises', if they are to be analysed as systems, must be broken down into subsystems. 'Coconut enterprise' is a good enough description if it refers to growing and selling coconuts; but if it includes selling some nuts, making coir from the husks of others, making and selling yam from this coir, and making and selling charcoal from the coconut shells etc., it will obviously be necessary to differentiate among these various subsystems of the coconut enterprise. This is best done by referring to all coconut-based subsystems in aggregate as an enterprise, and to each respective subsystem as a separate activity. Clearly, selling fresh coconuts will involve different resource inputs, product outputs and management problems than spinning coconut-husk yam. Thus a particular farm enterprise may involve one or more activities.

Second, some planning methods in farm-system analysis and construction (*e.g.*, budgeting and linear programming) require that the alternative tactics or technologies which can be used in the production of some resource or final product be specified. To take a very simple example, production of one hectare of paddy might require 100 kg of cattle manure or its equivalent as fertilizer. If the farmer has no manure, possible alternative tactics for obtaining it might be for him or her to buy NPK fertilizer, or to exchange labour with a neighbour for the needed manure, or to grow a green manure crop in the future paddy field, or to buy a cow. These alternative tactics (or any particular mixture of them) are each different activities which might be used to the same end of producing paddy. An important aspect of farm planning is thus to determine which technological activity or activities might best be used within each enterprise.

There are three ways in which 'activity' may be used as a technical term relative to the hierarchy of agricultural systems of Figure.

These are:

- To refer to a particular technology or process used at Order Level 1 or 2 in the farm system;
- To refer to a resource-generating subsystem of Order Level 3 in the farm system; and
- To distinguish at Order Levels 4 and 6
  - A particular method of producing the product of an enterprise from other methods of producing the same product or
  - The production of a particular product in an enterprise which has a variety of possible products. In general, which meaning should be given to the term 'activity' will be apparent from the context. Most often it will have the enterprise-related meaning pertinent to systems of Order Levels 4 and 6. Fuller consideration of the various types of activities relevant to the planning of farm systems is given.

ENTERPRISES

As noted above, an enterprise consists of a farm subsystem aimed at the output of final product. It may involve one or more activities in terms of the technologies used and the form of the final product.

ENTERPRISE BOUNDARIES

For farm management systems analysis in all Modes, an essential property of enterprises is that they be possible of identification and disaggregation from the whole-farm system context in which they occur, *i.e.* that their boundaries be defined and that their input-output relationships be measurable.

Where the enterprises already exist as part of a mixed farm system this proceeds by the three sequential steps of:

- Examining the farm system to identify the main commodities being produced;
- Identifying the resources used in relation to each commodity; and
- Identifying and quantifying enterprise input-output relationships in the form of an enterprise budget table as outlined.

ENTERPRISE STRUCTURAL TYPES

In terms of their structure, enterprises may be broadly categorized as simple, composite or complex. A *simple enterprise* is one which can be readily identified within and disaggregated from a whole-farm system. The extreme case is found on mono-crop estates and single-enterprise farms (*e.g.*, Sri Lankan tea estates, Singaporean pig farms) where the enterprise subsystem is practically equivalent to the whole-farm system. Only slightly more difficult to identify/disaggregate/quantify are the buckwheat and apple enterprises on small Himalayan hill farms; but the disaggregation of, *e.g.*, cotton/wheat/paddy/livestock enterprises on a mixed Sind farm is usually more difficult because of the structural interrelationships among enterprises.

A *composite enterprise* is one which aggregates what structurally or logically should be considered as two or more different enterprise subsystems into a single composite enterprise for one of two reasons—the practical difficulties of disaggregation, or the fact that the work involved in disaggregation might not be warranted for the purpose at hand. An example would be the 'livestock' component of a typical Peshawar mixed farm where the livestock could consist of two cows (for milk, butter, ghee, cheese sale and/or consumption), two oxen for ploughing (but sometimes rented out), three young sale cattle, one camel and three donkeys for transport, six sheep for wool (to be sold or spun) and five goats for milk and meat. All these classes of stock would usually be run/pastured together most of the year, none receiving any special treatment. While the different classes of stock can be readily identified, it would be very difficult indeed to disaggregate them into seven separate livestock enterprises, *i.e.*, to define meaningful boundaries for each livestock species subsystem. For most planning purposes they could be regarded as a single composite 'livestock' enterprise.

A similar situation arises on the intensive vegetable farms in the mountain zones of Java, where five, six, seven... vegetable species occupy the same field simultaneously, some directly dependent on others for shade, wind protection or live trellis support, and where each relay of each crop is partly dependent on previous relays for residual fertilizer and pest reduction. It is very difficult to disaggregate the species into separate bean, maize, sweet potato... enterprises. Possibly the most difficult of all systems to disaggregate are the highly mixed forest-gardens of the wet tropics, partly because the mix of 15 or more species is continuously changing.

A *complex enterprise* is one in which there is more than one important product and where there is some considerable degree of cycling of resources within the same enterprise, usually via the farm resource pool. This is common in traditional agriculture as exemplified in Figures By comparison, most enterprises on modem commercial farms are structurally simple. Using wheat production as an example, the situations are compared in Figure.

As shown on the righthand side of Figure, on modem commercial farms most resources are typically purchased, wheat is often grown as a sole crop for grain which is sold, and that is the end of the matter. On the other hand, in the traditional Asian situation, wheat is usually combined with several other enterprises and most resources are farm-generated. Thus, in the lefthand-side example of Figure, wheat both uses and produces some of its resources (retained seed and stockfeed cycled as oxpower and manure fertilizer). The enterprise has several products: grain (for family sustenance, sale and farm use), retained seed, bhoosa (straw, some of which might be sold for use in brickmaking and some retained for use as livestock feed/ bedding), and stubble which will be used or sold to other villagers as grazing. In addition, the enterprise might provide the basis for kitchen-scale food processing/marketing activities. Figure clearly illustrates the complexity of what at first glance might seem a fairly simple enterprise.

ENTERPRISE AND ACTIVITY BUDGETS

An enterprise or activity is defined and quantified in terms of a budget table which, relative to some specific time span, defines the boundaries of the subsystem. A *budget* is essentially a listing of all resource inputs to an enterprise or activity and their costs, and all outputs and their values, both inputs and outputs being measured over some specified time period.

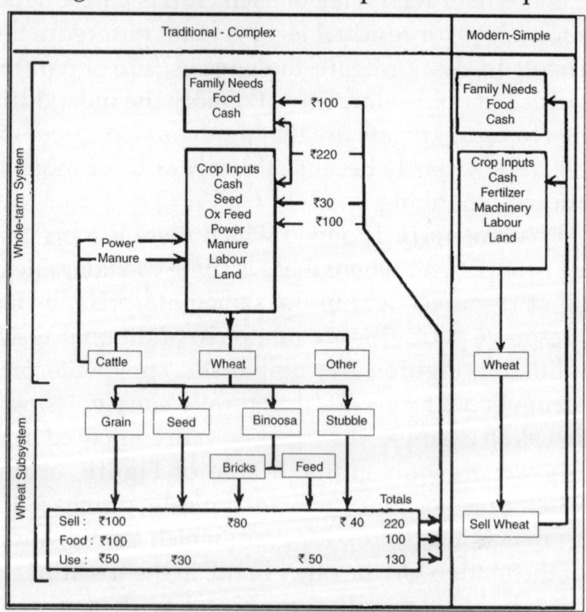

Fig 5.1 Comparative Structure of Traditional and Modern Wheat Enterprises

As appropriate, a budget can also show the difference between total costs and returns which is*enterprise net return* or, if no allowance is made for fixed costs, *enterprise gross margin*.

The time span to which the budget refers needs always to be specified and borne in mind. This period of time may be the production period of the output involved or some other period such as an annual cycle.

BUDGET TYPES AND PURPOSE

From a time perspective there are three kinds of budgets pertinent to enterprises and activities:

- *Planning budgets* are forward-looking projections of the resources which will be required to obtain some anticipated outcome. They are prepared as a basis for formulating an activity, enterprise or whole-farm production plan, usually for the next crop or seasonal or annual phase (if it is a long-term activity). They are concerned with what should happen.
- *Control budgets* are used to maintain a current check on and adjust resource supplies to an enterprise or activity once it is in operation, *i.e.*, once the planning budget has been activated. They are not used on small farms but are an important management tool on estates. Usually they take only a financial form and are designed to control fiscal expenditure in the activity or enterprise. The degree of control can be very high: *e.g.*, on Malaysian and Sri Lankan rubber, tea, oil-palm and coconut estates the daily-prepared control budget can show on any day of the operating year the amount of money spent on and the amount and value of product harvested from the enterprise, down to practically the last cent and kilogram. Control budgets are used for these and other continuous activities (such as on orchid, dairy, pig and poultry farms). Obviously, the shorter the production phase, the less need there is for budget control.
- *Evaluation budgets* are backward-looking summations of what did happen. They are essentially accounting documents intended to measure the past performance of an activity or enterprise over some period, usually the prior phase. They are better referred to as *operating*

statements because they state with certitude the facts they contain (inputs, outputs etc.). These might be intended only to offer an accounting of past results or, more analytically, to allow diagnosis of weaknesses within the system (or subsystem) and prescription of remedial action.

Table 5.1 Example of an Enterprise Planning Budget: Inputs, Costs and Returns for 2.5 Acres of Dryland Ginger in the Wet Zone of Sri Lanka[a]

	Real level (per 2.5 acres)				Per acre or unit level
Labour[b]					
Operation	**Timing**		**Labour days**	**Family or hired**	**Labour days**
Clear land	Mar		25	F	10
Clean drains	Mar		38	F	15
1st fork	Mar		125	H	50
2nd fork	Mar		88	H	35
3rd fork, smooth	Apr		63	H	25
Line for planting	Apr		5	F	2
Hole, plant, mulch	Apr		38	F	15
Fertilize	Apr		5	F	2
Weed once	May		25	F	10
Fertilize	Jul		5	F	2
Weed twice	Jul		40	F	16
Guard	Dec-Jan		75	F	30
Harvest	Jan		40	H	16
Total family labour			256		102
Total hired labour			316	₹ 3 160	₹ 1 264
					Materials
Item		**Amount**	**Price**	**Cost**	**Cost**
Seed	Mar-Apr	1 635 kg	₹ 5.90/kg	₹ 9 647	₹ 3 859
Tools	Mar-Apr			63	25
Watcher's hut	Mar-Apr			25	10
Fertilizer	Jul	340 kg	₹ 1.60/kg	544	218
Straw mulch	Jul	3 750 bundles	₹0.10/bundle	375	150
Crop storage	Jan	(already exists on farm)		0	0
Transport	Jan			63	25
Market sacks	Jan			250	100
Total materials				₹ 10 967	₹ 4 387
Total all costs[c]				₹ 14 127	₹ 5 651
Output					
Clean ginger		6 825 kg	₹ 4.50/kg	₹ 30 713	₹ 12 285
Gross margin				₹ 16 586	₹ 6 634

Note: [a]For purposes of later analysis related to Figure, note that these total costs are all variable costs. There are no fixed costs pertinent to this particular budget formulation.

Feedback

The use of evaluation budgets for diagnostic purposes

implies feedback from evaluation to planning budgets: adjustments to the system made on the basis of the former will occur via the planning budget prepared for the next operating phase.

Even if there are no weaknesses to correct, the actual enterprise outcome will seldom be exactly as predicted in the planning budget. Referring to Table, hired labour actually used might be 270 rather than 316 days and actual achieved yield might be 6 270 rather than 6 825 kg. These results would now flow back as guides to hopefully more accurate updated estimates in the next planning budget.

Data Content

In addition to summarizing likely enterprise or activity results, planning budgets are primarily concerned with identifying those resources and other factors which might limit or constrain production. Accordingly, in constructing them, it should be kept in mind that what might be apparently unimportant outputs (by-products) of one system might be critical inputs to another.

In control budgets the most important and often the sole data recorded might relate to flows of finance to the activity or enterprise; alternatively, the critical factor to control might be labour, or in an irrigated desert environment it might be water. Control budgets are not further discussed.

The basic data content of an evaluation budget depends on analytical circumstances, specifically the operating objectives of the enterprise or farm. If this is profit maximization, financial data alone will enable the evaluation; but if the objective is subsistence food production, the data will relate to resource inputs (mainly labour) in comparison with food outputs. But while either of these might be sufficient for only an accounting of what did happen, they would in themselves be practically useless if the analysis was in diagnostic mode. Evaluation budgets in this mode have the most extensive and detailed data requirements.

These are discussed in general terms in the remainder of this chapter and are applied in examples of systems' comparative analysis.

Hazards

The different types of budgets and their purposes will be clear enough. But budgets are not always what they seem. On one group of commercial farms it was routine office practice, until recently, to propose planning budgets for each enterprise in the approved way but then, at the operational stage, as the need arose, to allocate cash which had been budgeted for the wheat to the sheep, fertilizer budgeted for the pyrethrum to the wheat etc. In consequence, at the end-of-year evaluation stage, all that could be said was that some total amount of cash, fertilizer, labour etc. had disappeared somewhere into the farm, but as to the economics of the individual subsystems, or whether uneconomic enterprises should be curtailed or replaced by more efficient ones.

BUDGET STANDARDIZATION UNITS OF MEASUREMENT

For some purposes and modes of analysis (*e.g.*, description), the budget might be specified at *real level* (*i.e.*, at the actual levels of the input and output variables) and refer to the enterprise as it actually exists. But for most planning and evaluation purposes, since - *e.g.* - 2.5 acres of ginger cannot be directly compared with 1.9 hectares of paddy, it will be necessary to standardize the various enterprise or activity budgets by bringing them to a per acre or other *unit level* as in the righthand column of Table 5.1. Further, for purposes of comparison between enterprises or activities, these unit-level budgets must also refer to a common time basis such as, *e.g.*, per hectare per year.

Use of land area as the basis for standardizing crop and livestock budgets is not always appropriate or possible. The most appropriate standard unit to use will depend on the category to which the enterprise or activity belongs and the particular farm type/situation. Most field-crop and tree-crop budgets will in fact usually most appropriately be on a land-unit basis. So will budgets for the horticultural crops on large farms. But for small farms growing tree or vine crops and some horticultural crops (anthurium flowers in Sri Lanka, vanilla in Java), a more appropriate budget basis might be costs and returns per 100 plants or even per single tree (as for the houseyard farms of Java growing three or four high-value clove trees). Further, in the wet tropics the tree crops in particular are often grown in highly mixed stands: a forest-garden farm in Kerala or in Java might consist of six coconut palms, two breadfruit, three jackfruit, four coffee trees, three pepper vines, etc. These species-enterprises would be best budgeted/evaluated on a per tree or per vine basis (or for some purposes these various species might be consolidated into a single composite enterprise budget).

In other situations, even though a species might be present in large numbers as part of the whole of a farm system, it might be grown/managed/exploited without any regard to the land area it occupies—as in the case of nipah palms along the rivers of Trengganu, sago palms on village lands in Irian Jaya and palmyrah palms in the dry zone of Sri Lanka. Perhaps the extreme case is found in Kordofan where the baobab trees, each of which is the property of some family or clan and an important basis of their semi-nomadic existence, might be scattered along the clan's seasonal migration routes over a distance of 600 kilometres or so. Budgets for these and similar tree-crop enterprises could obviously not be expressed on a unit of land area basis; more appropriate would be inputs/outputs per family, or, since labour is a common factor in their control or exploitation, per labour day of effort expended in maintaining or exploiting some specified number of trees.

Livestock enterprises can present special problems in preparing standardized budgets for purposes of comparison. In some cases it will be possible to construct budgets for dairy cows, sheep etc. on a 'per hectare of land use' basis; but the yak herders of Haa and the camel people of Wajir would not have the slightest idea of the number of hectares over which they range.

Highly-mixed sedentary herds/flocks, as found in parts of Pakistan and North India, require standardization of two kinds (assuming they can be disaggregated). First, the separate species (cattle, camels, sheep etc.) and classes of each species have to be standardized in terms of some common animal unit (AU) basis[2] and then, as discussed above, the budgets for each of these (standardized) species-enterprises might have to be compared on the basis of some common input or production factor (such as land or labour or cash required or generated etc.).

In the following example, a farm's herd of five head of mixed cattle and a flock of 16 head of sheep are each standardized (on the basis of approximate feed requirements) by taking one lactating cow as equivalent to one animal unit (AU). Each other type of animal is then expressed as AU relative to a lactating cow, for example:

Cattle	Equivalence Factor	Sheep	Equivalence Factor
Milk Cow	1.0 AU	All types	0.15 AU
OX	0.9 AU		
Calves	0.3 AU		

Population equivalence in AU:
Cows: 2 head × 1.0 AU = 2.0 AU
Oxen: 2 head × 0.9 AU = 1.8 AU
Calves: 1 head × 0.3 AU = 0.3 AU
Total cattle in AU: = 4.1 AU
Sheep: 16 head × 0.15 = 2.4 AU
Total cattle and sheep in AU = 4.1 + 2.4 = 6.5 AU.

It is important to note, however, that from a farm management as opposed to an animal nutrition point of view, it may sometimes be more relevant to standardize livestock on some such basis as labour required by each species/type, or cash inputs required by each, etc. The above nutrition-based equivalence factors are for purposes of illustration only.

Long-term crop and livestock enterprises require a somewhat different approach in budgeting.

- Evaluation budgets of long-term enterprises (or activities) are usually prepared on an annual or seasonal basis and relate to the performance of the enterprise over its most recent operating phase. These single-phase budgets are the same as budgets prepared for short-term enterprises (or activities) and ignore what might have happened to the enterprise in earlier phases and what might happen to it in future phases.

- Planning budgets of long-term enterprises (or activities) are a different matter. Here the inputs/outputs of the enterprise (or activity) must usually be specified for each year of its future life—over 20 to 25 years for coffee, 20 to 40 years for cardamom, 60 to 70 years for coconut, etc.

LEVEL OF BUDGET DETAIL

The necessary degree of detail in a budget is determined by the mode and purpose of analysis. Thus Table 5.1 would probably be adequate for descriptive purposes and for planning purposes, but too detailed for accounting evaluation and too vague for diagnostic purposes.

Table 5.1 offers much information relating to labour: jobs to be done, monthly timing of operations, whether family or hired. This might or might not be necessary for planning. On the other hand, the budget says nothing about the type or quality of labour to be employed. Are these workers to be men, women or children?...or do the various tasks specifically require women or men? This would be important on an estate; or if the budget referred to a crop such as coffee requiring school children as harvesters. Regarding yield, 6 825 kg of good ginger is projected to be produced, but how much sub-standard ginger will also be obtained?... and would this be enough to provide a basis for a small kitchen-scale oil extraction activity?

Explicit and Implicit Information

In addition to offering explicit information, a budget should be amenable to implicit extension. Such measures as activity gross margin should permit derivation of further, more detailed measures: gross margin per hectare, per day of family labour, per ₹ 100 of operating capital etc. This is essential in comparative analysis.

UNIT BUDGETS

In order to apply some important planning methods, Table below contains too much information and is too awkward to be used directly. For such purposes, unit-vector budgets are needed.

These are simplified, stripped-down versions of a budget such as that of Table from which the following unit-vector budget for ginger has been developed:

Identification:			
	Date:		Feb. 93
	Crop:		Ginger
	Level:		One acre
	Production period:		11 months, Mar. 93 to Jan. 94
Gross margin:			6 634 ₹
Resource requirements:			
	Land		1 acre
	Family labour		
		Mar.	25 AME
		Apr.	19 AME
		May	10 AME
		Jul.	18 AME
		Dec.-Jan.	30 AME
	Operating capital		
		Mar.-Apr.	4 995 ₹
		Jul.	369 ₹
		Jan.	287 ₹
	Other		
		Storage	1 acre equivalent

In the above unit budget, the inputs of Table are consolidated under the headings 'land', 'family labour', 'operating capital' and 'other'. Labour and capital are given a time-dimension (for reasons discussed previously). Also, all information relating to costs versus returns is now consolidated into a single item 'gross margin ₹ 6 634', *i.e.*, no separate cost or return items are shown. Information relating to some items, *e.g.*, hired labour, is now discarded because item-specific costs have been consolidated in the single gross margin item.

All other data of Table are now discarded (but of course they would not be discarded if the purpose were detailed post-production evaluation rather than planning). On the other hand, some resources which might only have been implied in Table might now become important. Ginger storage was listed in Table but not the amount or quality of storage needed. If it is possible that these aspects of storage could prove limiting factors to future or expanded production, they would be entered as explicit resources in the unit-vector budget. Use of this type of budget in farm planning is illustrated.

EXTENDING BUDGET SCOPE PROCESSING AND MARKETING

In the conventional pre-systems approach to farm management, analysis was largely restricted to field production operations; the post-harvest aspects of an enterprise such as on-farm storage, kitchen processing, family consumption, transport and disposal of commodities beyond the farm gate were regarded as falling within the province of specialists in other fields - marketing experts, processing engineers, family nutritionists etc. Such a compartmentalized approach is possibly appropriate on those farm types where products are simply sold off the farm, *e.g.*, sugarcane to a mill or raw milk to a bottling plant.

However, as emphasized, such a level of structural simplicity is rare on small mixed Asian farms where products and by-products are used and disposed of in many different ways. Here, to define the boundaries of an enterprise as encompassing only field production operations would be quite inadequate. On Type 2 (semi-subsistence) farms it would tell only half the story and on Type 1 (subsistence-oriented) farms only a fraction of it. More specifically, it would overlook the possibilities for household income generation through on-farm or kitchen processing and local marketing, and at village level of establishing cottage industries, moreover, where agricultural resources are already exploited to their potential, local further processing of crop outputs often offers greater scope for rural development than does farm development *per se*.

A Bhutanese farm wife making corn cakes in her kitchen and selling them around the streets of Tashigang is as important a component of the farm's corn enterprise as her husband's corn-growing activity. In this hill country, too, it is not unusual to come across a group of farmers who have each carried out a sack of oranges or potatoes to the nearest road, maybe walking for two or three days, in the hope of selling them. Farm production problems become rather irrelevant. The people know these things; why not the universities?

Clearly, under these 'beyond-the-field' circumstances—and they are often the norm not the exception—if an enterprise is not to lose its 'pith and moment', a systems approach to farming and farm development is called for. But while systems concepts are increasingly accepted, their actual application in farm development projects is not remarkable. It remains at best a field in which the coconuts have only nodding acquaintance with the pineapples and the carp or tilapia, and at worst an arena in which the 'two and forty jarring sects confute'.

Flowcharts

As an aid in understanding the often complicated post-harvest flows of products and byproducts from an enterprise, a useful first step is to sketch them before attempting to incorporate their main elements into a budget.

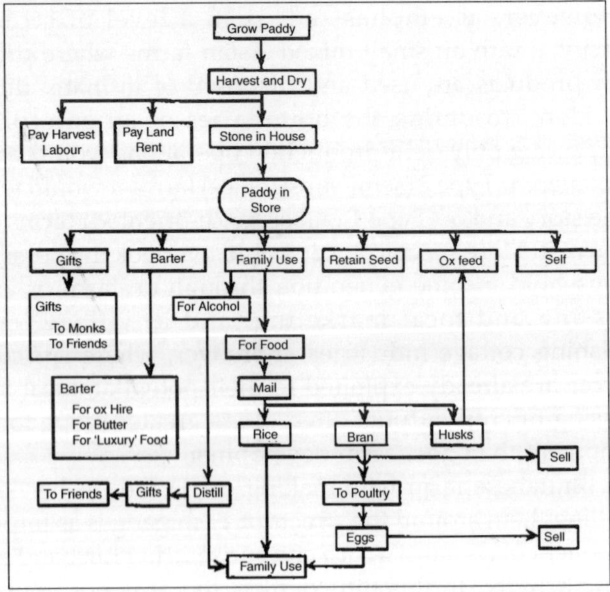

Fig 5.2 Example of a Flowchart Post-harvest Handling and Disposal of a Paddy Crop, Bhutan

An example is shown in the flowchart of Figure for post-harvested paddy on a small Type 2 farm in Bhutan. The chart emphasizes those portions of the paddy crop retained for family use; quantities are not indicated.

ECONOMIC AND FINANCIAL BUDGETS

Table 5.1 is an *Economic Budget.* As a planning budget, it lists all the planned inputs and outputs and their values whether or not these will incur actual out-of-pocket costs or will yield actual cash receipts.

For some purposes a *financial budget* will be required. This is an edited version of an economic budget which lists only actual financial outgoings (or costs) and income (or returns). For example, in Table 5.1 if the seed is to be retained from the previous crop and the tools are on hand, these economic 'costs' would now be excluded. Similarly if the cost of the watcher's hut in Table 5.1 is based on providing an annual depreciation amount for this capital item and is not an actual cash outlay, this also would be excluded from the financial budget.

On commercial farms, since all or most inputs are bought and outputs sold, economic and financial budgets are practically equivalent (except that non-cash charges such as depreciation are excluded from the latter). At the other extreme, on Type 1 farms there will be few if any purchased inputs and few sold outputs so that financial budgets are hardly relevant.

REAL AND IMPUTED INPUT COSTS AND OUTPUT VALUES

In a non commercial environment and where no actual markets exist for inputs or outputs, their values must be imputed. In Table 5.1 straw was valued at 10 cents per bundle. If the farm had not actually bought the straw this might be based on an estimate of what it was worth if used on some other crop (such as mushrooms) or what the farmer could have earned by working for a neighbour instead of staying home bundling straw for his ginger.

Usually the most important economic input is family labour. In Table 5.1 the 256 days of family labour cost nothing in terms of cash outlay and the enterprise gross margin is ₹ 16 586. This conveys an accurate picture only if family labour in fact has no value; but if some realistic value for family labour could be imputed (*e.g.*, by what it could earn off the farm or from the farm's roadside boutique) then Table conveys a false picture of ginger economics: *e.g.*, if family labour had a real value or opportunity cost of ₹ 10 per day, the gross margin would be decreased by ₹ 2 560.

On Type 1 and 2 farms there is often no reference point for the valuation of resources. In consequence, deciding on an appropriate opportunity cost or shadow price for labour, oxen, buildings etc. can be quite subjective. The facts alleged in a budget relating to subsistence-oriented farming, whether for a single farm or for the sector as a whole, will often not stand their ground. This is especially so in Fields C (*i.e.*, sectoral development) and D (*i.e.*, advice for policy making), and not infrequently—sad to say—the 'economies' of an enterprise (or farm or industry based upon it) are nudged up or down to serve a non-objective purpose.

BUDGET-BASED MEASURES OF PERFORMANCE

Depending on the purpose of analysis there are four ways in which an enterprise (or activity) can be evaluated, or four measures of economic performance which can be applied: enterprise net return *(NR)*, gross margin *(GM)*, operational gross margin (*OGM* or 'activity price') and cost of production *(COP)*. *NR, GM* and *OGM* are outlined in this section. *COP* is discussed.

Net Return

Net return *(NR)* is the most appropriate measure if the purpose is an accounting evaluation of past or future projected performance. It is obtained as *NR* = *TGR* - *TC* where *TGR, total gross return* of the enterprise, is the sum of all outputs times their prices, real or imputed, and *TC is* total enterprise cost, again real or imputed. *TGR* needs no further discussion.

TC consists of two components, total variable cost *(TVC)* and total fixed cost *(TFC)*. *Variable costs (VC)* are those of input items the amounts of which change (usually but not necessarily proportionally) with the size or level of output of the enterprise:

the labour, seed, fertilizer, etc. of Table 5.1 are examples. *Fixed costs (FC)* are those of input items, usually services rather than physical things, which remain constant regardless of the size or level of enterprise output: taxes on a barn used to store grain or other produce, the interest costs on an irrigation system, a depreciation amount set aside to eventually replace a cocoa dryer are examples. Fixed costs are further discussed in relation to whole-farm systems.

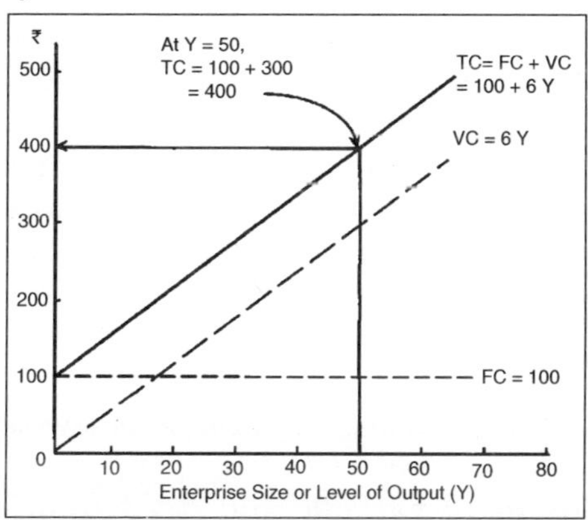

Fig 5.3 Example of Relationships between Level of Output and Fixed Costs, Variable Costs and Total Costs

The relationships between level of output and fixed, variable and total costs are exemplified in Figure. With zero output, variable costs are also zero, but increase as output or size of the enterprise is increased. Fixed costs are constant throughout (but some activities or enterprises will in fact incur no fixed costs). *TC* at any point over the output range is simply the sum of *VC* and *FC*; here, in this particular example, at an output level of 50 units, they are ₹ 300 + 100 = ₹ 400. Note that while *VC* will always increase (*i.e.*, slope upwards) as *Y* increases, the relationship between them need not be linear. This is in contrast to *FC* which will always be linear and parallel to the *Y* or output axis for a given configuration of the production system.

Gross Margin

Gross margin *(GM)* is the most appropriate measure of enterprise performance if the purpose is an operational rather than accounting one, *e.g.*, to make rapid comparisons among three, four, five... enterprises with a view to expanding some or contracting others. *Gross margin* is obtained as total gross returns less variable costs, *GM = TGR - VC, i.e.*, fixed costs are ignored since, by their nature, they have to be met whatever is produced (and even if nothing is produced). Justification for this is based on the fact that, by definition, farm fixed capital (ploughs, work oxen, irrigation, etc.) can usually be used by alternative crops; if it is currently used for cotton and cotton prices drop, the farmer will want to evaluate the possibilities of alternative crops—corn, sesame etc. In the short run he or she is stuck with whatever supply of fixed capital is on hand and can budget out the alternatives by considering only those input items which will change if he or she adjusts from cotton to wheat or sesame.

Operational Gross Margin

Operational gross margin *(OGM)* is somewhat equivalent to net return. *OGM = TGR - DC,* where DC is enterprise *direct costs* and consists of variable and fixed components. The difference is only one of emphasis; the *DC* of an enterprise consists of all costs directly associated with that enterprise, usually calculated on a per unit of enterprise basis (per hectare, per head of livestock, etc.). The *DC* of an enterprise thus consists of its variable costs plus some proportion of the farm's fixed costs which should logically be borne by the enterprise. The concept of *DC* is a piece of terminology used with linear programming. An example is discussed in situation (d) of Table below (*See Table 5.2 on page 184*).

Assignment Between Fixed and Variable Costs

The assignment of input items to the fixed or variable categories of enterprise total costs will usually present no problems. However, some items do not fall naturally into one or other category. Whether they should be put in the fixed or variable baskets will depend on circumstances. Four situations are shown in the budgets for a ginger enterprise in (a), (b), (c) and (d) of Table (*See Table on page 184*).

Situation:

(a) Is taken directly from Table. There are no storage costs, variable or fixed, and no other fixed costs, thus net returns of `16 586 are the same as gross margin. In situation

(b) The enterprise budget now contains a storage cost of 500. This consists of taxes paid on the storage shed which remain constant regardless of how much ginger is stored or grown. It is thus included as a fixed cost. In situation

(c) At a cost of `400, the farmer instead now rents storage on a cost per cubic unit basis; thus ginger storage is here a variable cost because if yield was twice as high or twice as many acres of ginger were to be grown, twice as much storage would be needed and its cost would be twice as much.

Situation (c) is also different in that where previously hired labour was a variable input of 316 days times `10 per day, labour is now not casual but permanently attached to the household and must be paid (at `10 per day) regardless of how much ginger is grown or its yield. Thus in (c), labour becomes a fixed cost to ginger. (This assumes that ginger is the only crop on the farm: if there were other crops, the fixed labour costs would be shared among them.) This is offered as a caution that some costs do not, simply because of their nature, always belong in either of the fixed or variable categories. An important variation of this occurs on estates where the resident labour force incurs both variable costs (a daily wage) and fixed costs (housing, clinic, worker insurance, retirement fund etc.).

Situation (d) is different again. Here the budget is to be used for planning aimed at selection of the best mix of several enterprises (ginger, corn, cotton etc.) and is on a per unit (acre) basis. Now the storage fixed costs, which were assigned wholly to ginger in situation (b) because this was the only crop on the farm or the only crop to need storage, are shared between ginger and some other storage-using crop, say corn, one fifth or ` 40 per acre to ginger and four fifths or ` 160 per acre to corn according to their likely relative use of this facility. In (d), the purpose of the budget is to obtain enterprise direct costs and thence the operating gross margin (*OGM* or enterprise net 'price') for use in formulating optimal combinations of several enterprises; the budget is not directed at the evaluation of past performance.

Table 5.2 Evaluation of a 2.5 Acre Dryland Ginger Enterprise Under Different Cost Conditions

For 2.5 acres of ginger		(a)	(b)	(c)
Variable Cost		(₹)	((₹)	((₹)
	Hired labour	3 160	3 160	(fixed)
	Seed	9 647	9 647	9 647
	Tools	63	63	63
	Watcher's hut	25	25	25
	Fertilizer	544	544	544
	Straw mulch	375	375	375
	Storage	0	0	400
	Transport	63	63	63
	Marketing	250	250	250
Total Variable Costs (*VC*)		14 127	14 127	11 367
Total Fixed Costs (*FC*)		0	500[a]	3 160[b]
Total Costs (*VC* + *FC*)		14 127	14 627	14 527
Gross Returns (*GR*)		30 713	30 713	30 713
Net Returns (*NR*)		16 586	16 086	16 186
Gross Margin (*GM*)		16 586	16 586	19 346
For 1 acre of ginger			(*d*)	
Gross Returns (*GR*)			12 285	
Total Costs without storage			5 651	
Total Costs with storage of Rs 40			5 691	
Total Direct Costs (*DC*)			5 691	
Operating Gross Margin (*OGM*)			6 594	

[a]For storage
[b]For hired labour

EXTENSION OF ENTERPRISE OR ACTIVITY BUDGETS TO WHOLE-FARM BUDGETS

A *whole-farm budget* is the structural parallel of an enterprise or activity budget, with budgets of the several enterprise and activity subsystems now aggregated. There is only one change: those fixed costs which cannot be logically assigned to any activity are now included as whole-farm fixed or common or *overhead costs (OC)*. This latter term is preferable because it distinguishes more clearly between fixed costs that are specific to an enterprise or activity and those fixed costs which are accrued on a whole-farm basis.

Overhead costs consist of land, water and road taxes, insurance and repair costs of buildings which cannot be assigned to specific activities, and all other input costs relating to the upkeep and maintenance of the whole farm. These overhead costs can be both fixed and operational: *e.g.*, both the annual tax paid on a farm water-supply pump and the fuel costs of operating it. The relevant criterion is that they cannot be logically charged against specific activities or enterprises.

The derivation of a whole-farm budget from the budgets of its constituent enterprises is shown in Table 5.3. In this simple case there are only three enterprises on the farm. This might convey an impression that enterprises can be clearly separated with well-defined boundaries. On small farms, however, there will usually be a ragtag of miscellaneous activities directed to supplying feed for the oxen, fertility for cash crops etc., so that budgets must be prepared for these also even if they do not generate a final product or positive (imputed or real) gross margin; or they can be aggregated into a smaller number of composite activities; or, when neither of these is possible, they must be included as whole-farm costs.

Table 5.3 Whole-farm Evaluation Budget Derived from Enterprise Budgets

Item	Gingar 2.5 acres (₹)	Cotton 1 acre (₹)	Soybeans 0.7 acres (₹)	Whole Farm (₹)
Gross Returns (*GR*)	30 713	20 000	10 000	60 713
Variable Costs (*VC*)	14 127	10 000	5 000	29 127
Fixed Costs (*FC*)	0	3 000	2 000	5 000
Overhead Costs (*OC*)				8 000
Total Costs (*TC*)	14 127	13 000	7000	42 127
Gross Margin (*GR* - *VC*)	16 586	10 000	5 000	31 586
Net Returns (*GR* - *TC*)	16 586	7 000	3 000	18 586
Household Non-farm Income				3 000
Household Total Income				21 586

Whole-farm budgets are used primarily as end-of-year accounting statements or summaries of farm performance over that or some other operating period. They are generally not operational tools, except when used to project whole-farm performance over several years, *e.g.*, to project the total results of a five, six, seven... year farm-development programme.

EXTENSION OF WHOLE-FARM BUDGETS TO THE HOUSEHOLD

At the whole-farm budget level, one other important element can now be introduced, namely household non-farm income. In Table this is included to obtain household total income. Where the purpose of analysis is not agro-technical farm planning but rather to ascertain the economic wellbeing of the farm household, the next step would be to analyse household outgo or expenditure on non-farm items necessary to keep the whole farm-household system operational—family expenditure on medical services, food, clothing, children's schooling, meeting social obligations etc.

But this step is seldom taken in formal farm management economics (which by-and-large remains preoccupied with agro-technics). This is a pity because it leaves one with an incomplete picture of what is really going on within the most important system component, the household. In particular, it gives no knowledge at all about which beneficiaries are getting what from the system... and, at the end of the day, this of course is what it is all about.

COST OF PRODUCTION

An enterprise or product-producing activity can also be evaluated in terms of its unit Cost of Production *(CoP)*. This is obtained as its total costs divided by the quantity of output achieved with those costs, *i.e., TC/Y*. In Table ginger CoP is ₹ 14 127/6 825 kg or ₹ 2.07 per kg.

CoP is usually not a relevant measure of enterprise performance in providing advice to farmers (Field A), especially on small farms where interest is in (net) income rather than what it costs to obtain that income. But in other fields *CoP* can be the most appropriate measure of performance. In Field C the manager of a milk bottling plant will want to know what the milk*CoP* is on farms supplying raw milk to his or her plant (as a basis for setting his or her buying and selling prices and consequent profit margin); he or she will not be interested in farmers' incomes as such.

In Field D, policy makers in Fiji will want to know what the copra *CoP* is on Fijian farms in comparison with Indonesia, Philippines, Malaysia etc. in order to establish sound industry research and development policies—and perhaps even to decide if the Fijian industry has a viable long-term future.

One area where *CoP* is important in Field A is on tea, rubber, cocoa, coconut and other estates where *CoP* rather than net returns or gross margin is the conventional measure of estate performance, both on the same estate over time and in comparison with other estates. But taken by itself *CoP* conveys no information, except perhaps by implication, of the real economics on these estates.

In the 1960s, due largely to political instability, those tea estates of Sri Lanka with the lowest *CoP* per pound of made tea were the worst estates in every other respect, the low *CoP* being due to the fact that the green tea was just being harvested and processed, with little or no expenditure on field or factory or other estate maintenance. In those circumstances *CoP* was, if anything, only a measure of the degree of current system exploitation. (The phase was only a temporary one.)

ACTIVITIES

As noted previously, an enterprise—or any parallel activities of Order Level 4 or 6 making up an enterprise—is a production process directed to the production of one or more final products for sale or consumption (but it might also indirectly generate some amount of resources). All other types of activities in a farm system (*i.e.*, those of Order Level 1, 2 or especially 3) are directed in one way or another to the generation of resources for use on the farm: but they might incidentally also generate some final products.

As with enterprises, these resource-generating activities have to be quantified and evaluated. This requires the construction of activity budgets which are in all essential respects similar to the enterprise budgets discussed above.

TYPES OF RESOURCE-GENERATING ACTIVITIES

The main types of resource-generating activities are now briefly discussed..

Activities and Enterprises as Resource Generators

Those enterprises or activities which also generate some amount of resources fall into three categories:

They Might Generate the Resource

- For their own use or
- For the specific use of some other enterprise or
- For general non-specific use by other enterprises. In the sketch of Figure, situation
  - Exists in the dairy enterprise: enough of the female calves produced are retained to replace the older cows as these are culled from the herd. In regard to this resource the enterprise is essentially self-perpetuating. Situation
  - Is represented by the second enterprise, maintaining a beef cattle herd in parallel with the dairy herd in which the latter generates male calves for the specific use of the beef enterprise. Situation
  - Is represented by the flow of another resource, dairy cow manure, into the general farm resource pool for use by any of the farm's crop enterprises/activities. In all these cases the resource-generation aspects of the dairy cows are incidental to their main purpose of producing a final product, milk. This type of enterprise (dairy cows) as a resource-generator would be quantified/budgeted/evaluated as was the ginger enterprise of Table 5.1; its total output value would include the value of calves and manure.

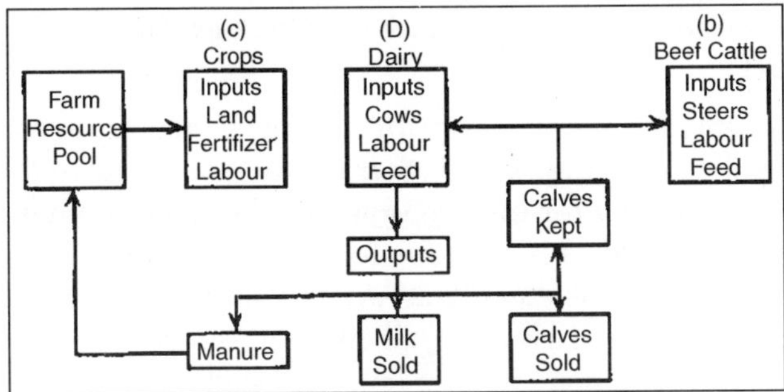

Fig 5.4 Example of Enterprises as Resource Generators

Major Resource-generating Activities

On mixed farms, particularly livestock farms, most resource-generating activities consist of substantial sets of inputs and operations which are similar in all respects to main enterprises except that the main output now is a resource for use on the farm, *i.e.*, an intermediate product rather than a final product. Common examples are a fodder crop grown for dairy cows and a legume crop grown to enhance fertility for some following cash crop.

When financial evaluation of such activities is required, this will proceed as in Table. If no final product is generated, the results of this evaluation will be a negative 'net return' or gross margin equivalent to activity total costs. If some final product is incidentally produced, the value of this will partly offset activity costs; in some activities, costs might be fully offset by the value of final products.

Budget evaluation of resource-generating activities will be necessary in two situations: first, when the activity as a resource generator is to be compared with alternative activities generating the same resource; and second, when cost and return data for all enterprises and activities on a farm, which have been evaluated separately, are to be pooled to enable a whole-farm budget to be constructed.

As with enterprises, it is sometimes not possible to define the boundaries of resource-generating activities, in which case several might have to be aggregated as a composite, or even accounted for on a whole-farm basis.

Resource Generation by Purchase or Barter-exchange Activities

Probably the simplest way for a farmer to acquire a resource is to buy it or exchange some other product or resource for it—payment of money for the use of a parcel of land, exchange of family labour with a neighbour for use of her oxen etc. Such purchase or barter is equally an activity and is quantified and evaluated in terms of a budget, albeit a very simple one. Budgets for two such activities - renting land and exchanging labour for ox draught power.

Table 5.4 Example of Budgets for Resource Generation by Purchase or Barter-exchange Activities

Budget Item		Activity
	Rent land oxpower	Exchange labour for
Input cost	₹600	20 Labour days
Output return	0.25 ha land	4 Ox days
Gross margin	-₹ 600	₹ 0

In the case of renting land, considering the activity only as an activity (and not considering any eventual recovery of the rental cost from the future sale of the crop to be grown on the land), the activity result is an annual cost of ₹600 or a net return or gross margin of -₹ 600 per unit (0.25 ha) of activity. This conceptual approach is appropriate where there are several alternative ways of acquiring land (by rent, lease, outright purchase, clearing jungle etc.) and the costs or returns of each have to be evaluated regardless of what might actually be produced on the land. However, if the renting of land is a normal cost of growing some specific crop, 'renting land' would then be only a normal cost item in the budget for such an enterprise and no separate land-renting activity budget would be necessary.

This also applies to the case of exchanging labour for oxpower. The only difference between the two cases is that the gross margin of exchanging labour is zero because it is assumed that the value of labour exchanged is equal to the value of ox days received (at least in the eye of the farmer). Again, it should be stressed that these resource-generating activities are here quantified and evaluated as activities; if they happen to be integral parts of some specific enterprise then no separate budgets are needed.

ACTIVITY BUDGETS IN LINEAR PROGRAMMING FORMAT

For one important method of analysis used in prescriptive farm planning, *i.e.*, Linear Programming (LP), such budgets as those of Table are reduced yet further. As shown in Table, they are re-written and couched, with slight rearranging, in relation to the farm's resource pool. The *GM* of each activity is the same as before and indicates the money amount by which the value of output of the farm system increases or decreases due to one unit of the respective activity being included as a resource generator in the farm production plan: renting land as an activity in itself would reduce annual farm income by ₹ 600; exchanging labour would have no direct effect. (However, both would have a later indirect effect when actually used in some enterprise.)

Table 5.5 Example of Resource-generating Activity Budgets in Linear Programming Format

Budget Item		Activity
	Rent land	Exchange labour for oxpower
Gross margin ₹	-600	0
Resource pool		
Land (ha)	-0.25	
Labour (days)		20
Oxpower (days)		-4

In LP format the input and output items of the budgets are stated in terms of their effect on or demand for those corresponding resources shown in the resource pool. Renting land has a negative demand on land in that it contributes to rather than detracts from whatever supply of land is available. Similarly the budget of the labour exchange activity indicates that this barter activity would require or use 20 days of farm labour and that it would generate four days of oxpower. The above activities and their 'budgets' are of an operational nature; their use in whole-farm planning is illustrated.

Resource Generation by Transfer Activities

This again is a very simple kind of activity. It consists of transferring some particular resource now assigned to one activity/enterprise to use by some other activity or enterprise. The ginger enterprise of Table provides an example. About seven tonnes of ginger storage capacity is needed. If this does not presently exist on the farm, a storage shed could be built at some known cost, or alternatively the farmer might be able to convert part of his or her cow barn to storage space for ginger. This type of activity 'generates' resources by transferring them from activities/enterprises where they are not needed or where they have a low use-value to other activities/enterprises where they are needed or have a higher use-value.

Just as for other types of activities, for farm-planning purposes transfer activities need to be quantified in budget form. Thus the above examples of transfer of space from use by cows to ginger is quantified by the following simple budget of this transfer activity:

Budget Item	Transfer of space from cows to ginger
Gross margin of activity (₹)	0
Cow shelter lost (m^2)	1
Ginger storage gained (m^2)	-1

The above example might appear trivial, but resource generation by use-transfer is a powerful tool in more sophisticated analysis of farm systems using linear programming.

External Activities

All the activities noted so far have been internal to the farm. In addition, where the opportunities exist, households often supplement these on-farm activities by off-farm work and petty trading. However, such off-farm activities are usually undertaken more to supplement household income than to obtain resources for the farm component. An exception could be when an above-normal amount of resources is needed temporarily for farm development as distinct from routine farm production.

Application and Use of Resource-generating Activity Budgets

Budgets for the various types of resource-generating activities outlined above are applied in whole-farm planning.

FURTHER EXTENSIONS OF ENTERPRISE OR ACTIVITY BUDGETS

Using a budget such as that of Table 5.1 as a base, several extensions can be made from it for operational purposes, viz.:

- Preparing *partial budgets;*
- Developing *conditional* or *parametric budgets,* equations or graphs;
- Deriving further *performance factors* for use in *comparative analysis* of farm subsystems;
- Preparing *long-term evaluation budgets* for *ex ante* appraisal of investment in an activity or enterprise which extends over many years; and
- Assessing an enterprise or activity under *conditions of uncertainty.*

PARTIAL BUDGETING

As the term indicates, partial budgeting is concerned with the evaluation of only selected parts of a system—only parts of a process, activity, enterprise, farm service matrix or of the whole farm. In farm management in Field A (*i.e.,* advising farmers) partial budgeting is most commonly used to test possible adjustments to farm-level systems which are presently not working well. At higher levels it is widely used as the basis for structuring agricultural development projects (*e.g.,* to assess the impact which a dam or a new road system might have on some parts of existing farm-level systems).

In Table 5.6 partial budgeting is applied to the 2.5 acre ginger enterprise of Table to evaluate the likely impact which irrigation might have on this presently dryland enterprise. Part:

- Of Table is the base budget for this activity, the present 'without irrigation' situation. In making the comparison it is necessary to consider only those few elements or parameters which might change if irrigation were to be used. These changes comprise additional yield whose value is partly offset by additional labour, transport and marketing costs and the lower price for irrigated ginger. As shown in part

- Of Table, the net effect of these changes, *i.e.*, 'after' versus 'before', is an increase in gross margin of `4 422.

Table 5.6 Evaluation of Adjustments to an Enterprise or Activity by Partial Budgeting

(a) Base budget (unirrigated ginger)		Change from (a) to (b)	(b) Partial budget (irrigated ginger) showing changes in input costs and returns	
Input cost (₹)			Extra labour (₹)	
Hired labour	3 160	+	Water channels	700
Seed	9 647	0	Water application	600
Tools	63	0	Extra harvest	100
Watcher's hut	25	0		
Fertilizer	544	0		
Mulch	375	0		
Storage	0	0		
Transport	63	+	Extra transport (₹)	15
Marketing	250	+	Extra marketing (₹)	80
Total cost (₹)	14 127	+	Total extra costs (₹)	1 495
Output			Output changes	
Ginger (kg)	6 825	+	Extra ginger (kg)	1 500
Price (₹/kg)	4.50	-	Lower price (₹/kg)	4.40
Gross value (₹)	30 713	+	New gross value (₹)	36 630
Gross margin (₹)	16 586	+	New gross margin (₹)	21 008
			Extra gross margin (₹)	4 422

At process level, partial budgeting is a useful tool for adjusting systems of Order Level 1 and 2 which do not warrant the use of more sophisticated methods of response analysis. At whole-farm level, partial budgeting can be used for adjusting the enterprise or activity mix of a system if this does not warrant the use of the more powerful programming methods.

CONDITIONAL OR PARAMETRIC BUDGETING

The type of budget of Table refers to an activity as formulated at some specific point in time. Obviously it will cease to be valid if there are changes to prices, costs, technology or the underlying production conditions. In most situations such changes will in fact occur either through the influence of the market on prices and/or costs, through changes in technology introduced by the farmer causing changes in yield and cost, or through yield changes due to Nature. If the budget is going to be needed for future or continuing use, it is desirable to anticipate likely future changes in the relevant *critical parameters* and build these into the *base budget*. This is done by adding, at the time of budget construction, conditional (or parametric) extensions to it. On the other hand, one might not be concerned with future change but only with considering several alternative cost/price/ technical scenarios at the moment of budget construction (*e.g.*, What if costs were to double? What if yields increase/decrease by 20%?...). Conditional extensions to reflect such possible changes in critical parameters are a useful analytical tool.

SINGLE-PARAMETER EXTENSIONS

The steps in conditional extension of an enterprise or activity budget are straightforward, viz.:

- Identify the parameter which is most significant in terms of its impact on budget results and likelihood to change. In the example of Table 5.1 this is, say, ginger sale price.
- Specify the range over which this parameter is likely to change; here, say, from ₹ 3 to ₹ 6 per kg.
- Specify the budget result (*e.g.*, ginger gross margin per acre) as a simple equation in terms of the parameter of interest (*e.g.*, ginger price). Thus, for the particular example being used here, from Table.

Gross margin/acre = Total revenue/acre - Variable cost/acre, *i.e.*,

$GM = TR - VC =$ (Yield/acre)(Price/kg) $- VC = (Y)(p_y) - VC =$ 2 730p_y - 5651

where Y denotes ginger yield per acre in kg and p_y denotes ginger price per kg in ₹.

(iv) Graph the single-parameter equation from (iii) as shown in Figure and use this graph as an alternative to solving the equation for all likely prices. Such a parametric-budget approach permits the validity of the base budget to be maintained even though the variable of concern might change over time.

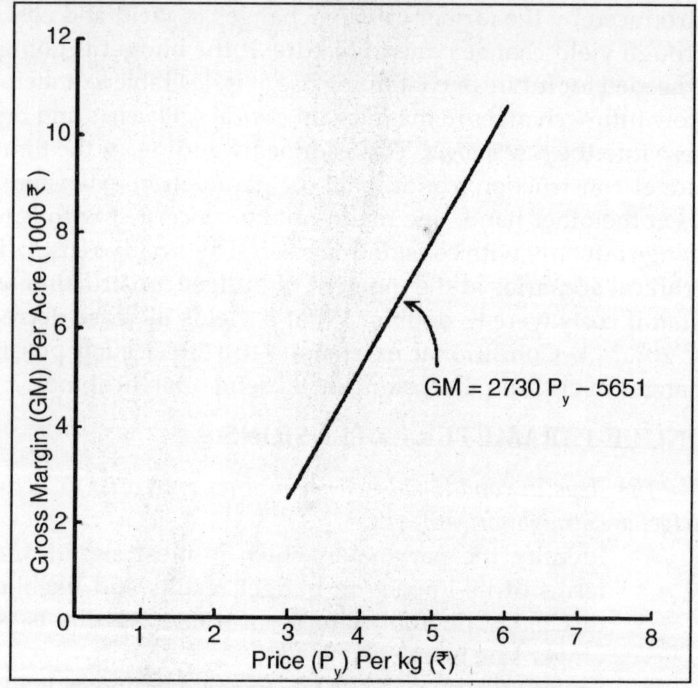

Fig 5.5 Example of a Single-variable Parametric Budget Showing Ginger Gross Margin Per Acre for Ginger Prices Ranging from 3 to 6 ₹/kg

TWO-AND THREE-PARAMETRE EXTENSIONS

Parametric budgeting is readily expanded to accommodate two or three variable parametres—beyond three variables, graphical presentation of results is usually too complicated. As an example, Figure 5.6 shows a three-variable parametric budget relating to the growing and chipping of cassava tubers by an estate for sale as livestock feed. The objective of this budget is to allow rapid determination of total estate net returns.

The unstable parameters of concern to management on this particular estate are: annual field yield of fresh cassava tubers per acre, the percentage of dry processed chips recovered per ton of wet tubers, and the sale price of dry chips. The graphs of Figure show how the results of a base budget for this enterprise might be parametrized in order for the budget to be 'solved' for any combination of the three unstable parameters: *e.g.*, at a yield of 10 tons per acre, with a chips recovery rate of 35 per cent and a chips sale price of \$13 per picul, total annual net returns for this particular West Malaysian estate would be approximately \$330 000. Analogously to the case of single-variable parametric budgeting (Figure), the graphs of Figure are based on the net returns equation,

$$NR = TR - TC = (Y) \rightarrow (p_y) - TC$$

where Y is tuber yield in tons per acre per year, r is the dry chips recovery coefficient and p_y is chips sale price per picul. Y, $r$and p_y are variable (*i.e.*, parametrized in the budget over their relevant ranges) and total costs are given.

Picul is a common weight measure in parts of South East Asia. It equals 100 catties of 1.3 pounds each and is thus equivalent to about 60 kg.

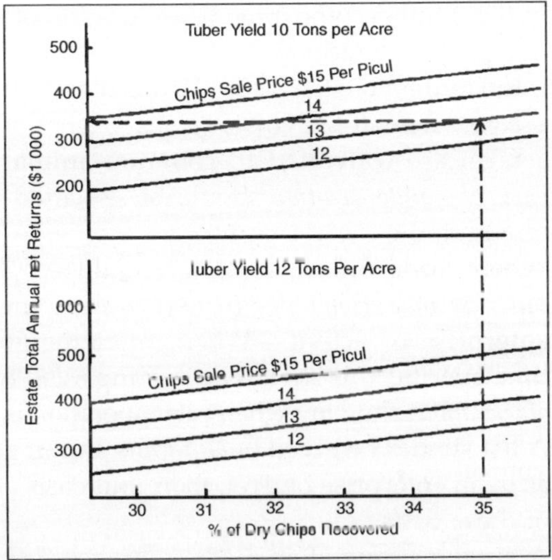

Fig 5.6 Example of a Three-variable Parametric Budget showing Annual Net Returns on a Cassava Estate by Tuber Yield, Dry Chips Recovery Rate and Sale Price

DO'S AND DONT'S OF ENTERPRISE AND ACTIVITY BUDGETING

Because budgets are the basis of most of the subsequent farm-household system analysis presented in the following chapters, it is appropriate to conclude this chapter with a list of do's and dont's as a guide to good budget construction.

This applies specifically to enterprise and activity budgets but also generally to other types of budgets such as whole-farm, partial, evaluations-over-time etc.

- The first requirement is for an accurate and unambiguous *heading* or *title* to the budget, *e.g.*, not just Tea' if reference is to some specific type of tea grown at a specific location and elevation.
- Specification should be given of the *level* or *size* of the enterprise or activity to which the budget data refer—*e.g.*, whether to one, two, six, seven or 100 hectares; or whether to one or 100 head of camels. It is not helpful when one encounters budgets headed simply 'Sheep' or 'Economics of Goats' etc. without indication of the number, type, breed and location of the animals under consideration.
- If the budget contains standardized or converted units —*e.g.*, when all the cows, calves, oxen, buffalo etc. on a farm are converted to common animal units—the *basis of standardization* should be specified in the table or a footnote.
- Where appropriate, a listing should be given of the *separate operations* performed within the budgeted enterprise or activity. When input requirements are time-specific, this should be accompanied by a *calendar of operations* showing when each operation is performed.
- A list should be given of *all inputs* and, if appropriate, as in an enterprise budget, their unit costs and the total of these costs.
- A similar *listing of all products generated* (by-products as well as main products), their respective unit prices if they are sold and the total value of the output should be given.

- The *manner of disposal* of the items mentioned in (6) above, together with the quantities disposed of by cash sale and various other means, should be shown. This is particularly important in traditional farming systems.
- *Grade and price classifications* should be given for that part of products sold. Sometimes a farmer will sell his or her produce ungraded, in which case an average price is appropriate. Often, however, he or she will do his or her own grading, resulting in two or more product categories, each with its respective price. This level of detail is often necessary in diagnostic analysis where it will serve as a pointer to specific system weaknesses.
- An aggregation should be given of cash sales to obtain total *cash returns* for the budgeted enterprise or activity.
- An aggregation should be given of all *economic returns* (cash receipts plus the real or imputed values of those parts of production which are used on the farm or bartered or given away). If only produce which is sold is considered, this might grossly underestimate actual total production and thus the real efficiency of an enterprise or activity.
- A statement should be given of enterprise *net returns* or *gross margin*, preferably both.
- A budget prepared for diagnostic purposes must obviously contain *sufficient detail to permit problem diagnosis*. To describe an input as 'fertilizer—100 kg' might be sufficient for some purposes but it would be near useless if a specific fertilizer problem exists on a farm and there is a need to know what kind of fertilizer is being used and perhaps even when it is being applied and how frequently.
- Although budgets prepared for financial accounting or economic evaluation need not contain *physical data*(*e.g.*, ox days used, kg of crop harvested etc.), it is generally desirable that they do so, especially if they

might be used at some future date to chart the progress of the farm over time. Because of price changes, inflation and devaluation, the information—drawn from comparison of 'then-and-now' budgets—that a Javanese paddy farmer advanced from having an income of ₹ 80 000 in 1975 to one of ₹ 300 000 in 1995 would be spurious; what would be important is whether his or her paddy yield increased or actually declined, and by how much.

- The *time-dimension* of the enterprise should be noted, preferably in the budget heading. This is often essential information in relation to short-term and annual field crops: a one-hectare bean crop which occupies the land for six weeks will, on an annual basis, require only one quarter of the land resources required by one hectare of a six-months paddy crop; and, other things equal, where land is in short supply a four-month paddy crop will be superior to a five-month crop. Some livestock enterprises also will require a time specification, *e.g.*, 10-, 11- or 12-week batches of broiler chickens. Most livestock enterprises, however, will be operated on a continuing indefinite basis and with these, as well as tree crops, the time basis of most budgets will usually be a one-year period.
- Finally, the *date of construction* and the *sources of data* contained in a budget should be indicated—whether from records of a single farm, from a survey of several farms or simply the analyst's estimates. This can serve two purposes. It will provide the opportunity for independent check of the data should this become necessary, and it will indicate at least implicitly the degree of reliability that can be attached to the respective data items and to the results of any analysis based upon them.

6

Processes, Structural Coefficients and Service

SYSTEMS OF ORDER LEVELS

Structurally, the main building blocks of a whole-farm system are its enterprises; these provide its income in cash or kind. Enterprises may stand alone or be supported by resource-providing activities. The building blocks of both enterprises and their enabling activities are agro-technical processes.

DEFINITION AND NATURE

A *process* is the specific way in which a production operation is done, together with the levels or amounts of resources used in doing it. A process specifies or implies the use of some operational technology, the types and levels of resources used in its operation, and the types and levels of its resultant outputs.

Processes present two general analytical or management problems:

- To select the 'best' or most appropriate technology; and
- To operate the selected technology at its optimal level in terms of inputs and outputs.

According to the general definition of a system, a process is itself a system. Its components are its technology, its inputs and its outputs. Interaction exists in the relationships among these inputs and outputs.

The (management) objective relative to a process system is to operate it:

- At a level which is optimal for the enterprise to which it contributes; and
- In such fashion as to achieve maximum efficiency in resource use, *i.e.*, maximum output for a given input, or minimum input for a given output. The boundaries of a process are defined by the specification of the process itself and, at least conceptually, a given process system can usually be disaggregated into successively smaller subsystems.

Before looking further at these problems it will be useful to consider some examples. Table 6.1 presents a typical activity budget for maize production. While Table (and similar activity or enterprise tables such as Table) would be adequate as the basis for financial evaluation of this activity, it is nonetheless a highly generalized statement: it offers little or no structural information about any of the seven operations which comprise the activity, *e.g.*, no information is given regarding how the field was ploughed (mule, bullock or tractor?), the number of times it was ploughed or the degree of tilth aimed at. Or considering operation (2), planting, no information is offered regarding the several variations possible in this operation which could affect crop yield, *e.g.*, depth of seed placement, in-row and between-row plant spacing, seasonality of planting, the moisture level of the field at planting time etc. Nor is any agro-technical information offered regarding any of the other operations beyond the bare fact that they were done and the inputs which were used in doing them.

The seven operations shown in Table 6.1 represent seven operational subsystems, one each relating to ploughing, planting, irrigating etc. However, due to the absence of data, it is not possible to judge whether or not these subsystems consist of the best of all possible technologies to use in each operation, nor whether each one is operated at maximum efficiency. Seven kilograms of seed are specified but would it be better to use six or nine kilograms? Forty kilograms of fertilizer are budgeted but might this better be 60 or 80 kilograms? In short, Table tells nothing about the optimality of resource use. Clearly, if interest is in ascertaining whether there are better ways of performing these separate operations and whether the resources to be used in them are being used to their maximum efficiency, these operations have to be examined in greater detail.

Table 6.1 Budget of a Maize-growing Activity Inputs Per Acre

Inputs per acre				
Operation	Materials	Labour (days)	Oxen (days)	Costs/returns (₹)
1. Ploughing		5	4	200
2. Planting	seed: 7 kg	1		240
3. Irrigating	water: 1 ac ft	1		50
4. Fertilizing	fert: 40 kg *N*	1		200
5. Weeding		3		30
6. Harvesting	sacks: 50	6		280
7. Drying	wood: 2 m	3		400
Total inputs and costs		20	4	1 400
Outputs per acre				
Item	grain: 1 t			3 000

The operations of Table 6.1 are listed again in Figure 6.1. This also shows, for each operation, the alternative technologies that might be employed in performing it and a range of input intensity levels at which each technology might be implemented. For example, the 'ploughing' operation could be done by tractor, by oxen or by spade; and whichever ploughing technology is chosen could be applied one, two, three or four times: further, whichever of these possible combinations is used, it could be applied to cultivate to a depth of 7, 14 or 21 centimetres. Alternative possible technologies and alternative possible technology intensities or input levels are also shown for the other of the seven production operations.

Each specific technology (*i.e.*, the way or means by which an operation is performed), operating with the application of one or more different kinds of (variable-level) inputs, is a *process*. The technology operates either as a single-variable input process or, if it is used with two, three, four... different kinds of inputs, as a multi-variable input process. In Figure, three possible technologies are shown for the planting operation: using two-row or four-row machines or doing this operation by hand. Whichever of these planting technologies is chosen by the farmer, it can be used with a variable amount or intensity level of seed (20-, 30- or 40-thousand seeds per acre). Each of the three planting technologies is thus a single-variable input process where the variable input is seed used in conjunction with a fixed input consisting of either a two-row, four-row or hand planter.

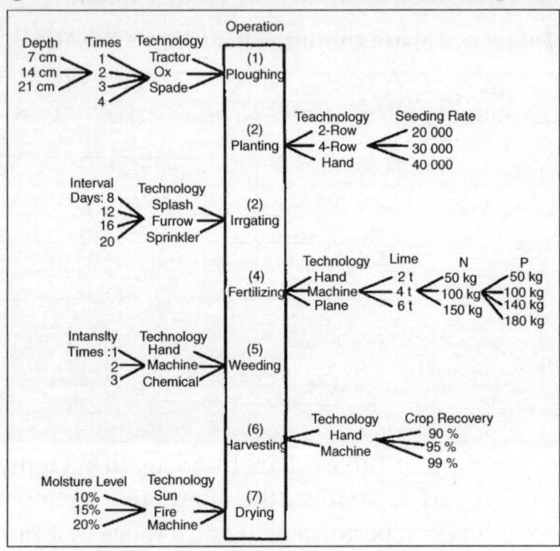

Fig 6.1 Example of Alternative Technologies in Maize Production (Per Acre Basis)

On the other hand, the operation 'ploughing' is a two-variable input process: each of the three possible ploughing technologies (doing this operation by tractor or by oxen or by hand) can be done or combined with some variable range of the two 'inputs' shown—depth to which the field can be ploughed and number of times it can be ploughed. Thus there are a total of three by three by three, or 27, combinations of ploughing technology by depth by frequency which could be applied to this operation.

Each of these 27 combinations could at least potentially result in a different crop yield as illustrated relative to number and depth of ploughings by the graphs in the lower half of Figure. For analytical purposes, such processes are usually described and quantified in mathematical terms as *response functions* or *production functions* which relate the output of a crop, livestock activity etc. to the inputs used in producing it. For a single-variable input process, they are specified by the general functional form $Y = f(S)$ which states that, *e.g.*, crop yield per ha (denoted by Y) is some function of the amount of seed used per ha (denoted by 5); or more realistically as a multi-variable input process, $Y = f(S, C)$ which states that yield is significantly determined by both the amount of seed and the number of times the field is cultivated (denoted by C); or more realistically still, $Y = f(S, C, N, P)$ where the effects of nitrogen fertilizer (N) and phosphate fertilizer (P) are also considered.

Figure 6.1 illustrates the concept of production functions. In the top figure, crop yield per ha (for some particular set of climatic, soil and husbandry conditions) is graphed as a function of the single input-variable seeding rate over the range from 10 000 to 50 000 seeds per ha. This depicts the response or production function $Y = f(S)$. In the lower figure, crop yield per ha (again for some particular set of climatic, soil and husbandry conditions - including seeding rate but excluding ploughing frequency and depth) is shown as a function of the two variable inputs depth (7, 14 or 21 cm) and number of ploughings (1, 2, 3, 4 or 5). This depicts the production function $Y = f(D, K)$ by the set of three single-variable input-output graphs $Y = f(K/D)$(for D respectively equal to 7, 14 or 21) where D and K respectively denote depth and number of ploughings and the symbolism K/D indicates that K is variable while D is fixed at some specified level.

NUMBER OF RELEVANT PROCESSES

The number of separate *operations* in an activity can be large (seven in the above example of Figure 6.1). The number of *processes* in an operation can also be large; *e.g.*, in the Figure three technologies are shown for the irrigation operation (the alternatives of splash, furrow or sprinkler application), each of these operating over some intensity range (days' interval between water applications). One could, if it were appropriate, list many more factors relating to irrigation which would have an effect on crop yield, *i.e.*, other dimensions in which irrigation could operate such as the amount of water applied at each irrigation, the quality/salinity of water used, the time of day at which irrigating is done etc.

However, such an examination of an operation in greater-and-greater detail by defining more-and-more dimensions in which it exists, if done for all operations in all farming environments, would be not far short of defining the total scope of all agricultural science. (Thus relative to the operations listed in Figure, 'planting' would encompass the realm of agronomists; 'harvesting' and 'drying' that of engineers; etc.) From the very large number of physical processes which do exist, farm management is concerned with selecting and analysing only that relatively small number which are of practical economic significance; or, in terms of the example of Figure, only those processes which have or are thought to have a significant (economic) impact on crop yield. Just which of these processes are 'significant' and thus to be subjected to economic analysis via *response analysis*, will depend on analytical circumstances. As a practical guide, farm management analysis would be confined to processes which have a relatively large effect on output or which are expensive or which require large inputs of scarce resources. In short, in such activities as those shown in Table 6.1 and Figure 6.1, there might be only two or three processes of sufficient importance to warrant full economic analysis.

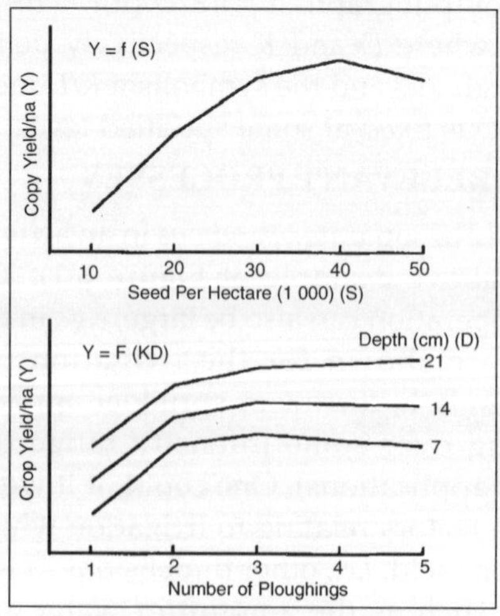

Fig 6.2 Graphical Examples of Single-variable Input and Two-variable Input Production Functions

Types of Processes

In agricultural production there are three broad types of processes:

- *Biological processes* are those in which the stimulus or input operates *directly* on the biological system of an animal or plant. Irrigation water applied to a crop root zone, feed digested by a dairy cow are examples. The great majority of economically relevant agricultural processes are of this type.
- *Bio-mechanical processes* are those in which the stimulus or input operates *indirectly* on a plant or animal, its direct or immediate effect being on the physical micro-environment in which the plant or animal exists. An example is the number of times a field is tilled. This will affect subsequent plant growth/yield, but will operate indirectly through changing the physical/ mechanical conditions in which plant growth occurs - *e.g.*, through changes to clod size, particle cohesiveness, water infiltration and soil moisture storage capacity etc. At a practical farming level these bio-mechanical processes are usually not distinguished from direct biological processes.
- *Mechanical processes* do not exist as part of a plant/ animal biological system, but act as physical/ mechanical support to such systems. Some of them can be operated at varying intensity levels, such as the delivery of feed to a herd of cows by a conveyor belt driven at varying speed. Here there might be some non-linear relationship between, say, fuel consumption and amount of feed conveyed by the belt, and the relationship would appear. In consequence, determination of optimal belt speed would be economically relevant. Many types of mechanically powered equipment—tractors, trucks, stationary motors—have such an optimal operating rate. But with others the relationship between fuel input/speed and work output is linear over some specified range; if the machine is operated beyond this range, it might simply disintegrate.

Shape of Input-output Process Relationships

Figure 6.3 illustrates some differently shaped production functions for the case of a single-variable input production process. Each graph shows the physical input-output relationship or total physical product curve as the level of the single variable input is increased with all other input factors held constant. Note that, in graphs A and B, the law of diminishing returns (sometimes called the law of variable proportions) prevails—beyond some point, as the level of the variable input increases with no change in the level of other input factors, increases in output occur at a diminishing rate (the marginal product is decreasing) and eventually, beyond the point of maximum output, output declines in absolute terms (the marginal product becomes negative).

In graph A of Figure 6.3, which is the classical depiction of a production function, all three theoretical stages of production are to be seen as the level of the variable input increases: first, an initial stage of increasing returns with output increasing at an increasing rate—maximum efficiency would never be achieved by operating the process in this stage since the marginal product is increasing; second, a middle stage of decreasing returns with output increasing at a decreasing rate (*i.e.*, marginal product is positive but declining); and, third, beyond some maximum level of output, a final stage where output declines (*i.e.*, marginal product is negative). Graph B is more realistic in showing only the second and third stages since increasing returns are not found in practice.

Graph C depicts a process in which output increases at a constant rate (*i.e.*, linearly) up to some maximum level and then remains constant (at least within the input range covered by the graph - it must be expected eventually to decline). While graphs A and B are non-linear, graph C is of (segmented) linear form. Note also that as depicted in all three graphs, output is zero when none of the variable input is used. This indicates that the variable input under consideration is essential to production (as, *e.g.*, seed in crop production). Often, however, some output may still be obtained when none of the variable input is used. In this case the input is to some extent optional (as, *e.g.*, chemical fertilizer in crop production).

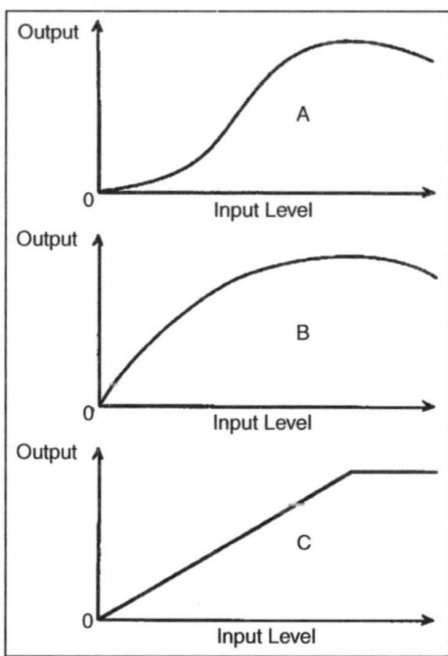

Fig 6.3 Stylized Production Functions or Input-Output Relationships for a Single Variable Input

The reasons why the use of some kinds of inputs beyond a certain level causes a decline in output will be intuitively obvious. As more and more water is added to a crop, keeping all other inputs constant (especially drainage capacity), the field will eventually become waterlogged and yield will decline; or as a crop is weeded with greater and greater frequency (*i.e.*, weeding labour inputs are increased), the point will be reached where workers will cause more damage in trampling the crop than benefit. Or again, as in curve C of Figure 6.3, offering more feed to a cow than she can consume might not cause actual milk output to decline, but beyond a certain level feed will be uneaten and go to waste (and the value of output will decline relative to the increasing cost of inputs).

ANALYTICAL PROBLEMS PRESENTED BY PROCESSES

As noted, processes present two problems in farm systems analysis:

- Selection of the 'best' technology or method of performing an operation; and
- Determination of the optimal level of intensity at which the process should be operated.

- *Technology:* Usually, selection of the 'best' process is not difficult on small farms; it is often determined by the socioeconomic environment. Selection of a two-row or four-row mechanical grain planter might present a real management problem in South Dakota, but there would be no such alternative possibilities among the hill farmers of Nepal where all field operations are done by hand. Where a farmer does face a management choice in technology selection, decisions can be made by budgeting out the costs and returns of the alternatives.
- *Optimization of input or intensity levels:* The second problem of operating the 'best' process at the 'best' level can be a little more complicated. If the choice is between two, three, four... discrete alternatives, this also can be made on the basis of comparative partial budgets. If the process is of such economic significance as to warrant more precision and if it relates to a continuous type of input, then it might require the more sophisticated methods of response analysis.

INTERRELATEDNESS OF SYSTEM COMPONENTS: *STRUCTURAL COEFFICIENTS*

The next element of a system to be examined is its structural coefficients. From the system definition, a necessary property of any system is the existence of interrelatedness among its components. In farm-household systems this takes the form of structural coefficients of two kinds. *Internal structural coefficients* exist and operate within individual production activities or other subsystems and define explicitly or implicitly the interrelatedness which exists between/among their several sub-components.

External structural coefficients are also often relevant for a given system, such as a production activity/enterprise, but their function here is to quantify relatedness between the given system or subsystem and other related systems or subsystems.

INTERRELATEDNESS WITHIN AN ACTIVITY INTERNAL STRUCTURAL COEFFICIENTS

Internal structural coefficients are those which 'tie together' or link the various components of a (crop, livestock or whole-farm) system. They are an especially important characteristic of those farm production activities which generate part of their own resources, *e.g.*, mixed livestock activities. The budget for one such activity, annual maintenance of a sheep flock to produce wool and lambs, is shown in the lower section of Table.

This flock budget would probably be adequate if the purpose is to evaluate the financial results of sheep production and perhaps compare such results with those of other activities.

Table 6.2 Internal Structural Coefficients and Annual Activity Budget for a Self-sustaining Flock of 100 Ewes

Internal Structural Coefficients	
Ewe mortality rate	0.05
Lamb birth rate	0.90
Lamb mortality	0.09
Rams: ewes	0.05
Ewe and ram replacement rate	0.20
Activity Budget	(₹)
Input costs	
Replacement rams	(bred)
Replacement ewes	(bred)
Feed	8000
Veterinary	300
Shearing	1900
Labour	2000
Marketing	800
Total direct costs	13000
Output returns	
Culled ewes and rams	9000
Male lambs	10000
Female lambs	5000
Wool	8000
Total returns	32000
Gross margin	19000

On the other hand, however, the budget tells practically nothing about the techno-economic structure of the activity, *i.e.*, how the various internal components of ewes, lambs and rams, and the technical performance of each, impact on each other and on the overall budget results.

Such interrelatedness must, of course, exist but in the budget itself it is only implied. To be of use for some analytical purpose - *e.g.*, analysis in problem-diagnostic mode—the implied coefficients have to be stated in explicit form. The relevant internal structural coefficients are shown in the upper section of Table. They indicate that in this example the normal death rate among ewes is five per cent annually; 90 lambs are born annually per 100 ewes; nine per cent of lambs do not survive; five rams are run per 100 ewes; 20 per cent of the (old) ewes and rams are replaced (by retained lambs) annually.

There are three main reasons for taking explicit note of these internal structural coefficients. First, they show at a glance the techno-economic conditions under which the results of an activity are achieved (in this example the results are a self-sustaining flock of 100 ewes yielding an annual gross margin of ₹19 000).

Second, they are essential information if the budget is intended for activity problem diagnosis. Third and of primary interest here, they provide a basis for closer examination of the interrelatedness of the various components of the activity—in this example between populations of and returns from the lamb and ewe components of the activity.

The objective might be to quantify the separate effects of sheep losses and sales on the annual maintenance of a constant-size flock of 100 ewes. Assuming that this particular aspect of the sheep system is to be examined, a flowchart such as that of Figure would be prepared showing the interrelatedness of components, in terms of animal numbers, in more detail. This is an elaboration of the relevant parts of the budget table. As noted, this flowchart refers to sheep populations. If some other aspect of interrelatedness is of interest (*e.g.*, feed supply *vs.* births/deaths etc.), a flowchart based on the relevant parameters would be prepared analogously to Figure 6.4.

STRUCTURAL COEFFICIENTS AS CRITICAL PARAMETERS

From the previous discussion of parametric budgets, most of the internal structural coefficients of Table will be recognized as 'critical parameters'. Such coefficients as lamb birth rates etc. are critical in the sense that any significant change from their present level would obviously flow through to alter the final result (sustainability and gross margin) of the activity. Such changes would be evaluated by making conditional or parametric extensions to the budget of Table.

However, it might be noted that while internal structural coefficients are similar to critical parameters, they are not exactly equivalent. Some factors, *e.g.*, lamb mortality rates, are both coefficients and critical parameters. But others, such as the amounts of wool cut from ewes and lambs and the prices received for these, are critical parameters although they might not involve interrelatedness among the several elements of the system and are therefore not internal structural coefficients. Similarly, some activity input/cost items such as labour and feed might be economically 'critical' but would have nothing to do with interrelatedness among activity components.

INTERRELATEDNESS AMONG ACTIVITIES EXTERNAL STRUCTURAL COEFFICIENTS

The second type of system interrelatedness, that which is quantified in terms of external structural coefficients between activities or enterprises, is illustrated by the example of Figure 6.4. This presents budgets for four integrated coconut activities: growing coconuts for direct sale, or alternatively using the nuts and by-products as inputs to the three related activities of making copra (from coconut flesh), making charcoal (from shells) and making coir fibre (from husks).

From the previous discussion, it is here useful to distinguish, on the one hand, between this set of four coconut-based operations as an enterprise and, on the other hand, each of the product-specific subsets of operations as activities. Note also that

Figure 6.4 encompasses only a small set of the great number of coconut activities that are possible.

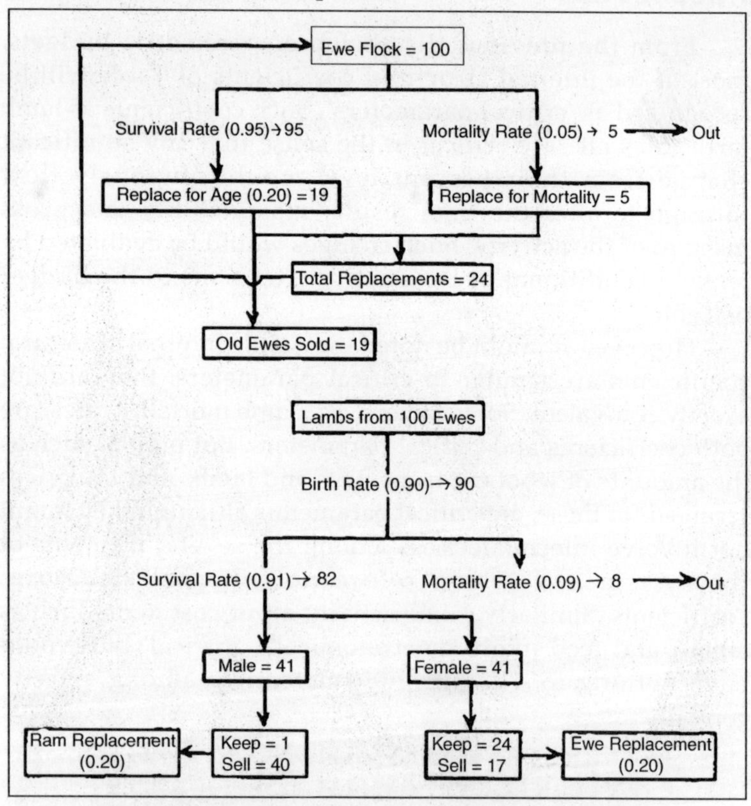

Fig 6.4 Flowchart depicting Role of Internal Structural Coefficients in Annual Maintenance of a Self-sustaining Flock of 100 Ewes

Activity budget 1 of Figure. which relates to producing 4000 nuts annually from the standard 64 palms per acre, would apply if these nuts are simply to be grown and sold. Budgets 2, 3 and 4 apply if instead the nuts are retained on the farm for further processing. They show operations, inputs, costs, outputs, gross returns and net returns for the respective activities (all of which are possible components of the overall coconut enterprise). For present purposes what are of interest are the external structural coefficients which link these several activities together. These coefficients are briefly explained.

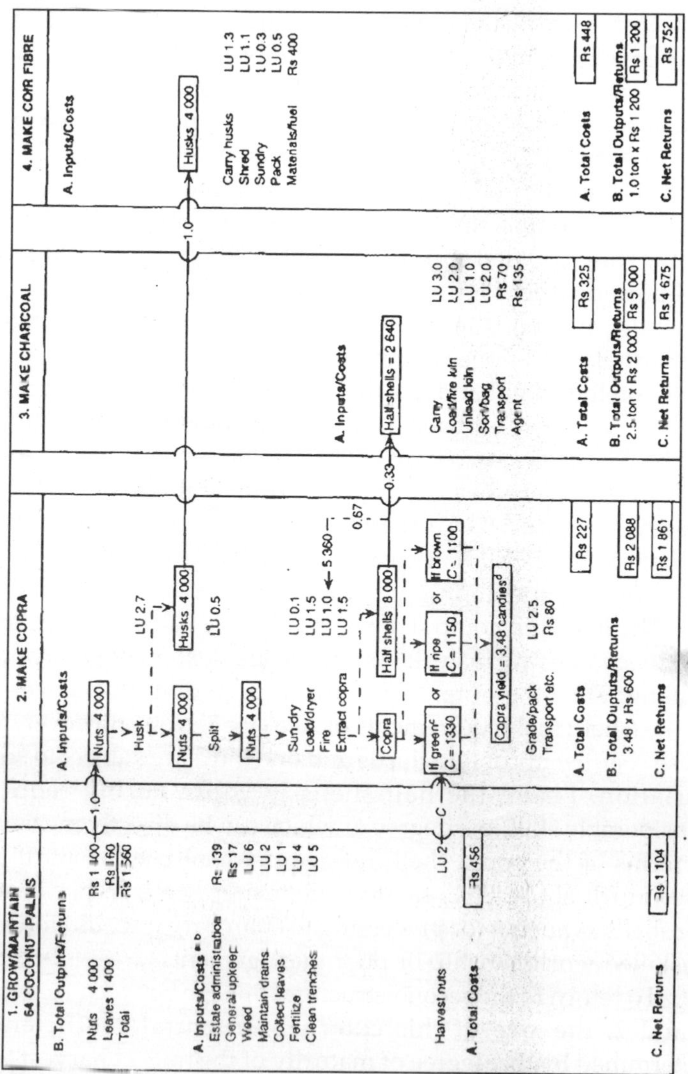

Fig 6.5 Structural Relationships among Four Coconut Activities (Per Acre Basis)

In Figure the first relationship between Activities 1 and 2 is through the output of nuts in Activity 1 as this determines the raw material available for Activity 2, copra making. This linking coefficient has a value of 1.0—all nuts are used for copra. But on some other farm the coefficient could be, say, 0.75 if three quarters of the nuts are processed and one quarter sold as nuts. This would occur, *e.g.*, if 25 per cent of nuts are first grade and sold as food, while all second-grade nuts are processed as copra.

In Activity 2, copra making, the first operation is husking 4 000 nuts, which produces 4 000 clean nuts plus 4 000 husks. The clean nuts are then split into halves which contain the (future) copra. These are first sun-dried for half a day then loaded into a fuel-burning drier for five days. After unloading, the cured copra is hand-extracted from the half-shells and is then subjected to the further operations shown under Activity 2. The now-empty shells, on the other hand, are disposed of in two ways: two thirds of them are recycled back as dryer fuel for curing some future batch of copra (*i.e.*, two thirds of the shells from any batch would provide sufficient heat to dry the copra of that batch). This is shown in Figure 6.5 as a coefficient value of 0.67 (of 8 000 half-shells) so that 5 360 half-shells are cycled back as fuel into the copra-drying operation.

The remaining output of one third of the half-shells, *i.e.*, 2640, becomes raw material input for the next activity, charcoal making. Thus the output of charcoal in Activity 3 is governed by the (shell) fuel requirements of Activity 2. Note, however, that these coefficients of two thirds and one third are subject to some variation. Firing the half-shells in copra curing requires considerable skill, the degree of which can be directly measured in terms of the copra-shell fuel requirement coefficient: if this rises much above 0.67, say to 0.75 (leaving only 25 per cent of the shells available for processing to charcoal), it would indicate unskilled workmanship or poor management.

To return to the second structural linkage between Activities 1 and 2: the size of this external structural coefficient is determined by the degree of maturity of the nuts at harvest time (coconut is usually harvested at two-month intervals). Maturity level affects the rate of recovery of copra. The recovery or nuts-to-copra conversion rates for three maturity conditions are shown as structural coefficients in Activity 2, but they are determined by the timing of the harvesting operation in Activity 1: the conversion rate, denoted here by C, will be 1 330 nuts required to make one 'candy' of copra (480 pounds, 218 kilograms) if nut harvesting is at the still-green stage. For ripe nuts, $C = 1\ 150$, and for brown nuts, $C = 1\ 100$. (Of course, other management practices such as palm fertilizer applied, weeding etc. will also affect the absolute level of nuts-to-copra conversion, but the relative recovery rates due to the maturity effect will still hold.)

Finally, Activity 4 consists of making coir fibre from the husks by-product generated in Activity 2. The structural coefficient relating these two activities has a value of unity since each nut for copra production provides one husk for making coir fibre. This is the only structural coefficient shown as providing linkage between Activity 4 and the other activities. However, on most estates another important linkage does in fact operate between Activities 1, 3 and 4: it consists of the common practice of retaining some proportion of the husks generated in Activity 2 and using them (buried in trenches alongside the palms) as a source of potash in the fertilizing operation of Activity 1. The proportion of husks used for this purpose, which will depend on the potash status of soils on any particular estate, will then govern coir production output in Activity 4. (The deciding factor between using husks as fertilizer or as an input to coir production will be the cost saved by using husks instead of artificial potash versus the income foregone by not making coir.)

In summary, the external linkage coefficients shown in Figure quantify the interrelatedness which exists between the various activity subsystems of this total coconut enterprise. Any full analysis of any one of these activities would also require consideration of its effects on the others.

FARM SERVICE MATRIX

The next element of a farm-household system to be considered is its farm service matrix. This is a system of Order Level 9. It consists of some set of material, labour and cash inputs which enables the farm-household to function as a system, but which is not specific to any particular production activity of the system. (If they are activity-specific they will be treated as costs of the appropriate activity.) This section thus continues the discussion of resources, capital and costs begun.

In their financial dimension these system-service inputs are referred to as *whole-farm overhead, common* or *farm fixed costs.* Such fixed costs must be included in the economic evaluation of a farming system for the two reasons that they influence both the profitability and the sustainability of the system.

There are two broad categories of overhead costs, *general charges* and *capital fixed costs.* General charges represent an actual money expenditure and as such, when included together with the aggregated direct costs of the production activities of the system, will determine its profitability. The second category of fixed costs (capital fixed costs, below), while not directly affecting immediate system profitability, will affect its sustainability.

GENERAL CHARGES

General charges are those fixed costs incurred in obtaining service inputs of an institutional nature which logically cannot be assigned to any specific production activity of the farm and which must be paid for. They represent an actual financial outlay. Some examples are: land tax payments, taxes on general-purpose livestock, water licence fees and vehicle registration fees.

Table provides an example of the general charges and capital fixed costs making up the annual fixed costs on a rubber estate. It illustrates the importance and wide range of general charges.

CAPITAL FIXED COSTS

Capital fixed costs are those costs incurred in the use of non-activity-specific physical farm capital and pertain to its maintenance, operation (in non activity-specific uses only) and provision for its eventual end-of-life replacement. Their payment is not mandatory—at least in the short run—and 'payment' is often in the nature of an internal bookkeeping transfer which is designed to provide—if indeed at all—only for the long-term sustainability of the system's fixed capital and for the eventual replacement of such capital as it wears out. Typical of these capital fixed costs are 'payments' or provisions for the maintenance, use and replacement of farm buildings, houses, fences, pumps and other machinery, paths, roads, farm bridges, ponds, irrigation and soil conservation systems, and breeding livestock.

Table6.3 Example Listing of Annual Total Fixed Costs on a Rubber Estate

Cost Item **General charges**	Amount ₹
Salaries	18 757
Staff allowances	600
Staff provident fund	1 012
Workers provident fund	11 462
Wage adjustment	673
Labour holidays	6 454
Food for functions	708
Medical, sanitation	3 635
All insurance	2 852
Office supplies	1 771
Commissions paid	1 005
Visiting agent	750
Rents, taxes	2 231
Vehicles	10 000
Watchmen	1 373
Retirement gifts	2 478
Capital fixed costs	
Housing upkeep	9 264
Labour-lines upkeep	1 857
Minor buildings	390
Roads, water supply	950
Total fixed costs	78 222
Total production (pounds weight)	276 600
Fixed cost/pound weight	0.28

The essential difference between general charges and such capital fixed costs is that payment for the former is mandatory, while cash disbursement for the latter is not. (The alternative, if no funds are put aside for capital replacement and no replacement is carried out, is to run down the farm capital structure, in which case it sooner or later ceases to be sustainable.)

RELATIVE IMPORTANCE OF TOTAL FARM FIXED COSTS

On most small farms, expenditure on fixed costs of both categories will be very low. Most fixed-capital costs (*i.e.*, for capital maintenance) will be 'paid' for in the form of family labour used to repair and eventually reconstruct fences, ponds, ox gear etc. Obviously, the importance of farm fixed costs will thus vary according to the farm type under consideration. The forest-garden farms of Kerala and Sri Lanka can practically ignore capital fixed costs (but not general charges such as land taxes), simply because apart from their trees, a few hand tools and the land itself, they have little capital.

On the other hand, on the intensively operated mixed crop-livestock farms of Sind, capital fixed costs (and total farm fixed costs) might be significant - but still much less so than on commercial estates.

The typical situation on these latter is summarized in Table which shows annual average direct, fixed and total Cost of Production *(CoP)* per pound of made rubber on a sample of 148 Sri Lankan estates. Total estate fixed costs (general charges plus capital costs, but, as noted, mainly general charges) are very significant and amount to about one third of total costs.

Table 6.4 Average Annual Costs of Production of Made Rubber for a Sample of Sri Lankan Rubber Estates (₹ per Pound Weight)

Sample	Direct costs			Fixed costs	Total *CoP*
	Cultural	Factory	Marketing		
36 sheet estates	0.402	0.088	0.030	0.249	0.769
86 crepe estates	0.430	0.147	0.045	0.293	0.915
26 mixed estates	0.450	0.117	0.049	0.289	0.905
All 148 estates	**0.430**	**0.138**	**0.044**	**0.289**	**0.901**

DETERMINATION OF CAPITAL FIXED COSTS

Obtaining the general charges of a farm or estate will usually present no problems. Table is an adequate guide to the types of cost items which may occur.

On the other hand, the evaluation of capital fixed costs will require a little arithmetic as exemplified by the illustrative schedule of Table. This is for a particular farm whose operating budget is presented later in Table. The schedule consists of a complete inventory listing of all the farm's fixed-capital items (including land) and their capital values as shown respectively in columns (1) and (2). The inventory is then assessed to obtain the annual fixed costs of replacing/repairing/operating these capital items as respectively listed in columns (4), (5) and (6).

These costs are aggregated in column (8) to give the annual fixed cost of each capital item. Column (7) is not needed immediately; it will be required later for economic evaluation of a farming system.

In calculating annual capital fixed costs as per Table, the values given to capital items in column (2) and hence their depreciation charge in column (4) should not be based on their initial purchase or construction cost. Capital items should be valued at their current *expected replacement cost.* The tractor, *e.g.*, might actually have cost ₹ 8 000 five years ago, but today the cost of replacing this five-year-old machine with a new one might be ₹10 000.

Whatever the initial cost or value might have been is of historical interest only and, except by coincidence, will no longer be of relevance in making provision for eventually replacing the item when that becomes necessary. Column (3) contains estimates of the years of useful service which can be expected of each item from the time of its initial purchase by the farmer. These are inevitably somewhat arbitrary. Land is assumed to be used sustainably and thus to have an indefinite useful life. Columns (4), (5) and (6) of Table show the individual components of the fixed-capital cost of each capital item, based on columns (2) and (3).

Table 6.5 Farm Capital Investment Inventory and Schedule for calculating Annual Capital Fixed Costs

Value based on current expected replacement cost. *'Land' includes all fixed improvements (drains, levelling, earthworks etc.) and permanent tree crops in house yard.*

Capital investment inventory							
(1) Capital item	(2) Item value[a] (₹)	(3) Useful life (years)	(4) Deprec'n[b] (₹)	(5) Repairs (₹)	(6) Operating costs (₹)	(7) Interest at 10% (₹)	(8) Total (4)+(5)+(6) (₹)
Land	50 000	-		-	-	5 000	-
House, sheds	15 000	25	600	200	-	1 500	800
Tractor	10 000	10	1 000	400	-	1 000	1 400
Hand thresher	2 000	6	330	50	-	200	380
Cultivators	3 000	5	600	100	-	300	700
Livestock gear	600	3	200	50	-	60	250
Barn	5 000	20	250	200	-	500	450
Fences	6 000	30	200	400	-	600	600
Dam/pond	8 000	40	200	-	-	800	200
Water pump	4 000	8	500	200	800	400	1 500
Oxen	3 000	5	600	-	200	300	800
Total	106 600		4 480	1 600	1 000	10 660	7 080

Note: [b]Here the straight-line method of calculating depreciation is used and it is assumed that the capital items have no residual value at the end of their useful life.

Depreciation is the decline over time in the capacity of a capital item to provide the service expected of it and for which it is held. Depreciation is usually measured on an annual basis. Ideally, it would be measured in actual terms but that would involve inordinate record keeping. Instead, simpler rule-of-thumb procedures (as outlined are used. As well as through *wear and tear* arising from use of the capital item, depreciation also occurs through *technical obsolescence* as more modem machines or other items providing the same service but at lower unit cost become available.

While wear and tear may be relatively predictable and approximately constant over time, technical obsolescence may not be. In consequence, to be as correct as possible, annual depreciation should be calculated afresh each year. Whether or not it is economically worthwhile to do so will depend on the particular situation.

Column (4) of Table 6.5 provides some examples of depreciation. These amounts are measured as a constant pro rata proportion over each item's life of its expected replacement cost. In percentage terms this depreciation cost corresponds to 100 divided by the item's useful life. Consider the tractor valued at ₹10 000 which is estimated to have a total useful life of ten years. On a pro rata basis, the annual cost of obtaining this service is ₹10 000/10 or ₹ 1 000. Or to put it another way, based on the present assessment, if the farm's fixed capital is not to be depleted, a sum of ₹ 1 000 per year should be set aside to enable the tractor to be replaced when it finally wears out or, due to technological advance, becomes obsolescent (in five years' time if it is five years old now). (Hence the preference for basing item value in column (2) on current expected replacement cost rather than past/historical actual cost.)

Repairs refers to the sum of money which normally must be spent on maintaining each capital item in good repair. Note, however, that in spite of such repairs, the item (tractor, thresher, fences etc.) will sooner or later wear out or become obsolete, hence the need for its depreciation as well as its routine repair.

Operating costs are the costs of actually operating a capital item: *e.g.*, ₹ 800 for water-pump fuel, ₹ ₹ of feed and veterinary expenses for the oxen. In Table the tractor would, of course, also incur fuel and oil operating costs but in a typical farm situation it would be fairly easy to charge these against the separate specific activities (paddy, cotton etc.) which actually consume this fuel or incur such operating costs, rather than against the farm as a whole. Often, however, some capital operating costs will be incurred in non-specific farm work, in which case they should be included in column (6).

Interest as listed in column (7) of Table 6.5 is a bookkeeping charge levied on total farm capital - *i.e.*, all capital invested in the farm - in order to assess the productivity of the several farm resource categories or factors of production (land, labour and capital). It is not a 'cost' in the conventional sense of detracting from the value of farm net output (or family income).

For the moment, only the procedure of obtaining this item is of concern. Briefly, some appropriate rate of interest, here ten per cent, is applied to the assessed value of each/all of the capital investment items as listed in column (2) of Table 6.5. The appropriate interest rate is determined by the opportunity cost of similar capital items in their 'most likely most profitable most prudent' other use. Thus if the best alternative investment available were for the family to sell the farm and put the proceeds in a bank earning ten per cent annual interest, this would determine the *opportunity cost* of farm capital and thus the appropriate interest rate to apply in obtaining column (7). To conclude, one might state the obvious: these procedures for obtaining the interest costs of column (7) are full of practical pitfalls.

Is the replacement value of an item a proper representation of its value in use? If not, a more appropriate value should be used. Or, as is not infrequently done, items might be valued at the mid-point of their useful life with allowance made for any residual value they may possess at the end of their useful life. Thus the oxen of Table with a useful life of five years and, say, a residual value of ₹ 800 as meat would be valued at ₹(3 000 + 800)/2 = ₹ 1 900.

Is it sufficient to apply some rate of interest (say ten per cent, as above) uniformly to all capital items, or are the opportunity costs of some capital items greater than of others? (Probably yes, but precision must be weighed against the extra work required in obtaining the necessary information.) What is an appropriate alternative investment? Could money, instead of being put in the bank at ten per cent, be lent to a speculator in the souk at 50 per cent and still be regarded as a prudent alternative investment? (Probably not.).... Anyway, do realistic alternative uses of farm investment capital actually exist?

On the other hand, when concern is with small farms,

These practical difficulties are largely removed by the facts that

- The value of farm capital itself, and thus the level of fixed costs associated with it, will not be very great; and
- Most capital can be maintained and replaced by using (largely 'free') farm-generated resources and family labour. In short, while the effort that goes into the

construction of Table must inevitably be considerable if later analysis based on it is to be technically satisfactory, the actual data obtained within and subsequently from Table might not make much practical difference in the evaluation of small-farm performance.

To summarize the discussion of Table 6.5: total capital fixed costs on this farm, column (8), are the sum of the previous cost-item columns (4), (5) and (6)—in the example ₹ 7,080 annually. Total farm fixed costs are the sum of this item and the farm's general charges.

MANDATORY *VS.* OPTIONAL FARM FIXED COSTS

It was noted previously that payment of general charges is usually mandatory. Taxes and licence fees must be paid. It was also noted that payment of capital fixed costs might be considered optional, at least in the short run. In fact it would be more correct to say that some of the components of capital fixed costs are mandatory while others are optional. Again referring to Table 6.5, payments for running repairs and operation (*e.g.*, fuel, feed for the oxen) are in a large sense mandatory, while provision for depreciation is largely optional (in any one operating year). Depreciation (column 4) might be provided for in practice by setting aside ₹ 4,480 per year; or such an amount might be re-invested in the business to generate the necessary future replacement funds; or no provision at all might be made.

This third case implies that:

- Farm capital stock is being run down or depleted;
- To the extent that such depletion is occurring, real farm net income is being overestimated; and
- Sooner or later the farm will cease to be a sustainable system.

DEPRECIATION METHODS

Ideally, the annual depreciation of a capital item should be measured in terms of its actual wear and tear due to usage and the change in its degree of obsolescence. This would imply much inconvenient record keeping not worth its cost. Instead, it is assumed that usage of the item and the accompanying flow of service from it follow some regular pattern and depreciation is estimated accordingly. Thus there are four main methods of calculating annual depreciation 'cost' or the annual rate at which a capital item provides services and is thereby used up or becomes obsolete. Three of these methods are briefly discussed here.

Straight-line depreciation assumes a constant flow of service with consequent wear and tear and/or obsolescence during the item's useful life so that the value of the item will therefore decrease by a constant uniform annual amount over its life. This is the easiest method to apply. The formula for obtaining the annual straight-line depreciation amount, denoted by D, is $D = (PV - SV)/L$ where PV is the item's present value (*i.e.*, its expected future replacement cost at the moment of analysis), SV is its expected salvage or residual value at the end of its useful life and L is its expected total years of life. Thus annual depreciation on a cultivator with an expected replacement cost of ₹1 000 and which has an expected total useful life of ten years and can then be sold for ₹ 200 as scrap would be ₹ (1 000 - 200)/ 10 = ₹ 80; or if it has no salvage value, ₹ 1 000/10 = ₹ 100.

This method is probably most appropriate for small Asian farms where most capital items (pumps, cultivators, livestock gear etc.) suffer no loss in value due to obsolescence, are entirely used up in the production process, and do not have a residual value (*e.g.*, as the basis for trade-in on a new model). The results of applying this method are shown in the lefthand-side graph of Figure.

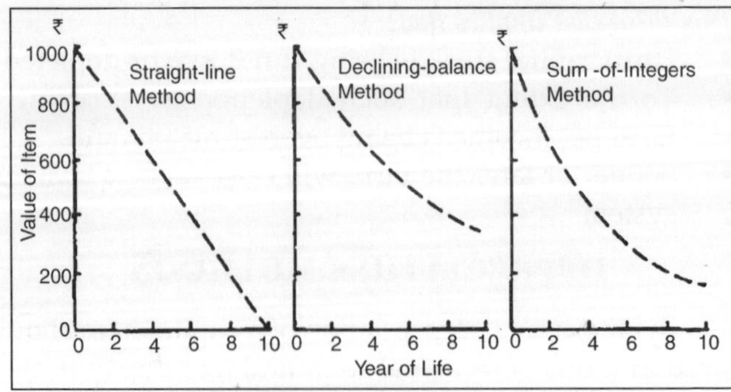

Fig 6.6 Example of Straight-line, Declining-balance and Sum-of- Integers Depreciation Methods Applied to an Item with an Initial Value of `1 000, a Ten-year Life and Zero Salvage Value

Declining-balance depreciation assumes that the item is used up and/or becomes obsolescent at a constant percentage rate of its annual starting value. Applied to the previous example with a zero salvage value and assuming an annual depreciation rate of ten per cent, this would result in an annual depreciation amount of ₹1 000 x 0.10 or ₹100 in year 1 of the item's life, ₹(1 000 - 100)0.10 or ₹ 90 in year 2, ₹(1 000 - 100 - 90)0.10 or ₹ 81 in year 3, ₹ 73 in year 4, etc. With declining-balance depreciation, the formula for calculating the annual depreciation 'cost' in year t, denoted by D_t is:

$$D_t = (V_{t-1})d$$

where V_{t-1} is the item's depreciated value at the end of year t-1, $V_{t-1} = (V_{t-2} - DT - 1)$, $V_0 = (PV_0 - SV)$ where PV_0 is the item's expected replacement cost at time zero, *i.e.*, at the start of the depreciation analysis, and d is the constant annual rate of depreciation.

Obviously, as illustrated by the middle graph of Figure 6.6, the procedure results in a lower and declining depreciation loss in later years. This is appropriate where the value loss is due to the 'planned obsolescence' of modem equipment (which is reflected in dealers' secondhand machinery and vehicle-buying price schedules as these are used in the West). Such obsolescence hardly exists on small Asian farms where, as noted, value loss is due to wear and tear from physical use. Note also from Figure 6.6 that, unlike straight-line depreciation, the declining-balance method does not lead to full write-down of an item at the end of its useful life.

Sum-of-integers depreciation is essentially similar to the declining-balance approach in that this method also results in less than full write-down and in a declining annual depreciation 'cost' which eventually becomes zero in the last year of life as shown by the righthand-side graph of Figure. Compared to the declining balance and straight-line methods, the sum-of integers method implies a more rapid initial depreciation but slower later depreciation. The formula for sum-of-integers depreciation is:

$D_t = (PV_{t=0} - SV)$ [Remaining years of life/Sum of integers of total life] where D_t is again depreciation for year *t* and $PV_{t=0}$ is the expected replacement value of the capital item at time zero, *i.e.*, at the start of the depreciation analysis. Using the previous example of the cultivator with a life of ten years and no salvage value (*i.e.*, $SV = 0$), the 'sum of the integers' would be (1 + 2 + 3..... + 10) or 55, and the annual depreciation 'cost' would be:

Year 1: ₹ 1 000 x 9/55 = ₹ 164
Year 2: ₹ 1 000 x 8/55 = ₹ 145
Year 3: ₹ 1 000 x 7/55 = ₹ 127
... ...
Year 9: ₹ 1 000 x 1/55 = ₹ 18
Year 10: ₹ 1 000 x 0/55 = ₹ 0.

Comparing the three depreciation methods outlined above, the straight-line approach is generally to be preferred on the grounds that it is less complicated and ensures full depreciation or write-down of the item.

7

Planning and Data Access

BACKGROUND

The National Action Plan on Climate Change (NAPCC) document has suggested 'Promoting Data Access', as one of the broad themes of its National Mission on Strategic Knowledge for Climate Change. This document lists that there are several database, which are relevant for climate research and suggests that the respective agencies that are responsible for collecting and supplying such data may take action to digitize data, maintain database of global quality, and streamline the procedures governing access there to.

It has further been suggested that the Ministry of Agriculture has to 'expand and improve the existing database' on

- Soil Profile;
- Area Under Cultivation;
- Production and Yield; and
- Cost of Cultivation.

OBJECTIVE

- To improve and expand the data bases on
  - Soil Profile;
  - Area Under Cultivation, Production and Yield; and
  - Cost of Cultivation.
- To digitize data, maintain database of global quality, and streamline the procedure governing access there to;

- To build public awareness through "National Portal" on agricultural Statistics.

STRATEGY

SOIL RESOURCE

The Department of Agriculture and Cooperation (DAC) has taken steps to digitize "the survey data as well as the relevant maps" by the Soil and Land Use Survey of India (SLUSI), in collaboration with National Informatics Centre (NIC).

The National Informatics Centre (NIC) has already published its village level dataset designed, for its Projects for grassroots development:

- DISNIC-PLAN Project: IT for Micro Level Planning and
- Agricultural Resources Information System (AgRIS) Project of Department of Agriculture and Cooperation pertains to Soil, Land, Groundwater and Environment parameters. Both these projects, DISNIC and AgRIS are under implementation in identified pilot districts.

However, the existing database on soil is inadequate to develop micro-level agricultural land use plan in the country, for which the needed scale of resolution is 1:4000/ 12500. The detailed digital database on soil (physical, chemical and biological) is a pre-requisite to address the various issues related to scientific Land Use Planning, soil reclamation; proper diagnosis of soils, judicious use of irrigation water and chemical fertilizers, nutrient deficiencies for maintenance of sound soil health and land productivity. The relevant soil parameters to be considered for such purposes are: soil type, elevation, type of land form, slope, geology (type of parent material), textural class, type of soil structure, soil water retentivity, soil pH, Electrical Conductivity (EC), Organic Carbon, $CaCO_3$, Fe %, Major oxides, available macro and micro nutrients, depth of water table, erosion class, drainage and run-off characteristics, land capability and irrigability etc.

An effective rural knowledge society and ICT system needs to be established in each gram Panchayat. This should be involve various stakeholders—farmers, development agents and agencies, knowledge generators and distributors (universities and public and private institutions) for steering a "knowledge-based Soil and Land Resource Management". Village Knowledge Centres (Gyan Chaupals) with extensive rural connectivity, including use of cell phones. This would empower the farmers to access database for site specific natural resource management. Data access through Common Services Centre (CSCs), VKCs and VRCs may be promoted.

LAND USE, AREA, PRODUCTION AND YIELD AND COST OF CULTIVATION

The State level entry of data in the existing database is undertaken by the SASAs, using the Software (LUS) developed by NIC.

In respect of Area, Production and Yield (APY) of Crops, the District-wise Crop Production Information System has been developed by NIC, facilitating on-line data entry by the States. Efforts for outsourcing for digitization of district-wise estimates of Area, Production and Yield pertaining to the last ten years.

So far as data on cost of cultivation is concerned, it is yet to be digitized. At present, the Cost of Cultivation data is generated State-wise for 19 States for various crops, every year since 1971-72. Along with cost of cultivation, costs of production data are also generated. The Government of India provides Grants-in-Aid to collect data on Cost of Cultivation through 12 Agricultural Universities, 1 Agriculture College and the Directorate of Tobacco Development (DTD). However, the data on land use, area, production, yield and cost of cultivation need to be collected and digitized and disseminated in a systematic manner.

PLAN OF ACTION

Following needs to be done to provide data up to Block/Tehsil level:

- Development of National Portal on Soil Resources including Detailed Soil Survey covering Block/Tehsil level data;
- Soil Resource Mapping and Land Use Planning
- To Develop a National Portal on 'Agricultural Statistics';

- Outsourcing of Block/Tehsil wise LUS data pertaining to the last ten years and their digitization;
- LUS data, under the nine-fold classification, at more disaggregated levels (*i.e.* at the Village/ Panchayat level) in pilot districts;
- Operationalising the LUS software at the State, District and Block level,
- Capacity Building through HRD for all Stakeholders of the System.

INSTITUTIONAL ARRANGEMENTS, COLLABORATING AGENCIES AND FINANCIAL OUTLAY

The institutional arrangements, collaborating agencies and financial requirements are proposed as follows:

DEVELOPMENT OF NATIONAL PORTAL ON SOIL RESOURCES

Timelines	2009-14 (Five Years)
Institutional arrangement (DES) Collaborating Agencies	NRM Divisions (ICAR & DAC), Directorate of Economics and Statistics – Ministry of Agriculture, and NIC SLUSI, NBSS&LUP, NRSA, NRAA, DOLR, NIC, State Land Use Boards, SASA, State Agricultural Universities, ICAR Institutes, Agricultural Colleges and Departments of Geography, etc Financial outlays ₹. 50.00 crore

DEVELOPMENT OF "DETAILED SOIL RESOURCE MAPPING" AND "LAND USE PLANNING" (1:4000/ 12500)

Timeliness	2009-12 and 2012-14 (5 Years)
Institutional arrangement Collaborating Agencies Agricultural	NRM and DES of DAC and Public-Private-Panchayat-Partnership (PPPP) Model SLUSI, NBSS&LUP, NRSA, NRAA, DOLR, NIC, State Land Use Boards, SASA, State Universities, ICAR Institutes,

(*Contd...*)

	Agricultural Colleges, Departments of Geography and Common Services Centres (CSCs) etc
Financial outlays	₹. 1000.00 crore

DEVELOPMENT OF NATIONAL PORTAL, IMPROVING QUALITY OF ESTIMATES, AND COST OF CULTIVATION

A tentative outlay of ₹ 10.00 crore per annum is required to fund the proposed action plan as detailed below:

Timelines	Eight years
Institutional arrangement	Directorate of Economics and
Statistics	
Collaborating Agencies	All Implementing Agencies/ SASAs
Monitoring and Evaluation (M&E)	Economic and Statistical Adviser
Financial outlays	₹. 90.00 crore

Grand Total (a+b+c) = ₹ 1,140.00 Crore

PLANNING AND OPERATING

There are basically two major farm-operating objectives, profit maximization on market-oriented farms and household sustenance on subsistence-oriented farms. By profit maximization is meant maximization of net gain measured as total benefit less total cost.

Profit maximization measured in money terms can generally be taken as the planning objective on farms of Type 5 (large commercial family farms) and Type 6 (estates) but this is increasingly constrained by external factors such as labour laws, health and safety regulations, and national policies to produce crops which will generate foreign exchange or serve as a basis for local industrialization

Internal constraints can also exist on such farms and take the form of management jealousy in protecting the 'mark' of their product even when production of lower quality produce might yield more profit, and spending more than the necessary amount of money on estate upkeep to maintain estate appearance and status. Profit maximization measured in money terms can also be the primary objective of some subtypes of Type 3 (small independent specialized) and Type 4 (small dependent specialized) farms.

Note that, strictly speaking, when uncertainty is present (as is usually the case), profit maximization is not a feasible objective. Under uncertainty, rather than a variety of sure profit options, the farmer faces a set of profit probability distributions corresponding one-to-one to the available decision options. For each of these risky choices with its corresponding probability distribution of profit, it can be argued that the farmer will have some equivalent sure profit or *certainty equivalent* such that he or she would be indifferent between

- Taking the risky option with its uncertain profit or
- Receiving the sure profit amount. The operating objective is thus to discover and implement that option which has the highest certainty equivalent. Thus, under uncertainty, profit maximization translates to certainty equivalent maximization. These matters are elaborated in.

Household sustenance through the production of food and fibre for household consumption provides the primary objective of all other (predominantly Type 1 and 2) farms but, as noted previously, it is increasingly modified by the need also to generate some level of cash income. Only some Type 6 farms (estates) and some Type 1 (subsistence) farms are found, respectively, at the extremes of aiming only for profit maximization or full subsistence; most farms of these and other types are located somewhere between these extremes along the profit-sustenance continuum as shown schematically in Figure.

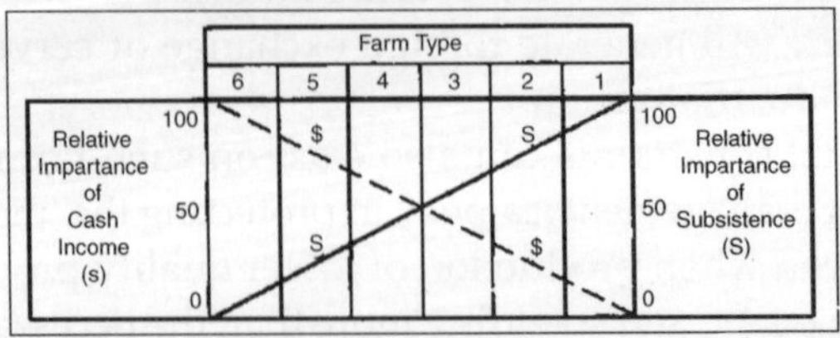

Fig 7.1 Stylized Representation of Relative Importance of Financial Profit and Subsistence by Farm Type

Beyond the priority objectives of ensuring sufficient food and cash for the farm household, Type 1 (subsistence) and Type 2 (semi-subsistence) farmers generally have a number of secondary objectives. These are likely to include such things as having security in their livelihood, having the opportunity to observe socio-cultural customs and obligations, and having a satisfactory amount of leisure time.

SYSTEM PROPERTIES AND PERFORMANCE CRITERIA

Given the two extremes in planning objectives and the relative weight which will be accorded to each for the various farm types, there are eight main properties a system might possess, thus requiring a set of eight criteria by which these system properties may be assessed. Each of these properties and its associated assessment criterion apply both to whole-farm Order Level 10 systems and to constituent activity/enterprise subsystems of Order Levels 3, 4 and 6. They are relevant to evaluation and planning both at farm-household level and at a broader social level.

The eight properties of farm systems and activities which need to be assessed are:

- Productivity
- Profitability
- Stability
- Diversity
- Flexibility
- Time-dispersion
- Sustainability
- Complementarity and environmental compatibility.

AT FARM LEVEL

These system properties can be quantified (at least conceptually; see below). They are all 'desirable' or at least neutral in the sense that an individual farm which ranks highly with respect to productivity, profitability, stability etc. represents a superior system to a farm on which productivity, profitability etc. are low. When applied to a specific farm only a few of these properties might be thought relevant by the farm family or other decision maker. One farm manager might have a purely profit objective and would wish his or her performance to be evaluated in terms of profit. A second manager on the same type of farm might seek some balance of profitability-stability-sustainability so that criteria relating to these three properties would then need to be applied. In both cases, however, the analyst/adviser would be wise to review the farm system relative to all eight criteria and to proffer relevant advice.

It would be an error to evaluate both farms according to a criterion which is relevant to only the first farm. However, at a more general level, this is what often happens when Asian farms are evaluated by Western-oriented economists as being 'inefficient', 'backward' and of low productivity etc. on the grounds that they perform poorly according to the conventional Western criterion of money profitability. In following sections the above eight properties and their associated performance criteria are examined in relation to their use at farm level in Field A (*i.e.*, on-farm problem solving and advice)—which is not to say that they are not relevant to farm management analysis in Fields B, C and D; indeed, particularly in Fields C (industry and sector-level analysis) and D (policy-making), they will often be highly relevant.

AT SOCIAL LEVEL

Apart from farmers, society has a vital long-term interest in how rural resources are used and how farm systems perform. When farm management operates in Fields C and D (*i.e.*, playing a contributing role in planning new settlements, irrigation projects etc., and in government policy guidance), it must also be cognizant of the several properties of farm systems. Some of these, particularly productivity, stability and sustainability, might well be more important from a social than from a private-household viewpoint.

To plan new farms which will be profitable is one thing; to plan profitable farms which also make optimal sustainable use of what are finally social resources is yet another. Even more difficult and increasingly important is to develop new or restructured farm systems which have all these desirable properties and, in addition, are compatible with the social environment and not destructive of the physical environment. Also, as evidenced by increasing interest in gender analysis, equity within farm-household systems may also be important from a societal view.

PRODUCTIVITY

Productivity is primarily a measure of the relative suitability of a system or activity in a particular agro-ecological environment. On commercial farms it is an indicator of relative efficiency of resource use and management performance. It is an underlying condition for profitability but should not necessarily be taken as a desirable attribute or objective in itself. On non-commercial farms, productivity is a necessary condition for achieving family sustainability—but only to a limit. Production beyond what a family can consume or store or barter becomes irrational and may even be undesirable.

At some places in the Himalayan hills (such as eastern Bhutan) up to 30 per cent of the maize crop is surplus to food requirements and, in the absence of programmes to develop alternative uses, is converted to alcohol with the most unfortunate social consequences. Yet in such areas it is not uncommon to find programmes to 'improve' maize production as a road to farm 'development'. A more rational approach would be based on crop development within the context of the farm and village socioeconomic system. This might well aim at reduction in some crop production and reformulation of the whole farming system.

Productivity is conventionally measured in terms of such units, *e.g.*, as tons, kilograms or litres of output respectively per acre, hectare or animal unit employed over some relevant time unit (typically a year). Or, if desired, it may be measured in financial terms over some relevant timespan as the ratio of total revenue to total cost, *i.e.*, the value of output per unit of cost. Productivity is an appropriate measure of system and activity performance when applied to single-output enterprises or mono-product systems. However, as one moves from commercial to increasingly sustenance-oriented farm types (Figure), there is a tendency for by-products to become more numerous and important. This introduces difficulties in the measurement of output and productivity. In a commercial situation, productivity can usually be measured as a single variable. However, in a quasi-subsistence situation, it might require the construction of a table of output items such as exemplified by Table 7.1. This shows the main and secondary products of a range of tree and vine crops commonly grown on forest-garden farms in Sri Lanka and Java and the relative importance of the products of each crop as assessed by the household head (which assessment, of course, would vary among individual households).

Product mixes from some single crops can be considerably more complex than Table suggests, *e.g.*, as with rubber. On an estate there will be no measurement difficulties: output is simply the number of kilograms of made rubber per hectare. In contrast, on a mixed smallholding, 'output' might consist of latex for sale, seed from the annual seedfall, shade for associated crops such as cacao and yams, live supports for such climbers as pepper, and prunings or branchfall for household fuel. Some of these products can be measured (latex, seed, fuel), some cannot (the shade effect and the contribution of rubber trees to the micro-environment for use by associated crops). If the separate outputs and inputs can be measured, the crop can be evaluated as a set of (related) activities; if they cannot, it will need to be evaluated as a composite enterprise.

Table 7.1 Relative Importance of Main and Secondary Products of Some Crops on a Sample of Forest-garden Farms

Crop	Main Product		Secondary Products					
Pepper	Pepper	1.00						
Rubber	Latex	0.78	Timber	0.09	Fuel	0.10	Seed	0.03
Tea	Leaf	0.85	Fuel	0.15				
Coconut	Copra	0.78	Husks	0.15	Charcoal	0.06	Leaf	0.01
Cloves	Buds	0.74	Stems	0.25	Dust	0.01		
Nutmeg	Nutmeg	0.70	Mace	0.30				
Jackfruit	Flesh	0.75	Seeds	0.20	Fuel	0.05		

PROFITABILITY

Financial profitability of activities/enterprises and of the whole-farm system are already discussed in this chapter. As shown in Figure 7.1, financial profitability becomes a less important performance criterion as analysis moves towards the subsistence end of the farm-type continuum. In particular, money profit or gross margin as a measure of performance of activities is typically both not possible and largely irrelevant for Type 1 (*i.e.*, subsistence) farms and often, to a significant degree, for Type 2 (*i.e.*, semi-subsistence) farms because of their lack of market interaction.

Financial profit as a criterion for measuring the performance of farm-household systems is often unreliable. This is because, on small farms, money profit is often generated at the expense of weakening or distorting the system through such factors as increasing household exposure to debt for purchased farm inputs, the danger of fostering an exploitative and non-sustainable rate of resource use (causing soil degradation), reduction in the level of reliability of household food supply and increasing risk. Nevertheless, many farm-economic surveys undertaken to measure the performance of small farms continue to gauge this solely in terms of financial profit, even when these farms might have quite different objectives (as discussed below).

Profit is normally measured in money terms as gross financial revenue minus total financial cost per period. Note, however, that it may—if need be—also be assessed subjectively in qualitative terms as net gain, *i.e.*, as total benefit less total cost however measured. Such an approach might be used in assessing the performance of Type 1 (subsistence) farms having no significant market interaction, leading to qualitative assessment of a Type 1 system as, *e.g.*, profitable or not profitable. Associated with profitability, however measured, is the matter of farm-size adequacy. Clearly, a prime requirement of any whole-farm system is that it be of sufficient size to satisfy the farm-based needs of its primary beneficiaries. Small farms should thus be assessed in terms of *income adequacy*, *i.e.*, their ability to sustain the farm household's need for income in cash and/or kind without causing resource or environmental degradation. Income adequacy is thus an important aspect of profitability.

STABILITY

System stability refers to the absence or minimization of

year-to-year fluctuations in either production or value of output. (The latter also implies either stability in input costs, yields and prices or counterbalancing movements in these influences on value of output.) Where conditions are favourable, price and production instability can often be countered by more careful activity selection (*e.g.*, of drought-tolerant varieties, pest-immune crops); by diversification of activities; by seeking greater flexibility in product use or disposal; by multiple cropping over both space and time; and by increasing on-farm storage capacity and post-harvest handling efficiency. In some situations the most direct strategy for stabilization is simply to increase production/ income to a level which allows an annual surplus to be retained/ invested in good years to cover deficiencies in poor years. This is generally possible on farms of Type 5 (large commercial family farms) and Type 6 (estates). (The classical tea/rubber/oilpalm/ coconut estate systems are generally production-stable but price-unstable.) Many variations of such a strategy are possible.

Around Ponorogo in the Madium Valley of Java a common practice among farmers growing sugarcane, paddy and palawija crops (*i.e.*, food crops other than rice) is to invest the proceeds of the (relatively stable) sugar crop in gold, then later sell this to finance the following (relatively unstable) subsistence food crops. In the hills of eastern Bhutan where mono-crop maize is the stable food and monsoon rains are erratic, the common stabilizing strategy is to plant 30 to 40 per cent more maize than will actually be required if the season turns out well which—since the crop requires no cash inputs but only family labour and oxen—is an insurance premium willingly paid. (But the social costs of this were noted in Section above.)

The magnitude of year-to-year variation in yield varies widely among crops and locations. The data presented in Table 7.2 for two common Sri Lankan tree crops, clove and coconut, illustrate the magnitude of possible yield fluctuations and the importance of the production (and income) instability problem which faces the smallholder clove growers in comparison with the growers of such stable crops as coconut. While cloves are often a very profitable crop, this would be partly offset by their high level of price and income instability. As would be expected, this usually leads small farms to combine cloves with other lower value/lower risk crops in order to achieve greater stability in the farm system as a whole.

Measuring Stability/Instability

Price/yield/income stability is most conveniently measured in terms of the *coefficient of variation,* denoted by *CV,* which expresses the standard deviation, denoted by *SD,* or positive square root of the variance (V) of a sample of observations on a variable *X* as a percentage of the sample's mean value $\overline{X}$. Thus,

$$CV = 100(SD/\overline{X}) = 100\left(V^{1/2}/\overline{X}\right) = 100$$

$$\left[\sum_{i-1}^{n}(X_i - \overline{X})^2/(n-1)\right]^{1/2}\left(\sum_{i-1}^{n} X/n\right)$$

where *n* is the number of observations, X_i is the *i*-th observation and S denotes the sum of the following values for *i* from 1 to*n*. The set of observations X_1, X_2...X_n may come from a sample generated across time or space or both. Thus the lower section of Table gives an annual time-series set of observations on copra yield per acre on a particular estate in Sri Lanka for the 13 years 1960 to 1972. In Table the *CV* of this sample of copra yields is calculated as 11.5 per cent. The upper section of Table gives a set of data on clove yield which is both of a time-series (years 1967 to 1972) and spatial (cross-section for five farms) nature.

Table 7.2 Year-to-year Variation in Clove and Coconut Yield

Clove: Relative annual yield over time on five farms, Sri Lanka (1972 base)					
Farm no:	(1)	(2)	(3)	(4)	(5)
1972	100	100	100	100	100
1971	0	2	0	40	600
1970	70	457	5	13	0
1969	93	71	30	100	0
1968	70	-	-	-	75
1967	0	-	-	-	-

Coconut: Annual copra yield from astand of mature trees, Sri Lanka (piculs per acre)			
1960	14.0	1967	11.6
1961	12.4	1968	12.5
1962	10.8	1969	10.0
1963	10.5	1970	12.6
1964	9.5	1971	11.4
1965	9.9	1972	11.8
1966	10.5		

Because *CV* is a pure number, it can be used to compare the relative stability of different activities/systems. For example, the *CV* of clove yield based on the 23 observations of Table is 157 per cent, implying that income on a clove-only farm - due to the yield effect and ignoring possible price effects and differences in flexibility of product use after harvest - is some 13 times less stable than income from coconuts. Likewise, comparison of the *CV* values for the clove-yield sample data of farms (1) and (5) of Table indicates yield is twice as unstable on farm (5) with a *CV* of 163 per cent as on farm (1) with a*CV* of 80 per cent.

Of course, a stable system or activity is not necessarily superior to an unstable one. Depending on relative costs/prices, an unstable activity may still be preferable to a stable one on grounds of long-run relative profit. But, other things being equal, stability will usually be chosen over instability, especially in subsistence situations where the goal is food rather than money, and where a high *CV* for yield might be synonymous with recurring famine. In addition to the inclusion of system-stabilizing activities in the farm system, there are other means of reducing system instability. These relate to the diversification of activities and their products; to achieving flexibility in the post-harvest use/disposal of products; and to the time-pattern of income receival. These approaches to mitigating instability are discussed below.

Table 7.3 Calculation of the Coefficient of Variation (*CV*) for the Copra Yield Data of Table

Year	Copra Yield (X_i)	Deviation ($X_i-\overline{X}$)	Squared deviation $(X_i-\overline{X})^2$
1960	14.0	2.65	7.02
1961	12.4	1.05	1.10
1962	10.8	-0.55	0.30
1963	10.5	-0.88	0.72
1964	9.5	-1.85	3.42
1965	9.9	-1.45	2.10
1966	10.5	-0.85	0.72
1967	11.6	0.25	0.06
1968	12.5	1.15	1.32
1969	10.0	-1.35	1.82
1970	12.6	1.25	1.56
1971	11.4	0.05	0.01
1972	11.8	0.45	0.21

$$\text{Mean}(\overline{X}) = \sum_{i-1}^{n} X_i / n = 147.50/13 = 11.35$$

Standard deviation,

$$(\text{SD}) = V^{1/2} = \left[\sum_{i=1}^{n}(X_i - \overline{X})^2/(n-1)\right]^{1/2} = (20.36/12)^{1/2} = 1.30$$

Coefficient of variation,

$$(\text{CV}) = 100(\text{SD}/\overline{X}) = (100)(1.30)/11.35 = 11.5\%$$

DIVERSITY

Diversity corresponds to 'not having all one's eggs in a single basket.'

It refers to a strategy of increasing the number of activities in a system and/or their separate products in order

- To reduce overall system risk of income or family-sustenance failure and/or
- To increase overall production/profit (averaged over time) through a better use of available resources. A high diversity level is conducive to system stability (but diversity might conceivably be achieved at the cost of a reduction in average profit).

Activity Diversity

As noted, in terms of activities the most diversified farms are the small subsistence and semi-subsistence farms of Types 1 and 2, respectively—*e.g.*, the irrigated crop-livestock-orchard farms of North India and Pakistan, the clover-wheat-barley—sheep-rabbit-poultry-scorpion-vegetable farms of China's Loess Plateau, the small mixed crop-livestock farms of South China and Taiwan, and the forest-garden farms of the wet tropics. The possibilities for diversification are relatively limited on Type 3 farms, *i.e.*, small specialist farms growing a single traditional crop such as the paddy farms of Java. Diversification is not a strategy generally available on Type 4 farms, *i.e.*, those growing an industrial crop under conditions dictated by a landlord or factory. While the possibility often exists (*e.g.*, growing food/cash crops within sugarcane rows or in the intervals between cane plantings, as in Mauritius), it is negated by such practical factors as lack of equipment suitable for other than the main crop; or lack of markets; or simply by opposition on the part of landlords or sugar mills to developments which would diminish their power over the tenants.

The three elements contributing to the overall diversity of a farm system are:

- The number of tree/crop/animal species present;
- The number of their respective products; and
- The number of ways in which these products can be used or disposed of (*i.e.*, the degree of flexibility they provide. These three elements of diversity exist in both physical and economic (value) dimensions, either or both of which might be relevant to a particular analysis of farm-system diversity.

If diversity comparisons are to be made within or between groups of farms, it may sometimes be sufficient to express diversity level as simply the number of species of trees, crops and livestock present. Generally, however, this would be a poor measure: the species (and their associated activities) need somehow to be weighted according to their relative importance, *e.g.*, in terms of the number of individuals within each species, or of the areas occupied by the various crops, or the amounts or values of outputs from the various activities. One relatively simple measure suited to such assessment is*Simpson's diversity index*. This is defined as

$$DI = 1 - \sum_{i=1}^{S} (n_i / N)^2$$

where S is the number of species or activities that are present; n_i (for $i = 1$ to S) is the number of individuals in the i-th species, or area devoted to the i-th species or activity, or income or value of the i-th species or activity; and N ($= \Sigma\, n_i$) is the total population of all individuals, or total area across all activities, or total farm income or value across all species or activities.

For a farm system with no diversity (*i.e.*, having only a single species or activity so that $S = 1$ and $n_1 = N$), DI is zero. As farm diversity increases, DI approaches unity, *e.g.*, for a farm with 20 crops each occupying three units of the total farm area of 60 units, $DI = 0.95$.

Calculating DI values for a small South East Asian mixed-farm system is exemplified by the worksheet of Table. DIvalues are calculated:

- On a species/activities or physical diversity basis and
- On an income basis. In its physical or structural dimension the farm system of Table is dominated by tree crops, particularly coffee. Note that difficulties arise in the calculation of *DI* on a species basis for those crops and livestock activities for which the individuals cannot be enumerated, *e.g.*, as with rice and other field crops or with pond fish. *DI* might then best be calculated, from a physical perspective, on the basis of the area devoted to each species or its associated activity.

Product Diversity

This refers to the number of separate final products of a system or activity. Some of the main outputs from a range of tree/vine crops were listed in Table 7.4. These can be disposed of in a range of ways which also represent an avenue to diversification. As shown in Figure 7.2, a single simple crop such as maize in Java can be significantly product-diversified by the way in which it is managed.

Table 7.4 Worksheet Calculation of Simpson's Diversity Index for a South East Asian Mixed-farm System in Terms of (A) Species and (B) Income

Farm structure	(A) Species or physical diversity		(B) Economic or value diversity	
Species/activity	No. of individuals (n_i)	$(n_i/N)^2$ $(S = 9)$	Annual income ($\$n_i$)	$(n_i/N)^2$ $(S = 11)$
1. Areca	50	0.0151	50	0.0011
2. Jackfruit	25	0.0038	70	0.0022
3. Coffee	200	0.2415	50	0.0011
4. Pepper	20	0.0024	50	0.0011
5. Coconut	50	0.0151	50	0.0011
6. Banana	30	0.0054	50	0.0011
7. Cloves	15	0.0014	100	0.0046
8. Papaya	15	0.0014	40	0.0007
9. Vegetables	?	?	70	0.0022
10. Cows	2	0.0000	850	0.3298
11. Fishpond	?	?	100	0.0046
Sum	$N = 407$	0.2861	$N = \$1480$	0.3496
$DI = 1 - \sum_{i=1}^{S} (n_i/n)^2$		0.7139		0.6504

Considering the range of crops grown on many small farms (*e.g.*, up to six or more on Sind farms, up to 25 or 30 or more on forest-garden farms), the possibilities of integrating different classes of livestock with these crops, and the total number of crop or livestock products which can be generated, it is apparent that diversification can reach very high levels. Small farms producing 40 or 50 or more final outputs are not uncommon.

In general, large commercial family farms and commercial estates (farm Types 5 and 6, respectively) remain undiversified in spite of the many opportunities which theoretically exist. Partly this is because it is felt that diversification would divert management effort away from the traditional main commercial crop. It is probably also due to an overly technical orientation in research to date, *e.g.*, cattle grazed among young rubber trees (failed because of neglect of cattle management practices to prevent damage to the trees); cacao-under-rubber (failed because of crop competition for labour and unwillingness to sacrifice some rubber population); food and grain crops among coconut and rubber trees (agronomically successful but has not reached its potential because of lack of a marketing element in the research programme).

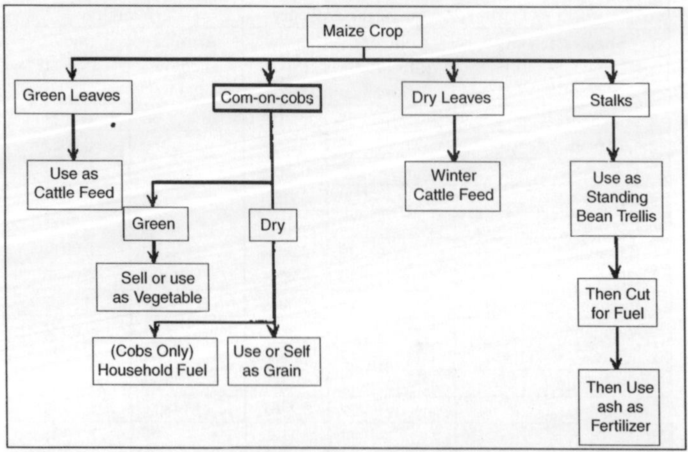

Fig 7.2 Product Diversification from a Maize Crop on a Javanese Farm

Income Diversity

As exemplified in Table, Simpson's *DI* can also be calculated relative to income. The calculated *DI* values of 0.7139 for species and 0.6504 for income indicate the farm is more diversified in physical terms than it is in economic terms. The$(n_i/N)^2$ values also indicate that while the farm's physical structure is dominated by coffee, its economic structure is dominated by the herd of two cows. Another convenient measure of income diversity is given by the *income diversity ratio,*

$$R=\left(\sum_{i=1}^{n} R_i\right)2/\sum_{i=1}^{n} R_I^2$$

where R_i (i = 1 to n) is the income from the i-th activity. Note that $1 \leq R \leq n$ for $R \geq 0$; and the larger the value of R, the higher the degree of income diversity. For the farm of Table, R_i = 2.86. In contrast, if the 11 enterprises of this farm had contributed equally to total income (*i.e.*, R_i = \$134.55), then the level of the income diversity index R would have been 11.

FLEXIBILITY

The property of flexibility of product use provides a second dimension to diversification: it refers to the availability of alternative ways of product disposal. There are a maximum of four ways: consume/use, sell/barter, store or process. A product for which all of these possibilities exist is intuitively preferable, other things equal, to one which can only be eaten or must be immediately sold. Further, the quality of processability permits repetition of the consume-sell-store-process alternatives at second, third or higher degree, but very few agricultural products are in fact farm-processed beyond a second-degree stage.

Thus, *e.g.*, the sap of coconut/palmyrah/nipah/kital palm is drawn off and farm-processed to make palm sugar or fermented to be drunk as toddy and, less frequently, toddy is further distilled to arrack, but hardly ever is arrack processed beyond this second stage. This also applies to such animal products as milk/butter, skins/leather and wool/cloth.

Farms of Type 4 (small dependent specialized family farms growing a cash crop such as cotton, tobacco, commercial sugarcane etc.) have least flexibility in product use since they have no alternative other than sale. Small subsistence and semi-subsistence farms of Types 1 and 2 usually have the highest overall system flexibility because of the type and number of items produced. Flexibility is well illustrated by the range of ways by which jackfruit are commonly disposed of on a Kandy farm. The family will consume some (as the carbohydrate staple in place of bread or rice), sell some for cash, barter some in the village for a chicken, then clean and dice the remainder to smoke-cure and store for use over the off-season. Further, they will probably extract the seeds and consume these; or sun-dry and barter them for some other food item; or water-store them (for up to eight or nine months) for eventual consumption or sale or barter. Even greater flexibility is possible in the disposal of the many products of the coconut palm.

TIME-DISPERSION

Time-dispersion of production or income refers to the degree to which a given production or income pattern is predictably dispersed (or, conversely, concentrated) over time - over a season or, more usually, the operating year. It is a measure of the uniformity of within-year production/income flow. Time-dispersion is a basis for distinguishing systems from which the product or income is received as a lump amount at one point in the operating year (*e.g.*, in a single harvest month) from systems which yield a uniform flow over the operating period.

The two extremes are:

- A product/income which is perfectly dispersed (*e.g.*, received as 12 equal monthly amounts over the operating year each equivalent to 8.3 per cent of the annual total amount); and
- A product/income which is all received as a single quantity in only one month of the year.

Table 7.5 shows the monthly time-dispersion of total annual production for a sample of tree and vine crops at selected locations in Malaysia and Sri Lanka. As these data show, such crops as tea and rubber are highly time-dispersed; others, *e.g.*, kapok, have far more time-concentrated patterns of production. The table could obviously be extended to include annual or short-term crops and livestock products.

When grown at any particular location, all crops fall into one of three categories in terms of time-dispersion of their products, viz.:

- Naturally time-dispersed crops (*e.g.*, rubber, tea, cacao, cinnamon)
- Naturally time-concentrated crops (*e.g.* most fruit, vegetables, field crops)
- Crops which are time-dispersed by management (*e.g.*, relay-planted, stored-in-ground).

On small farms a high level of time-dispersion (or low level of time-concentration) of production/income is usually desirable for the following four reasons:

- *Regularity/Reliability of Food Supply:* The important dimension in production of perishable food items (fruits, vegetables, animal products) on family-sustenance farms and where storage is not possible is regular and reliable availability rather than the amount of total annual product. A sufficient quantity of jackfruit, milk, eggs etc. available in each month of the year is superior to a larger volume of produce occurring in only one month of the year.
- *Avoidance of storage costs and losses:* Although simple storage methods are generally available (*e.g.*, rodent-proof granaries, anti-weevil grain treatment, smoke-curing or drying), they have not been adopted by many farmers and post-harvest losses continue to range from 20 to 40 per cent. Lack of household supervision of stored produce continues as a major cause of food loss, even when the cost of safe storage is within the reach of the poorest families. Thus, where it can be achieved, a time-pattern of food production which avoids or minimizes the necessity for storage is an alternative which is superior to storage as a means of ensuring food availability.

- *Minimization of family debt:* Near-perpetual indebtedness of small-farm families to landlords, moneylenders and/or shopkeepers is a serious problem throughout much of Asia. Debt is incurred for two main purposes: as credit for family food and material requirements during lean periods, and to meet socio-cultural obligations (weddings, deaths, festivals). Farm systems which yield income only once a year (*e.g.*, tenant-operated sugar farms) are almost sure to enter into indebtedness—all too often under onerous conditions—as a normal part of their existence. Other things being equal, the need for such indebtedness is minimized if the farm system can be so structured as to generate a uniform flow of food and cash income throughout the year.
- *Technical and economic efficiency:* The relatively high efficiency of farm Types 5 and 6 (*i.e.*, large commercial family farms and estates) is due largely to their organization along industrial lines. Processing is an integral part of their operations and efficient processing requires continuous-flow rather than batch-type operation. To achieve this, estates deal with crops (*e.g.*, tea, rubber, cocoa, coconut) which naturally give a highly time-dispersed flow of production over the year. Alternatively, they produce crops which, although each production unit (*e.g.*, hectare) may be time-concentrated, can be sequentially harvested to give a uniform flow of operations and product over the year (*e.g.*, cassava, sisal).

The annual time-pattern of production (as opposed to total annual production) has been a largely neglected aspect of agricultural research in relation to small-farm development.

These considerations of estate structure indicate corresponding weaknesses on many small farms, *e.g.*, dryland crop farms operated according to seasonal conditions. While such small farms must have a basic set of farm equipment, this equipment might not be used for more than two or three months of the year. (Such excess capital cost will not be great in absolute terms since most equipment will be farm-made, but nevertheless the highly time-concentrated production pattern will require a capital stock some three or four times greater than would be the case if the production pattern was time-dispersed.)

Table 4.5 Monthly Distribution of Production of Some Tropical Tree and Vine Crops at Selected Locations in Malaysia (M) and Sri Lanka (SL)

Crop and Location	Per Cent Annual Production in Each Month											
	J	F	M	A	M	J	J	A	S	O	N	D
Cacao (Perak M)	17	10	15	7	4	2	3	4	7	8	11	12
Cacao (Matale SL)	3	2	2	5	9	5	3	2	5	20	29	15
Arecanut (Kandy SL)	15	35	15	15	0	0	0	0	0	5	5	10
Cardamom (SL)	6	5	3	4	4	10	10	10	10	12	15	11
Cloves (Kandy SL)	25	28	32	10	2	0	0	0	0	0	0	3
Coconut (Negambo SL)	6	6	6	7	10	11	11	12	10	9	6	6
Nutmeg (Kandy SL)	2	1	45	10	1	1	35	1	1	1	1	1
Pepper (Matale SL)	20	10	2	0	2	7	12	3	2	3	14	25
Kapok (Matale SL)	0	0	0	0	80	20	0	0	0	0	0	0
Rubber (South SL)	13	9	9	8	5	4	7	7	11	7	11	9
Tea (High Country SL)	8	8	11	12	13	8	7	5	4	6	7	11

A related weakness consists of the time-bunching in the demand for farm labour relative to the supply-flow of family labour. Total labour supply on a small farm on an aggregated annual basis might commonly exceed annual requirements by 50, 100, 200... per cent, but labour shortage at critical periods (planting, weeding, harvesting) might still impose a major production constraint. This is commonly the case on dryland hill farms operated without draught animals, especially where there is only a short wet-period for land preparation and planting. But the problem is also serious across the great monsoon paddy lands where little can be done in the fields before the irrigation channels begin to flow.

The Western answer to similar problems with highly time-concentrated farm systems—almost an automatic reflex - has been farm mechanization. But other counter—strategies are possible on Asian farms: cooperative work-sharing (such as the 'bawon' harvest system of Indonesia); changing the structure of the system to include crops less sensitive to harvest or planting date; or by making more fundamental structural changes to the system by which labour-intensive field crops are at least partly replaced by near zero-labour food tree crops (such as jackfruit, breadfruit and coconut).

Measurement of Production/Income Time-dispersion

There is no generally recognized measure of time-dispersion of production or income but a useful index of relative dispersion can be constructed on the basis of the dispersion of individual monthly values of production or income relative to their annual totals. Examples are offered below.

Time-concentration of Single Activities

Table 7.6 shows monthly relative production (or income) for four crops - kapok, pepper, rubber and single-crop rice - on a Sri Lankan farm. For each crop, the coefficient of variation (*CV*) of its monthly production. As shown for single-crop rice, annual production (or income) of any crop which occurs wholly within a single month represents complete time-concentration and has a *CV* of 347 per cent. With production (or income) measured on a monthly basis, a *relative time-concentration (RTC)* index of any other crop relative to such a perfectly concentrated crop can be obtained as the ratio of its *CV* to the *CV* of 347 per cent for the perfectly concentrated crop. This results in an *RTC* index of 0.81, 0.28 and 0.09 for kapok, pepper and rubber, respectively, while the completely time-concentrated single-crop rice has an *RTC* index of one. The *relative time-dispersion (RTD)* of production (or income) from an activity or system can then be measured as one minus its relative concentration, *i.e.*, *RTD* = 1 - *RTC*, giving *RTD* values of 0.19 for kapok, 0.72 for pepper, 0.91 for rubber and zero for single-crop rice. (Note that a perfectly time-dispersed crop would have a CV of zero, an *RTC* index of zero and an *RTD* value of unity.)

Time-concentration of Systems

Discussion so far has related to separate crops or activities which are the components of systems. The relative time-dispersion of a whole-farm system also can be obtained as the sum of the relative time-dispersion *(RTD)* values of the productive components which comprise the farm system, weighted according to their individual importance. Consider the pepper-rubber-kapok growers around Matale in the Kandy Hills of Sri Lanka. Here a common crop system consists of old rubber trees thinned out to about 40 per acre which are tapped for latex, but the main function of which is to support pepper vines, at two vines per tree. The rubber-pepper fields are enclosed by live fences of kapok, yielding floss and (oil) seed, which also support pepper.

Thus the products of this system are latex, pepper, kapok floss and seed (and kapok pods for household fuel). The annual value of production per acre is some ₹ 2 400 for pepper, ₹ 800 for rubber and ₹ 600 for kapok or ₹ 3 800 in total. Using these product values as relative weights for the three crop components of the system and taking their relative time-dispersion values from Table 6.6, the system as a whole would have a relative time-dispersion (of production and income) index value of: 0.72 (2400/3800) + 0.91 (800/3800) + 0.19 (600/3800) = 0.68.

For the several reasons discussed above, the time-dispersion of income, and especially of sustenance food production, is an important dimension of small-farm system performance. Note also that the time-dispersion of more complex systems generating even more products can be quantified by the method outlined.

Table 7.6 Relative Monthly Production (or Income) and Relative Time-concentration and Relative Time-dispersion of Four Crops on a Sri Lankan Farm

Month and statistics[a]	Monthly production (or income) as a percentage of annual total by crop			
	Kapok	Pepper	Rubber	Single paddy
January	0	20	13	0
February	0	10	9	100
March	0	2	9	0
April	0	0	8	0
May	80	2	5	0
June	20	7	4	0
July	0	12	7	0
August	0	3	7	0
September	0	2	11	0
October	0	3	7	0
November	0	14	11	0
December	0	25	9	0
$\overline{X}$	8.33	8.33	8.33	8.33
V	542.42	64.61	6.61	833.39
SD	23.29	8.04	2.57	28.87
CV	280%	96%	31%	347%
RTC	0.81	0.28	0.09	1.00
RTD	0.19	0.72	0.91	0.00

Note: [a] The statistical measures $\overline{X}$, *V*, *SD* and *CV* are derived as already explained earlier.

SUSTAINABILITY

By sustainability is meant the capacity of a system to maintain its productivity/profitability at a satisfactory level over a long or indefinite time period regardless of year-to-year fluctuations (*i.e.*, of its short-term instability). In an agricultural production context, sustainability is relevant to farming systems of whatever composition, but not necessarily to the individual production phases of short-term crops. The concept involves the evaluation of farm activities and systems in terms of their (interrelated) ecological, economic and socio-cultural sustainability over long time periods of many years.

From a national or agroecoregional perspective, reference may be made to the *spiral of unsustainability*. As depicted in

Figure, under the pressure of increasing population and inappropriate policies, this is a downward spiral of diminishing resource availability, deteriorating environmental quality and increasing poverty leading to economic, social and political instability. Farmers, especially small farmers of Types 1 (subsistence) and 2 (semi-subsistence), are both possible victims of and contributors to this spiral of unsustainability should it occur. Conversely, through the management of their resources in a sustainable way, farmers can help to prevent its occurrence. Sustainability is thus a very important criterion in assessing the performance of existing and potential farm activities and systems.

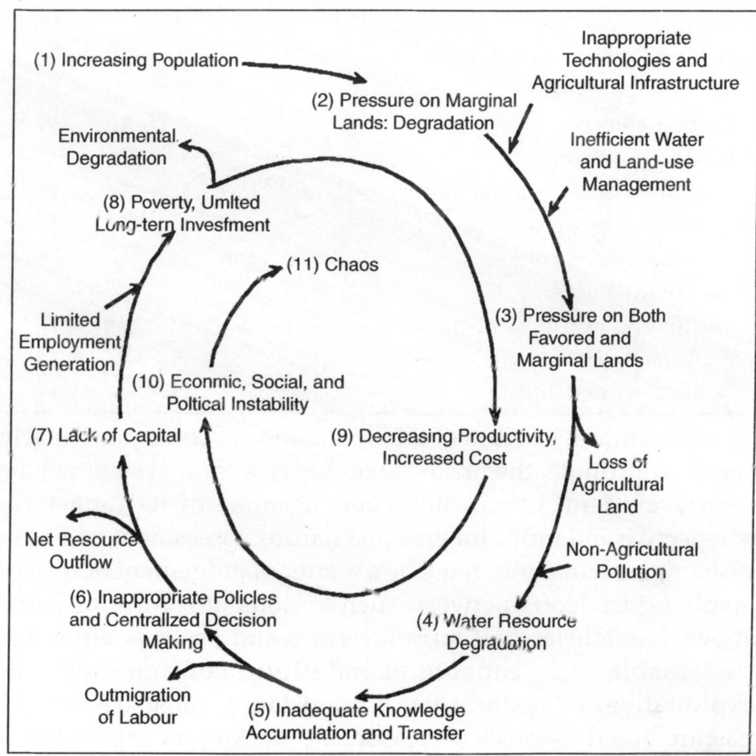

Fig 7.3 The Spiral of Unsustainability

Sustainability is a multidimensional concept. In the context of farm systems it may relate to physical, biological, economic and social attributes. Assessment of the sustainability of a particular farm system from both a private and a public view might involve judgements as to its merits in terms of such characteristics as listed below.

To exemplify this listing, intensive cropping

- On good soil/slope conditions; and
- On poor soil/slope conditions; and
- Perennial tree crop plantations are rated high (H), medium (M) or low (L) relative to each attribute.

	(1)	(2)	(3)
Biophysical attributes:			
Nutrient cycling capacity	M	L	H
Soil and water conservation capacity	M	L	M
Stability to pests and diseases	L	L	L
Level of biodiversity	L	L	L
Carbon storage	L	L	M
Economic attributes:			
Requirement for external inputs	H	M	H
Provision of employment	H	M	M
Generation of income	H	L	H
Social attributes:			
Health and nutritional benefits	M	M	L
Cultural and communal viability	H	M	M
Political acceptability	H	M	H

Sometimes, because of the dominance of some particularly negative attribute, the unsustainability of a farm system will be clearly evident. Often, however, because of its long-term perspective and multidimensional nature, assessment of a farm system's sustainability must be a matter of judgement or degree involving tradeoffs between such various attributes as listed above. Nonetheless, all farm activities and systems are either sustainable—*i.e.*, capable of indefinite continuation - or exploitative, or restorative. By-and-large, most tree crops, pasture-based livestock (at reasonable stocking rates), sawah or terraced paddy at reasonable intensity, and field-crop systems with a long ley phase are sustainable.

Many nutmeg groves in the Kandy Hills are still producing at about 100 years of age. In the same area there are clove plantations which naturally regenerate themselves from seed-fall and thus have an indefinite life. In the Sri Lankan mid-country there are many tea fields with over 100 years of recorded production (but many others, exploitatively managed in the past, have long since had to be abandoned). Vacancies which occur in row-planted cinnamon are usually in-filled to give this crop an indefinite life. Old coconut is commonly inter-planted with young palms with the same result. At their traditional levels of land-use intensity, these are sustainable systems.

On the other hand, as evidenced by Byerlee and Gill, 'continuous' intensive rice or wheat systems even on good irrigated lands are probably not indefinitely sustainable. The more or less continuous row cropping of clean-cultivated cassava, maize, oilseeds and cotton on lands of significant slope, with the now common annual 'fix' of urea, is certainly not sustainable. In Java, most of the remaining farm systems of the Slendro hills, the southern flanks of Mt Lawu and the karst tracts skirting the Indian Ocean are little more than monuments to systems that have been pushed beyond their limits, as are many of those in the Himalayan foothills. The people cling to them because they have no choice... 'Bare ruined choirs where late the sweet birds sang'.

Causes of farm Unsustainability

Beyond the pressure on the agricultural resource base induced by such primary social causes as population pressure and poverty,

farm systems may become unsustainable due to many factors of which the following are probably the most important:

- *Soil loss* due to sheet/rill/gully erosion if unchecked will remove the physical base for plant production. By and large, engineering methods of soil conservation (terraces except on wet paddy lands, contour drains, diversions, strip cropping etc.) have not been successful in Asia (or Africa) except when installed by estates or authoritarian governments. Thus the only practical approach to sustainable land use is through less intensive crops and less demanding (but not necessarily less productive) farming systems combined with a farming systems development approach to soil conservation and sustainability as argued by Norman and Douglas.

- *Soil structure deterioration and nutrient loss* through leaching and over-cropping, especially when combined with actual soil loss (above), will also necessitate eventual abandonment of the system (or the land), or the application of ever-increasing quantities of artificial external inputs—leading eventually to the same consequence, often together with adverse downstream effects and watertable pollution.
- *Declining terms of trade* or long-run adverse movements in agricultural commodity prices relative to input costs (especially of imported inputs) are increasingly a prospect facing much tropical and sub-tropical produce (*e.g.*, some oilseeds, cassava chips, sisal and the other coarse fibres). At some point some of these crops might well not be sustainable in marginal producing areas and will have to be abandoned for economic reasons. To the extent that they form components of systems, these systems will have to be restructured. Increasingly, economic pressures for change are also reinforced by socio-political factors: *e.g.*, the liquidation of sub-marginal tea estates in Sri Lanka for village settlement; the growing pressures for inter-row production of food crops on Malaysian cash-crop estates; pressures for diversification and food production on Mauritian sugar estates.
- *Government failure* through the introduction of inappropriate policies affecting agricultural production and resource use or the failure to introduce appropriate policies for the protection of natural resources and the environment (Pinstrup-Andersen and Pandye-Lorch; Scherr and Yadav). Historically, many developing countries have had food price policies favouring urban consumers at the expense of producers. This has undoubtedly engendered poverty and resource degradation among marginal producers. Likewise, many countries have inadequate controls on the use of

agricultural chemicals whose indiscriminate use has often caused widespread environmental pollution.

- *Biological factors* (disease, pest outbreaks) have on more than one occasion led to the decimation of crops and farm systems, and to the impossibility of restructuring these under conditions which could be economically sustained (*e.g.*, the abandonment of coffee in Sri Lanka in the 1880s due to rust).
- *Inequitable research and development* relating to a crop in one geographical area not infrequently reduces its economic sustainability in other areas. To the extent that improved varieties and technologies are developed in countries already enjoying a comparative advantage (*e.g.*, coconut in Philippines, rubber and oil palm in Malaysia, specialist tea in China), this will force changes in the farming systems of less advantaged countries, and lead either to their abandonment of these particular crops or, more likely, restructuring of their farming systems into mixed and probably more complex systems.
- *Regional interrelatedness*, whether physical, economic or political, provides another set of factors that can lead to unsustainability The causes of unsustainability noted in (1) and (2) above, soil erosion and degradation, arise on an individual farm or local group of farms and can (at least theoretically) be removed by local action on a watershed basis. But the non-maritime floods which increasingly devastate the delta farms of Bangladesh arise from causes (*e.g.*, deforestation of the Himalaya chain) located in other up-stream provinces—or indeed in other countries—and these, not amenable to local action, are affecting the sustainability of downstream agriculture on a vast scale. Acid rain in Europe, chemical pollution in the Mississippi, the Nile, the Vistula and some of the East African lakes—these are other examples of real threats to farm system sustainability which arise

beyond the farm gate and often beyond the national border.

Alternative System-management Strategies

Alternative on-farm management strategies towards resource and system sustainability or exploitation are illustrated by the examples depicted in Figure 7.4 Curve.

- Represents a uniform and sustainable system producing 60 income units ($) annually. A second possible system such as depicted by curve
- Might yield an initially higher income, but one which declines over time (*e.g.*, because of erosion, salinity, chemical pollution) until the system becomes economically unsustainable after 20 years.

From a social viewpoint, farmers should select system(1).

However, there are many reasons why in fact they often choose the exploitative system (2):

- The need for maximum current income (as distinct from future income) because of poverty, debt, exploitation by landlords, conditions of tenancy etc.;
- Limited length of farmer planning horizons (although system (2) is not sustainable, it yields greater total returns if the planning horizon is less than 20 years);
- Failure to recognize the fact that the declining income of system (2) is caused by resource exploitation (environmental damage is gradual and insidious);
- Ignorance that a better, sustainable system might exist; and
- Selection of system (2) as a deliberate choice, but with the intention to later—when family income needs decline, when the sons are educated, when the daughters are married—switch to a less exploitative system, or even to a restorative one as represented by curve (2a).

Consideration of these factors leads to the conclusion that the presence of a conservation programme in a particular area and the engineering knowledge this implies in designing contour banks, grass waterways, avoiding soil salinity etc. is only one of several necessary conditions for sustainable land use. The others are economic, social and political. The rate of accumulation of engineering and scientific knowledge needed for conservation has long exceeded rates of change in public attitudes towards conservation, without which such engineering solutions cannot be applied—or, if imposed, maintained.

The third alternative, adoption of a restorative system or one which improves the initial productivity conditions, is represented by curve (3). The accumulated income from system (3) exceeds that from system (1) but only after 20 years. System (3) is therefore a rational farmer alternative only for farm families with long planning horizons or who are free from the exploitative pressures of debt and poverty and can afford to wait. From a social viewpoint, however, system (3) will always be a superior alternative.

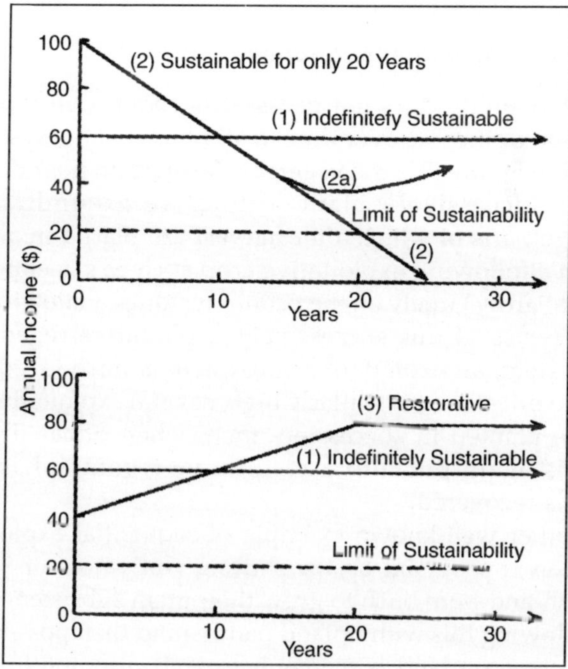

Fig 7.4 Illustrative Income Flow of Sustainable and Unsustainable Systems

There are many examples of restorative or resource-creating systems – though not as many as of exploitative systems. They are of two broad types. The first seeks to convert some previously exploitative system into a sustainable one. In Sri Lanka several thousand families have been settled on farms growing restorative soil-protecting tree crops in dense stands on old eroded tea lands (without removing the tea). There also some of the estates have been converting from (exploitative) tea to (regenerative) cloves and cardamom, again by interplanting. The second type of restorative system seeks to so improve some initially poor resource base that a sustainable fanning system becomes possible. In Malaysia and Philippines, the nipah palm, planted in saline mud flats, is used to dry out these coastal tracts and create conditions under which more productive species—coconut, breadfruit, jackfruit—can be established as the basis of future settlement farms. Likewise, in the arid zones of Australia and southern Africa, the shrub saltbush is used to remove soil salts and up-grade grazing systems.

Sequential Exploitation-restoration

Sustainability does not necessarily require uniformity of production or income over time in all phases of the system. As depicted in Figure 7.5 , the vegetable farmers on poor clay soils in Johor successively plant restorative groundnuts, the vegetative parts of which after harvest are placed in a trench, and then a following exploitative crop such as sweet potato is planted to grow largely on the peanut residues. Following three or four cycles of this successively exploitative-regenerative phase system, an exploitative subsystem is introduced: when vegetable prices are particularly high, several exploitative crops might be planted in succession; then, when prices drop, the system is again put into a restorative legume-phase until fertility is recovered.

Another well-known example of sequential exploitation-restoration is provided by the shifting cultivators of Sarawak who slash-and-bum bush to grow their main subsistence maize crop, following this with upland paddy (and then possibly with a cassava crop if land is scarce) before abandoning the site to bush for a six-, seven-, eight-... year restorative phase. The system consists of the successive exploitation or run-down of six, seven, eight... individual land parcels which comprise the 'farm'. In former times it was stable.

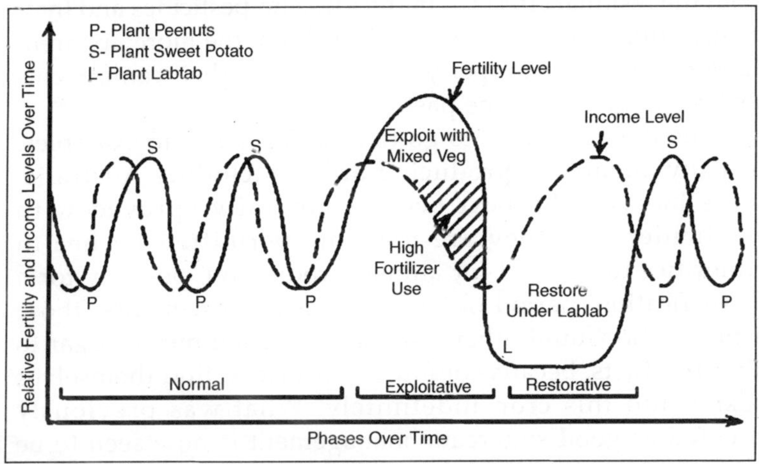

Fig 7.5 Successive Exploitative and Regenerative Phases in a Johor Vegetable Production System

Exploitation over all parcels was in balance with restoration. But now, in many areas of Sarawak, Kalimantan, the southern dry zone of Sri Lanka and parts of Africa, the restorative phase in such slash-and bum systems has had to be reduced due to population pressure and the exploitative phase prolonged. Because also of the temptation to produce cash crops in addition to food, the exploitative phase is now much intensified and such slash-and-bum systems are breaking down.

COMPLEMENTARITY AND ENVIRONMENTAL COMPATIBILITY

When applied to activities, this last of the eight properties requires that any crop or livestock component of a system be capable of structural integration with all other components of the system and its environment in terms of management practices, resources and technologies used, and disposal of products/by-products.

Such structural integration is especially important in relation to long-term activities where bad decisions made regarding one activity and their adverse effects on other activities might not be easily rectified. This probably is a statement of the obvious. However, the more that is learned about the residual effects of herbicides and pesticides and their further effects lower down the food chain, the more apparent it becomes that this property of systems and their components has been neglected in the past.

One does not have to go to Asia for concrete examples. In many sugarcane producing areas, including Australia, fields have in the past been so liberally sprayed with weedicides that they are not now permitted by health authorities to be used for animal production, possibly for a 'detoxification' period of 20 years. As a consequence, those farmers who would otherwise have adjusted out of sugar to other products, because of low sugar prices, find themselves locked into this crop indefinitely. What was previously accepted as good sugarcane management is now seen to be incompatible with other alternative activities.

When applied to whole-farm systems the requirement is that each of these be at least not incompatible with other systems in the village or area (for purposes of obtaining inputs and disposing of products). Although the subject has been largely ignored in farming systems development research, there are often close complementary relationships between groups of systems, *e.g.*, in neighbouring villages, without which each would be weaker.

In the Solo Valley of Java, the farms of Batan (where they grow only paddy and cannot keep cattle) complement those of nearby Boyalali (where they cannot grow paddy but have many draught cattle). This type of inter-village or inter-system complementarity is common throughout Asia. Where it exists, development efforts which remain preoccupied with the optimization of systems in technical and social isolation are likely to achieve no great success.

A related requirement is that both whole-farm and activity systems be compatible with the wider physical, biological and socio-religious-cultural environment. This desirable system property of environmental friendliness appears so obvious that examples should not be necessary.

Nevertheless, it is frequently overlooked in farm-systems development. The tale of rice schemes (planned for non-rice eaters)—of mechanization schemes (in areas without a mechanical tradition and with surplus labour) - of chemically-based crop production projects (which would obliterate a thousand years of village culture).... if it were told, this tale would be a long and doleful one.

SUMMARY

It now remains to consider how the criteria outlined in earlier sections of this chapter 6.2.1 to 8 above would be applied in specific analytical situations. Such application of the criteria might be considered from the perspective of, first, necessity and, second, desirability.

In terms of necessity, to use only one criterion to assess system performance will sometimes be sufficient. Commonly, for commercial farms, this is some aspect of profit, *e.g.*, gross margin or net farm income. But the use of some other single criterion may also sometimes be necessary: *e.g.*, analysis in support of planning a farm credit programme in Field C (*i.e.*, analysis oriented to systems above the farm-household level) might be concerned primarily with the need for credit as determined by the time-dispersion patterns of farm income, and for this purpose most of the other system properties might be ignored.

More often it will be necessary to work with some subset of the eight properties and their criteria. In relatively few situations it might be necessary to consider all eight factors, *e.g.*, in planning comprehensive general-purpose rural development projects. As noted above, most of the properties are capable of quantitative measurement; those that may present difficulties, such as sustainability and compatibility, might have to be assessed subjectively.

So much for what may be necessary. In terms of desirability, from both a private and a public view, the aim should be to have farm-household systems that are sustainable and environmentally friendly. Any farm management analyst worth his or her salt will therefore always endeavour to appraise farm and farm-household systems in terms of these two overarching criteria.

Table 7.7 Summary of Farm-household System Objectives by Farm Type and Performance Criteria Operating Objectives

Farm Type	Primary Objectives
(1) Small, largely subsistence, family	Subsistence
(2) Small, part commercial, family income	Sustenance and some cash
(3) Small, independent, specialized, family	Cash-based sustenance
(4) Small, dependent, specialized, family	Cash-based sustenance
(5) Large, commercial, family	Mainly profit
(6) Commercial estate	Profit

SYSTEM PROPERTIES AND CRITERIA FOR MEASUREMENT OF PERFORMANCE

Property	Criterion
1. Productivity	Yield per land unit or animal unit or other unit of resource or the value of output per unit of cost.
2. Profitability	In financial terms or measured subjectively as net benefits.
- of activities	Gross margin.
- of whole farms	Measures discussed in Chs 5 and 7.
3. *Stability*	Coefficient of variation (CV).
4. *Diversity*	Simpson's diversity index (DI)
- of activities	Number of activities in system.
- of products	Number of products of system.
- of income	Income diversity ratio (R).
5. Flexibility - of a single product - of all system products	Number of first, second ... degree uses to which products can be put (sold, consumed, processed, stored).
6. Time-dispersion - of production - of income - of whole-farm system	Relative dispersion of generation over the operating period (usually year) on a daily/weekly/monthly/quarterly basis as measured by the relative time-dispersion index (RTD).
7. *Sustainability*	No single general quantitative measure. Measurement would relate to physical, biological, economic and social factors with reference to the number of years over which a given system may be operated before its continuation becomes infeasible or inadequate.
8. *Complementarity and environmental compatibility* - of activities in a system - of systems in the environment	No cardinal measure but an ordinal measure ranking activities or systems on a scale of high, low, neutral or negative relative to their physical, biological, socio-economic, cultural and religious environmental friendliness could be used.

Bibliography

Bennett, J.: *Irrigation of Agricultural Crops,* Madison: American Press,1994.

Black, A.: *Soil Erosion and Productivity,* Madison: American Press, 1998.

Boserup, E.: *The Conditions of Agricultural Growth,* New York: Aldine Publishing, 2001.

Bowden, L.: *Agriculture in Semi–arid Environments,* Berlin: Springer, 2001.

Boyce, K.: *Challenges in Dryland Agriculture,* USA: Oxford, 1998.

Burnett, E.: *Water and Water Policy in World Food Supplies,* Texas: University, 2005.

Cornish, P.: *Dryland Farming,* Australia : University Press , 2002.

Dregne, H.: *Dryland Soil Resources,* Washington: Oxford, 2004.

Hargreaves, M.: *Dry Farming in the Northern Great Plains,* Cambridge: Harvard University Press, 2001.

Hegde, B.: *Dryland Agriculture,* Jodhpur: Scientific Publishers, 1995.

Hegde, B.: *Dryland Farming: Past Progress and Future Prospects,* Jodhpur: Scientific Publishers, 1997.

Hurni, H.: *World Soil Erosion and Conservation,* Cambridge: University Press, 1995.

Kerr, J.: *An Evaluation of Dryland Watershed Development in India,* Washington: Thomson Nelson, 2000.

Koohafkan A.: *Challenges and Strategies for Dryland Agriculture*, Madison: *CSSA Publication*, 2004.

Lascano, R.: *Irrigation of Agricultural*, USA: American Press, 2006.

Ma Shijun: *Challenges in Dryland Agriculture: A Global Perspective*, USA: Texas, 2004.

Mann, T.L.J.: *Dryland Farming: A Systems Approach*, South Melbourne: Sydney University Press, 1998.

O.R. and Unger, P.: *Agriculture and Environmental Challenges*, Washington: Srivastava Press, 1998.

Pieri, C.: *Soil Management: Experimental Basis for Sustainability and Environmental Quality*, Africa: CRC Press, 1997.

Radder, G.: *Sustainable Development of Dryland Agriculture in India*, Jodhpur: Scientific Publishers, 1997.

Scoones, I.: *Sustaining the Soil: Indigenous Soil and Water Conservation*, Africa: Earthscan Publications, 1996.

Singh, R.: *Dryland Agricultural Research in India*, Jodhpur: Scientific Publishers, 2002.

Steiner, J.: *Dryland Agriculture: Strategies for Sustainability*, New York: Springer, 1995.

Stern, N.: *The Economics of Climate Change*, U.K: Cambridge University Press, 2007.

Stewart, B.,: *Water Conservation Technology in Rainfed and Dryland Agriculture*, USA: University Press, 2005.

Index